GROUPS THAT WORK

GROUPS THAT WORK

Structure and Process

2ND EDITION

PAUL H. EPHROSS AND THOMAS V. VASSIL

COLUMBIA UNIVERSITY PRESS   NEW YORK

COLUMBIA UNIVERSITY PRESS
Publishers Since 1893
NEW YORK   CHICHESTER, WEST SUSSEX

Library of Congress Cataloging-in-Publication Data

Ephross, Paul H.
    Groups that work : structure and process / Paul H. Ephross and Thomas V. Vassil.—
2nd ed.
        p. cm.
    Includes bibliographical references and index.
        ISBN 0-231-11508-3 (cloth : alk. paper)
        ISBN 0-231-11509-1 (paper : alk. paper)
        1. Social work administration. 2. Health services administration. 3. Small groups.
    4. Social service—Teamwork. 5. Organizational effectiveness. I. Vassil, Thomas V. II. Title.

HV40.E64   2005
361.3'068—dc22   2004056031

Columbia University Press books are printed on permanent and durable acid-free paper.
Printed in the United States of America
c 10 9 8 7 6 5 4 3 2 1
p 10 9 8 7 6 5 4 3 2 1

CONTENTS

PREFACE TO THE SECOND EDITION

THIS SECOND EDITION is revised and expanded from the first edition of *Groups That Work: Structure and Process*, published in 1988. Over the past decade, we have been teaching, writing, and practicing group work in a variety of social work venues. Our thinking and reflection prompted us to expand our work on leadership, increase the number of cases with analyses, and rework material on boards of directors and on teams. We added detailed profiles of five distinctive group cultures and expanded the organic metaphor regarding organizations to consider them as interactional and transactional associations of small groups.

In the beginning of the twenty-first century and for the foreseeable future, our vision is that the small group in large and small organizations and neighborhoods can be a focal point that revitalizes democratic principles in various combinations of instrumental and interpersonal influences. In this regard, we note the contributions of the Association for the Advancement of Social Work with Groups in reviving the importance—indeed, the primacy—of the small group in social work.

Much has changed since the first edition. What has changed is not so much the nature of groups but rather our understanding of them, of the organizations that are composed of ecologies of small groups, and the world in which these groups and organizations live.

We acknowledge the supportive atmosphere set by Dean Jesse J. Harris of the University of Maryland School of Social Work for his effective leadership and unchanging civility at a time when both are in short supply in many organizations. We thank John S. Glaser, an excellent social worker and community activist, for his insight into small groups and processes in organization. Joan C. Weiss contributed cogent observations about the increasing power within organizations of information technology and of people skilled in its use. Raymie Wayne contributed a case study of leadership that lets us shine some light on the relationship between a staff person and the indigenous leadership within a group.

Our special thanks to Gwen Young for keyboarding the text and numerous revisions with her usual skill and good humor.

A privilege we shared was to experience teachers who cared deeply both about groups and about their students. There were too many to mention them all, but we refer especially to the late Saul Bernstein, Herbert Thelen, and Mary Louis Somers. What's useful about this new edition is the result of the foundation we got from them, other teachers, colleagues, our students, and the groups in which we have worked.

As in the first edition, the authors share equal responsibility for the words and ideas in this text, an experience that will be remembered with a smile.

GROUPS THAT WORK

I

WORKING IN GROUPS

THIS BOOK IS ABOUT working groups that are concerned with producing a product of some kind external to themselves. Such groups are composed of people who are members because of their professional and occupational responsibilities, their interest as citizens in creating some sort of a product, or making a difference in the community or the broader world, or a combination of the two. Working groups do not aim primarily at changing the attitudes or behaviors of their own members but rather form in order to generate some external product, develop policies, or participate in decision-making processes. It is this focus on producing or influencing something external to itself that defines the essence of a working group. Others have used terms such as *task group* to differentiate working groups from those formed for clinical treatment of their members.

Suppose you were to spend a week with a nurse-administrator, an executive director of a social agency, an educational planner, a department head in a hospital, or a human services administrator in a state government. You might ask the question, "What does this person actually do?" If you try to answer this question by directly observing the person and noting the amount of time he or she spends performing various kinds of activities during the week, you would find that a large number of working hours are spent participating in various roles in working groups such as staff meetings, committees, subcommittees, task forces, boards of directors, commissions, and subunits of these bodies. Some professionals, especially those who hold jobs with major administrative, planning, policy formation, or research components, may spend a majority of their working hours in activities connected with their memberships in such groups. These activities include preparation for group meetings, participation in the actual meetings, and following through on decisions reached during the meetings. Technically, of course, only some of these so-called groups deserve the name. Others are collectives or aggregations, or encounters, or whichever term one prefers for a collection of people who do not constitute a fully developed group. What meanings does participation in these groups have for members? For the professional being observed, the meaning may be broad and deep. Some of the events that are most important for members of various professions, and those whom they serve, take place within working groups. Points of view are accepted or rejected, modified or voted into effect. Decisions are reached that either enable or support, or frustrate and discourage the deepest purposes of professionals, their professions, their organizations, and individuals who compose them. Organizations, services, agencies, and projects are funded or ended as a result of decisions reached in groups. Particular targets of services are selected. Criteria for future decisions are developed. Group members learn a wide range of knowledge, attitudes, and skills. Judgments are made, hirings and firings planned and confirmed, influence strategies adopted, and rewards and sanctions distributed, all within the context of working groups in which professionals serve as members, chairs, staff, or sometimes all three.

Each of these terms deserves some attention to definitions. In this book, we will use the term *staff* to refer to professionals who carry responsibility for working with, advising, and following through on decisions made by various groups. Characteristically, such people hold administrative responsibility within organizations. We will use the term *chair* for an elected or subselected person whose responsibility it is to keep the group going, to keep the trains running on time, as the old expression has it. Generally, the chair is one of the members of the group. The staff person is not and is paid by the organization. It should be noted that professionals not only staff working groups but also serve as members of others. And, indeed, professionals also serve as chairs of working groups.

Community development and all forms of planning are carried on largely within the context of working groups. Funds are raised and allocated in the voluntary, not-for-profit, for-profit, and public sectors by groups that exist for these purposes. Administration involves a large and crucial component of group participation and group leadership. Even clinical practitioners in the various health and human service professions find, as their careers progress, that they spend a good deal of time in working groups such as staff groups, teams, and professional associations.

Working groups are as important in the lives of many citizens in their lay capacities as they are for professionals. Such groups occupy a great deal of time and attention of a wide range of people who participate in them as volunteers. What goes on in such groups makes a great deal of difference both in the inner lives of lay participants and in various organizations, institutions, and processes in society at large. The fabric of social living for many adults is woven of experiences in local unions and trade associations, charitable organizations, churches, synagogues, or other religious groups, community councils, political clubs, sports teams, community choruses, and ethnic organizations, each with its many committees and other subunits. All these groups are important in people's lives, though we shall consider in this book only those that are part of organizations connected with the delivery of health and human services.

Working groups are very much affected by and affect the processes of social change. Various writers have pointed out that today's work organizations in the twenty-first century are quite different in structure and in operation from the organizations that characterized our society in the past. Together with writers such as Lincoln (1985), we view organizations as ecologies of groups. The small group is the framer, the definer of issues and the decision maker. Organizations can be viewed as interlocking networks of small groups and groups as the parts of organizations that defines the relevance of other parts of the organization.

With the emphasis on creativity that characterizes the transformed work organization (see Bennis, Spreitzer, and Cummings, 2001), working groups can also be viewed as "charismatic enclaves." Small groups are the places within organizations in which new ideas, new views, new ways of defining problems, and new ways of finding solutions come about.

This new view of working groups and the vital function they perform for organizations is true, in the views of theorists, for all organizations. We shall point out repeatedly and from various angles that nowhere is this more the case than in organizations devoted to the provision of health and human services. In our view, health and human service organizations depend on the working groups of which they are composed for their existence, their development of resources, their allocation of resources, their standards of quality for providing services, and for the evaluation of success or failure that is so important a part of service delivery organizations. While leaving room for examples of individual creativity, the largest part of the work of health and human service professionals is and should be spent making contributions to the working groups that compose the organizations within which most professional lives are lived. We shall elaborate on this perspective in several chapters and illustrations in this book.

If working groups are so important, it might be expected that the various professions and programs of professional education would pay them lots of attention. One might expect that the skills required for both effective participation and effective leadership in such groups would be widely taught as part of the educational system that prepares people for citizenship and that the processes of working groups would be studied exhaustively through both formal research and informal means. Quite to the contrary, it seems to us that most people have experienced comparatively little formal teaching and learning about how to work together in groups. For the most part, our society has relied on catch-as-catch-can experiences and folk wisdom as sources of learning about working groups.

This book is an attempt to fill some gaps in readers' educations. Before we proceed, it may be helpful to look at some of the reasons that working groups haven't received as much attention as they deserve. A brief look at some of the history and sociology of approaches to work with groups may provide some answers.

Working Groups and the Sociology of Group Work Knowledge

Social workers and other applied social scientists have been aware of the importance of group work from the beginning. Late-nineteenth- and early-twentieth-century figures in the development of social work wrote about work with groups in general and about working groups in particular. Specifically, Mary Parker Follett was deeply committed to building democracy and developing citizenship through experiences in groups. In 1920 Follett wrote, "The group process contains the secret of collective life, it is the key to democracy, it is the master lesson for every individual to learn, it is our chief hope for the political, the social, the international life of the future."

During the 1930s and 1940s a steady stream of social and behavioral scientists seeking refuge from the horrors of Nazi Europe brought to this country a concern with teaching democracy at the grass roots. It was natural that many, including especially Kurt Lewin (1948), emphasized the potential value of learning to work together in small groups for teaching citizenship and inoculating society against the possibility of totalitarianism. The contributions of these refugees blended with the earlier, indigenous concerns of others to produce a sizable constituency of writers, theorists, and practitioners whose interests centered on group processes and group work.

During the postwar period, these interests produced two bodies of research and practice. The first, initially identified with social scientists who had been exposed to group theorists in their graduate education, developed within universities. This body of practice and research came generally to be known as "group dynamics." The second body of knowledge and practice came largely from social work, used the name "group work" or "social group work," and emphasized work with groups of children, adolescents, and adults, including older people, in neighborhood and community settings, and, later, patients in health care settings. It was somewhat unclear to what extent either group dynamics or social group work were fields, professions, methods, or processes that had relevance for all. Group workers formed their own association, the American Association for the Study of Group Work (later the American Association of Group Workers) during the 1930s and sought to decide whether they belonged in social work, in education, in recreation, or elsewhere. Ultimately, the decision was made to consider social group work as a part of social work, and the AAGW was one of the organizations that formed the National Association of Social Workers in 1956. The group dynamics idea grew to span boundaries, as it still does, among sociology, psychology, education, nursing, psychiatry, and at times political science as well. During the 1960s and 1970s the idea grew, entered the mainstream of American life through the mass media, became a topic of popular conversation and even a subject for parody, and was sometimes referred to as a growth industry.

Our concern is not so much with history per se as with a look at the development of knowledge about groups and group work. A quick tracing of group work in social work may be useful for understanding what has happened to knowledge about groups in other professions as well. The classical group work texts of the period from 1948 to 1972 (see Ephross, 1986) were clear on two points. All group work practice was viewed as having social goals content, sometimes implicit and sometimes explicit. The ultimate purpose of work with groups was viewed as contributing to the development of a better, more just, more equitable, more humanistic society. Equally important, group work skills were presented as applicable to a wide range of types of groups, including, explicitly, working groups. A very influential text of the postwar period (Wilson and Ryland, 1949) not only devoted a chapter to "administrative processes" but also began with the citation from Follett given above.

At the same time, group work was one of the very first of what may now be termed the "process disciplines." Groups' processes are intangible (though their products may not be), and perhaps for this reason expertise in group work sounded and felt a bit slippery in an earlier, industrial, production-oriented world. Now, when we are used to viewing with respect skills such as computer programming, information systems design, and arbitration and conflict management, earlier points of view may seem obsolete. For earlier decades, however, mere skill at guiding interpersonal relationships and group development lacked those elements of production that made for recognition and prestige. Further, since much early group work practice was not directed toward healing the sick, it lacked the quasi-medical aura that surrounded treatment and therapy. Finally, since much group work practice was directed toward members of low-power populations, such as children, immigrants, ethno-racial minorities, adolescents, the aged, and poor people, some stigmatizing probably tainted both the practitioners and the organizations that sponsored the practice. Such speculations are intriguing and await more rigorous historical study for further development.

Until the late 1960s group work in social work contained an emphasis on contributing to the building of society and a corollary emphasis on the importance of democratic group participation; group workers were to learn skills in working with citizens' groups, in particular. In our opinion, these emphases have been somewhat neglected over the past thirty years or so. Staffs and their processes, though omnipresent in service delivery organizations, have not received their proper share of attention. A steadily increasing concern with gaining skills in group methods in treatment, which is to be applauded, has not been accompanied by corresponding attention to working groups.

Related questions may be asked about group dynamics. Why has so much research been conducted with ad hoc nongroups, many of them temporary aggregations of college students that do not meet the criteria for being groups? Why has there been so little observation of existing groups in their natural habitats? To underscore these questions, we note that many articles and even some books use the general term "groups" to refer to just one particular type of group, usually the T (training) or experiential learning group. Other types of groups are often ignored.

Retrospect can be useful in several ways, not only to understand what has happened in the past but also to learn about our present dilemmas and enable us to chart a course for the future development of knowledge about groups and group work. It seems to us that, just when group work was establishing itself clearly as a major part of social work and group dynamics as a major part of applied social sciences, developments within human services in general and major social trends combined to divert attention away from the detailed study of what takes place in microsocial interactions among people. Some of this attention has been diverted toward greater concern with broad social goals and questions of societal direction. These concerns are genuine and need to continue. They may correct an earlier, somewhat naive, all-is-for-the-best stance that was part of the development of knowledge about groups (Feldman and Specht, 1968). It is time to return to a concern about what takes place within groups, particularly working groups, because of their importance in the lives of people, in the development of health and human services in our society, and in the effective delivery of such services to those who need them. In sum, it is our point of view that those who are concerned with social planning and social change are precisely the people who need to be concerned with what goes on in groups and how one can influence it.

Group processes influence the lives of citizens and professionals in many settings and throughout life. Only a small proportion of the population, relatively speaking, is involved in purposeful group experience for therapeutic or people-changing purposes under professional direction at any given time. A much larger proportion is involved in groups at work, in neighborhood organizations, or religious congregations. In order to influence large numbers of people, those who work with groups need to develop the skills needed to work with both naturally occurring groups and with formed working groups. Most of these groups exist in order to achieve purposes that are important to them, which they view as important ends in themselves. Personal growth that takes place for members of such groups, while vitally important for society in the long run, is a distinctly secondary motivation for most working groups' members. Achieving groups' purposes and succeeding at groups' tasks should be given full weight and respect by all concerned.

There are some hopeful signs that widely disparate voices are beginning to recognize the need for attention to be paid to working groups. The quality of people's experiences at work is now being widely recognized as an important topic for attention. This is true both in the broader society, by students of management (Oichi, 1981), and within the human service field (see Ephross, 1983), particularly by those who have defined the phenomenon of burnout (Edelwich and Brodsky, 1980). There are signs of a revival of interest in group work that stems directly from some of the historical developments alluded to above (Garvin, 1987:32—34). Perhaps most important, there seems to be growing recognition throughout the health and human service professions that service delivery and service system issues are important and should not be separated from issues of service effectiveness. That is, how a health or human service can be delivered, what kinds of organizations should deliver it, and what human resources and interpersonal structures and processes are needed may be as important to the welfare of the consumer or patient as the nature of the service or treatment itself. This perception is more and more widespread. In our view, it is accurate, and it underlies much of the material that follows in this book.

Throughout this book, we shall blend perspectives gained from practice, theory, and research and draw upon the insights of writers and practitioners educated in various professions and disciplines. We hope that readers will make the translations necessary to apply what we have written to their own work and their own professional identities; we have, however, tried to keep the need for such translations to a minimum.

SOCIAL TRENDS THAT AFFECT THE IMPORTANCE OF WORKING GROUPS

As we move into the body of the book, a list of major social trends at the beginning of the twenty-first century may provide a useful backdrop to understand the relationship between and among individuals, groups, organizations, and the broader society. We suggest the following list for discussion. It was developed for this book, based on a great variety of sources.

1. Changes in the Nature of Work. Most work is or will become connected with the use of information technology and/or provision of services. This is having a number of effects on organizations, including making race, gender, ethnicity, and age both less and more important: less important for effective task accomplishment; more important for effective work in groups. Most work in contemporary society requires education beyond the basic literacy that virtually all jobs require.

2. Information Technology. The widespread importance of information technology has resulted in increased organizational power for those skilled in its use and decreased power for those who are not. In addition, variations in horizontal and vertical communication within and across units can significantly alter organizational cultures.

3. Changes in the Nature of Organizations.
   a. There is still a clearly hierarchical quality to many organizations, including human service organizations. This quality is most plainly seen in overinflated salaries, options, and bonuses paid to CEOs.
   b. The increasing diversity of the work force results in an advantage for supervisors, managers, and peers who are culturally

competent and corresponding disadvantages for those who are not.

c. The organizations that are succeeding and growing—whether in business, government, or the military; in the reduced but still huge production sphere; or in health care or human service delivery—tend to be flatter. They value creativity at the expense of conformity. They set clear boundaries between employees' work and personal lives and refrain from trying to control the latter.

d. We think the organizations of the future will be made up of fairly stable small groups, with the keyword for work success being participation that is conscious, effective, and contributes to group productivity.

4. The Diversity of U.S. Population. The U.S. population has diversified at a rapid pace in the last several decades and is bringing and will continue to bring about a corresponding diversity within virtually all the institutions of society, as well as greater readiness to accept diversity in institutions previously thought of as homogeneous.

5. Major Changes in Gender Roles. Changes are still in process and include but are not limited to:

a. Greater acceptance of sexual minority behavior.

b. Sexuality primarily viewed as a means of establishing, maintaining, and changing relationships and as a means of self-expression.

c. The entry of more women in the workforce with higher levels of education and acceptance into professions, which has helped to produce greater variance in family structure, for example:

i. Both parents employed, contributing equally or nearly so to family income.

ii. Greater acceptance of single-parent families, both male- and female-headed and other diversities of family structure.

iii. Far greater use of out-of-home day care from infancy.

iv. Increased prevalence of divorce/remarriage/blended families, which has changed the modal life cycle (see below).

6. Quantitative and Qualitative Changes in Both the Modal and Normative Life Cycles.

a. Life expectancy has increased for all groups of the population, though there is still a lag for some minority groups.

b. Adolescence/young adulthood has been extended in parts of the population, accompanied by a significant increase in concerns about fertility for couples in their thirties and forties.

c. Divorce, followed by remarriage and establishment of blended families or less formal relationships, is both more common and more widespread.

d. Expectations for vigorous good health in middle and later years have increased. There is a growing tendency to go back to work, at least part time, after retirement.

e. "Science fiction" developments in diagnostic, surgical and pharmaceutical care, widely publicized, increase most people's expectations.

f. The crisis in paying for medical care and medications highlights the increasing inequality in what health care is available to particular parts of the population and what is not.

g. There has been a rapid increase in acceptance of a widespread need for therapy of various kinds and forms. The most recent boom is in "life coaching."

7. Capitalist Triumphalism.

a. The end of Soviet Union and radical shifts in the Chinese economy mean that the only real challenges to Western-style modified capitalism come from the premodern rather than radical side.

b. Rapid increases in environmental awareness, from energy use to diet, exist in a state of tension with a consumerism that is sometimes frenzied.

c. The range of income, from top to bottom of organizations and in society as a whole, is extremely high. In other words, inequality has increased.

8. Intergroup Relations.

a. Decreases in overt/de jure discrimination and racism make the covert de facto racism, whether individual, institutional, or cultural, all the more painful and destructive.

b. In the 2000 census, for the first time, people could identify themselves as being of "more than one race," with 6.826 million people identifying themselves this way. (U.S. Bureau of the Census, 2004).

9. Education. From preschool to graduate school, is education evolving or in a state of revolution?

10. Terrorism. At home and abroad, terrorism and its ramifications with respect to the military, governmental, and societal fabric have grown greatly in importance.
11. A collapse of the moral authority vested in CEOs and corporate boards of directors. This collapse has taken place simultaneously with the decline and disempowerment of employee and stakeholder rights.

The mixed picture facing the American public, in many forms and guises, presents formidable challenges that will surface in small group processes. At this juncture and for the foreseeable future, social work is in a unique position, as a profession with deep concerns for the democracy of group processes, to assume and exercise a leadership role in revitalizing interest, study, and practice in work groups as keys to change and stability.

2

Frames of Reference for Understanding Work Groups

THE STUDY OF GROUPS suffers from a surplus of terms to describe group phenomena and characteristics, so spending a little time on defining terms now may make what follows clearer for the reader. We label as "contracting" (Shulman, 2001; Garvin and Seabury, 1984) processes that others have referred to as clarifying and agreeing on individual and group goals (Coyle, 1954), setting group objectives (Zander, 1982), or defining the ground rules (Thelen, 1958). The group member who carries elected or appointed responsibilities for leadership and is so designated in public will be called the chair, though in various organizational settings this person may be known as president, chairman of the board, executive director, executive vice president, commander, department head, section chief, presiding officer, task force leader, or convener. Both staff and chair share leadership responsibilities for the group. As a group matures, so does each membership. As Mills (1984) and many others have pointed out, in a mature group all group members share responsibility for the group's executive function, which can be defined loosely as "making the group's wheels go round."

Whichever terms one uses to describe the processes and life of the group, each reader may be expected to have emotional reactions to them. For example, the term "worker," while comfortable enough for social workers, is an unknown and not necessarily positive term for nurses, physicians, or public administrators. The term "manager" is entirely acceptable to someone who thinks of himself as a business administrator; however, it may have unpleasant overtones for someone who is a physician or social worker. When it comes to working in groups, most of us grew up in a mode of thought that can best be described as prescientific. Many of us, however well educated we are in our respective professions, however technologically sophisticated, grew up with the same mingled reactions of mystification, prejudice, and resignation concerning what goes on in a working group that our medieval ancestors had regarding what goes on inside the human body. Like our ancestors, we are likely to view the workings of a group as predetermined. We are also likely to view what goes on in groups—and particularly the tendency of group meetings to consume our time—as a function of an unkind and random fate. The point of view of this book is that, while much of what goes on in groups is unknown, group phenomena can be comprehended to a large extent, can be studied, and can be affected through skilled and conscious participation.

CONTRACTING

One of the most important processes that takes place in any group is contracting. A contract has been defined as "an agreement, especially if legally binding" (New York Times 1982:14T). In groups, contracting means reaching an agreement about why a group exists, how long it will exist, what will be expected of the members, how and whether the group will be structured formally, what will be expected of a staff person (if there is one), what a group's relationships will be with other groups and with the organization that sponsors it (if there is such an organization), which behaviors are to be permitted and which not permitted, which outcomes should be considered successes and which failures, and often other matters as well (Shulman, 2001; Schwartz, 1976). In this book, we are concerned with working groups that often have professional staff resources to serve their executive functions. Thus we include in the elements of a contract the respective behaviors, authority, powers, and responsibilities of the staff person and the group members, and sometimes of the sponsoring organization as well.

Contracting in groups is a dynamic and flexible process that starts with the first glimmer of the group's conception and ends with the last ripple caused by the group's termination. The initial contracting process should be authentic and should have meaning for all concerned. Even so, the agreements reached initially will be reinterpreted in the light of changing circumstances as the group goes through its life and in their final form may themselves be considerably changed.

The evolution of the contract need not be smooth, but it does need to be ongoing. Many disagreements and conflicts within a group may surface and be addressed in the course of revising and renegotiating its contract. If these conflicts are handled well, the process will be one of the growth-inducing aspects of group life. Contracting should be an open and participatory process, known to all the group members. Secret, covert aspects of contracts kill group processes as effectively as anything can. A balance needs to be maintained between treating a contract as rigid and fixed, which is usually unrealistic, and spending frustrating amounts of time negotiating it. The second is usually a sign of group immaturity or a lack of integration of group members, group purposes, and organizational goals.

While we will discuss some specific contracting behaviors in chapter 6, contracting is such a basic process that some preliminary thoughts are in order. The contract as an agreement does not carry quite the force of a legal document. As a working framework, however, it spells out the expectations of the parties who have a stake in the problem. Among the initial framing planks of a contract, the following are important to consider:

1. What is expected of the members? Questions that arise commonly involve representation, the personal responsibilities of membership, membership as commitment, a sense of outcomes, and the time and length of meetings. In essence, members have to know what they have to do to be good group members. Therefore, expectations regarding membership need discussion.

2. What do potential members expect of the group and the experience?

3. What will the staff person do? Clear expectations regarding the staff role need to be spelled out. Such activities as keeping a discussion going, taking minutes, following up on group decisions between meetings, working with the chair, gathering and presenting information, and other tasks may be included here. More general responsibilities such as keeping an eye on general goals and scanning the group's environment for changes in the organizational, neighborhood, or community context may also be included. A group or an organization may need to revamp objectives in the face of economic constraints. A small organization may need to extend services to a satellite center, at the cost of altering its current services. Issues such as these entail weighing values and making choices. To the extent that these occur, then members' behaviors in the group may change. All these developments have implications for a staff person's role as well.

4. A third party to the contract is the host organization. This party is often introduced by the staff person, who generally represents the sponsoring organization. A staff person functions not only as a facilitator and doer in the group but also as a representative of the host organization, especially during the contracting process. The organi-

zation (if there is one) has a major stake in the contract the staff person and members work out. The staff person and the chair carry responsibility for translating an organization's purposes in sponsoring a group into operational terms to which the group can develop commitment. What makes this process complex is that organizational purposes tend to be expressed in generalities, while group contracts need to be as specific as possible. Purposes define plans; contracts need a compass.

In Example A below, "The Mayor's Task Force," the first charge to the group is to "survey existing services for the frail elderly." What this means for the task force in operational terms needs to be spelled out in the contract.

Public Aspects of a Group Contract

Why and when do contracts change? Neither staff nor each member will necessarily tell all or even listen to and incorporate all that is said in an early contractual situation. There are several reasons for this. First, some purposes are implicit and may never be spelled out. For example, staff persons are unlikely to state group cohesion as a goal at first because they think that this is not a purpose that is real for the members. Second, some purposes may not be known to the participants because they evolve in the course of the group's life (Luft, 1970). Competition between subgroups is an example of such a purpose. Third, and perhaps most important, the parties to the contract may not be ready initially to share in some long-term or controversial objectives. More personal objectives, such as achieving greater power or prestige in the group, may be more on members' minds at the beginning. Similarly, an organization may be using a group as a testing ground for its participants for future assignments. The organization may not be ready to share this purpose publicly or fully, at the outset or even later.

Contracts can also change with changes in group composition. For example, a group may expand to include one or more new members and thereby reactivate initial contracting processes. Any change in group composition alters the properties of the group at both the work and the levels.

Contracts can be revised. Two situations may be contrasted. In the first, which we view as legitimate, the agreed-upon parts of a contract are explicit but partial. This is the situation in most groups, at least at the beginning. Additional pieces can be added to the contract as the need for them arises. In the second situation, which we view as illegitimate, the stated contract is in fact the opposite of what one or more of the parties really intend. For example, the stated contract may be oriented toward involving all group members in decision making, while the real or operational purpose may be to concentrate decision-making power in a few individual group members. Groups that abuse contracts in this way do not easily grow to maturity, in our view. Such groups are often experienced by the members, and sometimes by the group's leadership, as games. They raise the discomfort level of participants. For example, committees that are formed just to meet predetermined outcomes can be destructive because they destroy faith not only in themselves but in groups in general.

Without sound and careful planning, groups, and sometimes subgroups or individual members, can subvert or abuse a contract in radical ways. One way this may happen is when the group acts to change its place in an organization. With thought and foresight, such adjustments can sometimes be powerful and revitalizing vehicles for change. Another way to subvert a contract is for the group to invite people to join simply to corrupt or to co-opt them. When a group invites new members whose presence neutralizes a special interest, such as that of residents of a housing project, the purpose really may be to prevent or forestall resistance rather than to have new members share in decision-making processes. Members may also abuse contracts by violating general standards of moral conduct or personal behavior.

When and why are contracts terminated? A natural termination occurs when the outcomes or goals have been achieved. When a work group has finished its assignment, its life is completed, unless there is agreement on other work for it to do. Other reasons for termination occur when members are either recalled by the organizations they represent or leave for personal reasons. These possibilities mean that the issue of commitment needs to be examined early in the group's life. Contracts can be terminated because there has been a gross violation of personal or organizational values or authority to the extent that one or more members cannot continue to be part of a group. Groups may also disband because they couldn't achieve their purposes. For example, a committee appointed to bring about an organizational merger may find itself unable to do so. Finally, a listless and apathetic group may, as a last resort, need to be helped to disband.

GROUP EXAMPLES

We turn next to summary descriptions of five diverse working groups. These examples will be designated as A, B, C, D, and E. They provide an overview of some of the diversities and similarities among different kinds of working groups. Throughout the book, we shall refer to these illustrations in order to clarify points and raise questions for further thought. Each example contains many elements drawn from the experiences of the writers, their students, and others with whom we have come in contact. Each example, however, is a fictional composite, and therefore none should be read as a description of an actual group or of a particular, extant organization.

EXAMPLE A: THE MAYOR'S TASK FORCE ON HEALTH AND HUMAN SERVICES FOR THE FRAIL ELDERLY

Stimulated both by public pressures arising out of a metropolitan newspaper's series of exposés on the frail elderly as crime victims and by a series of memoranda from the city's commissioner on health, the mayor of a large metropolitan Midwestern city has appointed the Task Force on Services to the Frail Elderly. The formation of this task force was announced at a well-publicized press conference attended by some forty public officials as well as by representatives of various church and civic groups, social welfare agencies, several leading elderly citizens, clergy of all faiths, and the chiefs of geriatric medicine at all three of the largest hospitals in the city. In his executive order establishing the task force, the mayor stated that its charge was to survey existing services for the frail elderly, to identify gaps in available services, and to develop and present a plan for coordinating both existing and new services so that no older resident of the city need live either in fear or in want of help. The task force has been given a year to prepare and present both its report and its plan. The office of the mayor has made a budget available, and staff services will be provided by a staff member on loan from the City Planning Department, Mary Ann O'Brian. The mayor has appointed as chair of the task force Dr. J. J. Wiley, retired president of the local branch of the state university, a man noted for his devotion to the needs of older persons throughout his lengthy educational career. In an editorial generally commending the mayor for establishing the task force, the largest metropolitan newspaper noted, somewhat acerbically, that it was to be hoped that it would be given the independence from political pressures necessary for it to accomplish its job within the allotted time and with due regard for all the city's elderly citizens.

Among the major issues to consider about example A are:

1. To what extent will the task force of twenty-two persons develop into a working group in any real sense? Is it intended to do so? Is there any real independence vested in the staff member who is supposed to take orders from the mayor's office?
2. Are there limits or biases that arise from the method by which group members have been selected? If so, do they operate to constrain the recommendations the task force may make?
3. What are the motivations of task force members in accepting appointment? How will their motivations affect the group's life and the group's product?
4. Will the consumer representation be real and effective?
5. What does the budgetary allocation mean for the task force and its work?

EXAMPLE B: THE AVON FRIENDLY SOCIETY BOARD OF DIRECTORS

The Friendly Society, established in 1841, is a nonsectarian family service agency that serves the city of Avon and its surrounding suburbs. The society is governed by a board of directors, which has traditionally included younger members of the first families of the community. In fact, after holding office on the board of directors of this agency, many past officers have gone on to become prominent on the boards of the United Way and other social, religious, and civic organizations in the metropolitan area. Some have referred to the board of directors as a training ground for civic leadership in metropolitan Avon. Over the past twenty years, both public and private pressures have been brought to bear in order to democratize the board of directors and to provide for representation on it from the growing minority communities, as well as from present and past consumers. There has also been some pressure, more sporadic in nature, to provide for consumer representation, that is, for representatives of the populations that use the agency's services to be seated on the board. The president of the board has been elected, each year, by passing a motion, usually prepared in advance, instructing the secretary at the annual meeting to recorded a unanimous ballot for the single slate proposed by the nominating committee. The current incumbent is a young, up-and-coming, African-American businessman, who is the first person of minority racial or ethnic background to be president of this board. The agency is faced with a serious financial squeeze, as are all voluntary agencies in metropolitan Avon, since the money raised by voluntary philanthropic drives in the area has not kept pace with the burgeoning demands for service experienced by the various agencies. Traditionally, the board of directors has conducted much of its work through committees that meet at lunch in various downtown and suburban locations. Board meetings have been largely pro forma and have consisted of ratifications of recommendations from the various committees. One controversial issue facing the agency is the extent to which it should become involved with refugee resettlement in the metropolitan area. The executive director, a social worker, is Jennings Bancroft. Mr. Bancroft is completing his twentieth year in this position.

Some issues raised by example B are:

1. The agency is an integral part of the city, and board membership has played a part in the careers of many prominent and wealthy Avonians. What do these facts mean for the way the board and its subunits operate, should operate, and will operate in the future?
2. How may the changes that have arisen as a result of sociopolitical trends in the broader society translate themselves into the interpersonal and group life of the board?
3. At both the value and practical day-to-day levels, how will the agency deal with the pressures for expansion or change of its function and services? What will happen to staff? What role ought Mr. Bancroft to take, and how should he operationalize this role in behavioral terms?
4. What is/ought/will be the executive director's role in influencing board composition?
5. Ought the board be doing strategic planning for resource development over the next five to ten years?

Example C: Mount Williams Community Hospital

The Mount Williams Community Hospital chiefs of service meet every Tuesday morning from 8:00 to 10:00 A.M. Present at these meetings are the nine chiefs of the various medical departments—internal medicine, surgery, pediatrics, psychiatry, orthopedics, obstetrics and gynecology, geriatric medicine, family practice, and ophthalmology—and the heads of the departments of nursing, social work, clinical psychology, and occupational and adjunctive therapies. Also present at these meetings are the hospital's director of security and the chief of the buildings and grounds department. Finally, the meeting always includes the hospital administrator and, occasionally, the hospital's development officer. The Mount Williams Hospital is a large metropolitan establishment, accredited for 845 beds. It has teaching affiliations with two of the medical schools located in the metropolitan area and serves as a training site for students of medicine, nursing, social work, occupational therapy, physical therapy, dentistry, clinical psychology, and health care administration. The meetings are chaired by the annually elected president of the group. This year, for the first time, that position is held by a woman, Dr. Jane Dudley, chief of the department of psychiatry. A good part of each meeting has been devoted, traditionally, to announcements by each of the participants. Although these announcements have been deprecatingly referred to, at times, as show-and-tell, many participants have said that this is the only chance anyone gets to find out what is going on in departments other than one's own. Periodically, the group of chiefs has requested earlier involvement in the budgeting process of the hospital, but this never became a reality until the current year, when, under increased pressure from a variety of sources, a series of informational sessions on the hospital's financial situation has been scheduled. Representatives of both public and private participants in paying for medical care will be taking part in these meetings.

The current membership of the group is as follows:

Chief of Internal Medicine: Charles Swain, M.D., formerly head of internal medicine at Smallville Hospital, age forty-three, is the author of *Swain's Principles of Internal Medicine* and a famed yachtsman. His scholarly interests result in a constant outpouring of articles in professional journals.

Chief of Surgery: William Lord, M.D., was "Physician of the Year" in Mount Williams after a local TV station ran a three-hour special on an innovative surgical technique he had developed. A persistent rumor within the hospital is that the technique was really developed by one of his assistants. He is fifty-seven years old, tall, distinguished looking, and related by marriage to the governor of the state.

Chief of Pediatrics: Jorge Guttierez, M.D., is in his first year in this position. He spent the previous ten years at a highly regarded community hospital located in a depressed and deprived area. He is forty-five.

Chief of Psychiatry: Jane Dudley, age fifty-five, born and brought up in Mount Williams and a member of the psychiatry department staff for twenty-three years, was one of nine female members of her medical school class at Princemouth. She is widely respected for her abilities to keep things on an even keel and deal with conflicts and tensions.

Chief of Orthopedics: Leon Marony, M.D., age sixty-six, is the senior member of the hospital's staff in point of service. He built his staff from scratch and has served three terms as chair of the chiefs of service group.

Chief of Ob/Gyn: Eliza McCracken, M.D., is a sixty-year-old Canadian who has authored a textbook entitled *Medical Practice: A Woman's View.* She is an active contributor to organizations that promote improved health care delivery for women.

Chief of Family Practice: Bradford Palmer, M.D., forty-four, is still remembered for his outstanding athletic exploits as a high school and college three-sport athlete. He went to medical school in preference to a proffered, lucrative professional baseball career. As a young faculty member at the State University Medical School, he was a strong advocate of the concept of family practice, and he is the first chair of that department, established at the hospital ten years before.

Chief of Geriatric Medicine: Daniel Wong, M.D., M.P.H., a native of Hawaii, heads this newest medical department at the hospital. Its establishment was for several years a favorite project of the dean, himself an internationally prominent geriatrician.

Chief of Ophthalmology: Dr. Horst Schmidt, age forty-two, is an ambitious department head in his second year. Brilliant and acerbic, he has embarked on a program to market his hospital's ophthalmology services to various state and county institutions. On his desk is an award entitled "Only the Best."

Head of Nursing: Heather Tomlinson, R.N., M.S.N., age fifty, is the first African American chief of nursing services. Her driving ambition is to expand the hospital's affiliation with the local university's school of nursing. She is highly respected for her budgetary sophistication.

Head of Social Work: James Myers, D.S.W., forty-nine years old, is one of two males and three African Americans among the hospital's sixteen social workers. The search committee that recommended his appointment five years before thought it important that the chief of social work hold a doctorate and interact as an equal with the other chairs.

Head of Clinical Psychology: Dr. Frank Berger, age thirty-seven, is noted for his informal manner and particular interest in adolescent patients. His favorite compliment is to call a program "innovative."

Head of Occupational and Adjunctive Therapies: Norma Nelson, M.S., OTR, age forty-six, directs the work of seventeen occupational therapists, audiologists, speech pathologists, and recreational therapists. She is a widely known local artist and benefactor of social welfare/philanthropic causes.

Director of Security: Hugh Delaney, age sixty-two, retired five years before from the Mount Williams Police Department, with the rank of lieutenant of detectives, to assume his current position. He directs a staff of thirty security employees and regales them with stories of his eleven beloved grandchildren.

Chief of Building and Grounds: William Sobranski, age fifty-eight, director of plant operations, is a retired navy warrant officer. His entire adult life has been spent working in hospitals, both in the service and as a civilian.

Hospital Administrator: Nick Dellajoio, M.B.A., M.H.S., age forty-three, has been administrator of the hospital for ten years, the period that it has taken the hospital to occupy its new buildings. He introduced to the hospital a computerized system of budget control and cost accounting.

Development Officer: T. Linda Hill was director of a highly successful fundraising campaign for the Mount Williams Art Museum. At age thirty-seven, she is in her third year in her current position. She reports directly to the hospital administrator.

Among the issues raised by example C are:

1. What are the latent and manifest purposes of the group? Why do members attend?
2. Group members have different backgrounds, statuses, and functions within the organization. How do these affect group life?
3. Does the hospital administrator function as staff or as executive of the group? Why (or why not)?
4. To what extent, if any, do differences in age, racial/ethnic origin, sex, or personal/family background affect what goes on in this group? Should they?
5. How does the history of this group affect its present, given that some members have been part of the group for many years and others have not?
6. How much of what goes on in this group may be expected to be setting specific, that is, a result of the fact that it is a group of chiefs of service and department heads of a hospital?

EXAMPLE D: THE LONG-RANGE PLANNING COMMITTEE OF THE JEWISH FEDERATION OF METROPOLITAN AVON

The board of directors of the Jewish Federation of Metropolitan Avon is composed of thirty members who, under the organization's bylaws, serve two-year terms. Each member can serve one additional two-year term but must then not be a member of the board for a two-year period. The full board meets monthly, except for August, in a luncheon format. A detailed agenda is distributed to members by mail in advance, as is an extensive monthly packet of committee reports and recommendations and other materials deemed relevant by either senior staff or the executive committee. The federation conducts an extensive and well-organized campaign that seeks to raise, annually, a sizable amount of money to support Jewish social welfare activities overseas and a network of local Jewish human services, social welfare, and educational agencies in the metropolitan Avon community. In addition, it allocates small amounts of money to support national Jewish organizations and multisectarian local and state social welfare causes. For the current campaign, the goal has been set at $9.7 million. The professional staff of the federation includes a total of twelve employees. The major work of the federation is carried on through a network of standing and ad hoc committees.

A well-established staff-and-committee structure has developed over the last decade in this highly regarded, medium-sized federation. In recent years, there has been a growing sense, both in the professional literature and in the informal discussions within the federation, that the younger people—in many cases, the children of old, established families, previously themselves major donors to the federation—now take a different view of their role. They are concerned with having personal impact on particular projects, having a voice in how their donations are to be used, and examining and influencing the trends of use of philanthropic money throughout the community and the world.

In the face of greatly increased needs, collections through established groups, including the federation, have remained relatively flat while there has been a tremendous growth in the development of family foundations, largely governed by these younger members of traditional philanthropic families. Donors have been less willing to adopt an overall view of the traditional philanthropic responsibilities of organizations such as the federation and more concerned with particular activities.

The Long-Range Planning Committee is composed of the board's chair and three vice-chairs, the chairs of the boards of four constituent agencies who are major recipients of funds for local services, the immediate past chair of the federation's board, and two lay members of the community, each of whom is a professor at a local university. It is staffed by the vice president for planning and budgeting; meetings are usually attended by the CEO (president) as well. Its charge is to develop a listing of priorities for funding local services for the federation over the next five to ten years. This listing is to be based on an assessment of the service needs of the metropolitan Jewish community over the next decade. In addition to telephone calls from the board's president inquiring about prospective members' willingness to serve, formal letters were sent to the members, pointing out both the intensive work to be required of the committee and its importance for the future of the organization and the community.

Among example D's illustrative issues are:

1. How may this group's dynamics be affected by the many and long-standing interrelationships among various members of the committee, some of them going back several decades?
2. What are the variables that may affect the role behaviors of the highly skilled, professional staff members in this group?
3. How do values, visions, and views of the future act as data for such a planning group? What happens if these come into conflict with real data, such as demographic developments?
4. How, if at all, will the life processes and patterns of the LRPC be affected by the sectarian nature of the sponsoring organization and its goals?

EXAMPLE E: THE WINTERSET ADVISORY COMMITTEE

The committee is composed of five members of the board of the local neighborhood center (the Neighborhood House) and five residents of the Winterset Housing Project. The committee was formed in order to provide a channel of communication between the agency, whose board was instrumental in getting the project built and in maintaining adequate budgeting for it, and the community, which is largely made up of lower-income black and Hispanic residents, including a large proportion of aged individuals and couples. The Neighborhood House was originally skeptical about the need for such a committee, but gradually and grudgingly it came to accept that some sort of mechanism was needed. The reasons for the changed perception included increasing signs of tension and alienation between the housing project's residents and the board, staff, and spokespersons for the Neighborhood House, who were supposed to act and operate in the interests of all. Members of the advisory committee on the residents' side were elected in a rather heavily publicized election held as part of the annual housing project fair. Members of the committee from the Neighborhood House were selected by the executive committee of the board of directors at two meetings attended by the executive director and the advisory council of past board presidents. Members of the committee as finally constituted were:

Board Members	Residents
John Throckmorton	Betty Judge
Elizabeth Frothingham	Virginia Lopez
William McDevitt	Enrique Mantilla
Jonathan Mifflin	Lincoln Ellis
Wilhelmina Loring	Althea Smith

Issues to be considered regarding example E include:

1. Can a group whose membership is divided into sub-populations of diverse social backgrounds form as a group? How? With what kinds of help?
2. To what extent can a group engage in problem solving if it does not control its own resources?
3. Can such a group agree on the nature of problems or the nature of possible solutions to them?

These five examples do not, of course, exhaust the great range of types of working groups. They do, however, give an indication of the diversity of compositions, purposes, structures, and responsibilities that characterizes such groups. The group in example A, the Mayor's Task Force, is an ad hoc body, with a specific charge that comes from the mayor, a specific time frame, and a product—a report and program design—that it is to produce. Example B's group, the board of the Avon Friendly Society, is a voluntary, fiduciary group with an elaborated structure of governance and legal, as well as moral responsibilities. The staff chiefs and department heads of the Mount Williams Hospital form an administrative group that has clear governance responsibilities relative to the services provided by the professional staff of the hospital and to the mission of the hospital itself. The authority of the members derives from their respective professional competencies and responsibilities within the organization. The group in example D, the Long-Range Planning Committee of the Jewish Federation, is an organ of the board of directors. The board is charged by the bylaws of the organization with serving a function of stewardship, and the Long-Range Planning Committee is a subunit of that body, created for the purpose of fulfilling one of the board's overall functions. The Winterset Advisory Committee of example E is characteristic of a large number of working groups whose functions are advisory. Such groups often have as their major tasks interorganizational linkage and communication. How they resolve the issues inherent in being advisory rather than having specific powers included in their charge is one of the interesting aspects of their life courses.

Each of these groups is quite different from the others. What goes on in each is affected by its specific setting, composition, charge, time frame, and organizational location. In addition, prevailing societal trends, issues, and modes affect the meaning that membership in each group has for its participants. For example, the Winterset Advisory Committee may take on one meaning if it comes into being during a period of high social tension and quite another meaning if it comes into existence during a period of relatively low tension among groups, age cohorts, or ethnic communities. The differences among the examples are important. Participation in such groups, whether as staff, chair, or member, without attention to the specifics and uniqueness of each group would severely limit a member's ability to influence in a meaningful way what goes on there. On the other hand, each of these groups also shares certain characteristics, processes, and developmental problems with the others. Tracing these similarities, as well as the uniqueness, is the task of the chapters that follow. First, however, it may be helpful to step back and develop a model of some of the conceptual parameters that we think can be helpful in understanding the processes of all working groups. The similarities are abstractions that are useful in understanding the processes of specific groups. Specific groups do not experience themselves as abstractions, however, but as ongoing realities with significance and salience both for their members and for the organizations of which they are part.

3

TOWARD A MODEL OF WORKING GROUPS

I N THIS CHAPTER, we shall attempt to approach a model of working groups from two perspectives. First, we will present individual concepts that we think form part of our model of working groups. We shall discuss fourteen concepts, sometimes individually and sometimes in pairs in developing a model. We shall then develop some ideas regarding the group as a whole and ways of thinking about this extraordinary phenomenon that we call a group.

We propose that the following conceptual features, each linked to the nature of group life, need to be taken into account for the purposes of guiding assessment and practice.[1] Together, the concepts to be discussed form a framework through which the lives of groups can be analyzed and understood.

TEMPORARY/PERMANENT SYSTEMS

Time-limited, temporary groups can bring about conditions of trust, experimentation, novelty, and productivity. For short periods of time, members may take more chances and put up with more discomforts than they might in a long-term group (Miles, 1964). They may also work harder. Mechanisms can develop within a temporary group to prevent individuals' needs from blocking the accomplishment of the group's task. Various members may take on the responsibility of reminding the group of a deadline that it may face or of other constraints. A temporary group is likely to be concerned with maintaining its boundaries. Members of temporary groups can often examine the emotional, personal, interpersonal, and social sources that motivate participation patterns without getting too deeply invested in such analyses. The extent to which a group is perceived by its members as time limited, separate from their "real" lives, needs to be taken into account in understanding its processes.

A relatively long-term group poses a different set of circumstances. Belonging to a long-term group encourages many members to invest themselves in a major way in their membership. All other things being equal, the more permanent a group is, the more likely it is that what happens in it will be important to each member. The first concept to be applied in understanding the life of a group is the time frame within which the group is operating.

In example B, the board of the Friendly Society of Avon represents a group where membership continues for a long time. In fact, members of some Avon families have been board members for generations. By way of contrast, in example A, the Mayor's Task Force is scheduled to exist for only a year and has not yet begun its work. For both examples, subcommittees are likely to be formed, and the clarity of goals and time limitations present dynamics that can be useful in arriving at decisions.

STRUCTURE AND PROCESS

"Structure" and "process" refer respectively to the stable and emerging characteristics that form the identities of groups. Ongoing group processes such as opinion and information exchange, social comparisons, direct and vicarious social reinforcement, decision making, and support generate more stable patterns such as roles, norms, subgroups, affectional ties, and patterns of conflict management. We view these stable patterns as structural properties, since they change relatively little over time. Structure and process can be viewed as two complementary aspects of the same realities of group life. Process refers to those aspects that change from minute to minute or even from second to second within a group. The distinction between the two concepts is useful because worker interventions differ at both levels. Altering seating patterns is a structural concept. Supporting a member's point of view in the immediate discussion is a process concept.

What connects processes to structure is the patterning of group behavior. Patterns are segments of behavior that can be observed and described, repeat themselves over time, and can be classified for purposes of analysis and theory building. For example, one member may consistently defer to the suggestions of another. When this pattern of behavior has shown itself several times, the relationship between the two can be considered as a part of the structure of the group. The interaction between the two is also part of the communication processes of the group. Were one concerned with analyzing the behavior of an individual only, one might describe the behavior of the deferential member as dependent. In a group perspective, what is important is that the structure of the group contains a dyadic subgroup. This is to be viewed as a superior-subordinate relationship responsive to a group issue or dynamic rather than as a personality factor.

> In example E, Betty Judge developed in the Winterset Advisory Committee a pattern of deferring consistently to John Throckmorton. Ms. Judge is a new member of the committee, while Mr. Throckmorton has been a member of the board for ten years. Once this pattern of behavior was established, the dyadic interaction between Ms. Judge and Mr. Throckmorton became part of the structure of the group and needed to be taken into account both for group analysis and for planning staff participation in the group, especially in the context of an agency in the middle of dealing with a housing project in transition and representing diverse constituencies.

Public and Private Sentiments

Giving opinions, suggesting ideas, seeking cooperation, making plans, and responding to the ideas and feelings of others together constitute a good deal of the processes of groups. These activities are sometimes lumped together under the rubric "discussion." Publicly expressed communications in groups, both verbal and nonverbal, often subsume other, more private feelings and ideas. This private content may be consciously withheld or may be nonrational and habitual in nature. A member's private content may also stem from deeply rooted sentiments that are potent underlying determinants of behavior of which both staff and member are unaware (Goleman, 2000). Persistent and stubborn patterns of feeling in groups may be helpful or debilitating to the group as a whole, depending on their perceived relevance to the group's tasks and their acceptance or rejection by various members of the group. Both public and private sentiments in various combinations, held by group members and/or by the group as a whole, are sources for actions that become group products. The temporary or permanent nature of a group may have a good deal to do with an individual member's willingness to expose private feelings or desire to conceal them.

> In example D, the members of the Long-Range Planning Committee differ considerably with regard to the extent to which their roles within the Jewish community are salient aspects of their personal and social identities.

One member of the committee, Mr. Snyder, is the son of a Holocaust survivor. He feels issues regarding the future of the Jewish community with extraordinary depth. He thinks that the other members of the committee understand why he gets so emotional about certain issues but is not sure that he wants to stimulate an open discussion of his private sentiments for the whole committee to participate in.

BONDING

Bonding refers to attachments and alliances made between and among members in groups. In our view, three different types of bonds can be identified. They vary in strength, direction (symmetrical or asymmetrical), duration, and effects on participants. All three can be lost and recaptured over and over again in the life of a group, and a member's option to participate in one or more, singly or in combination, is greatest when the group is mature and a democratic microcosm (see below) is in full operation.[2]

A "simple" bond is one in which there is informational exchange between two or more group members.[3] Member A wants information, and member B supplies it. This exchange of information can occur more than once and with more than one person.

A more complex bond, which we call "covalent," involves the exchange of more than one item of information, with both parties being affected by the exchange. There is a measure of reciprocity in such an exchange that implies an investment in sharing in a common, valued outcome. An example is an exchange of support for an idea or proposal, one idea building on someone else's input. Coalitions within groups are other examples of covalent bonds. An experience may be provided by member C that is accepted, tried, and found useful by members D and E. This process is akin to what Schwartz (1976) and many others have called "mutual aid."

We call the third type of bond "coordinate covalent." This bond, which may or may not arise from one of the first: two types, involves a transformation of behavior in the two or more parties involved in the transaction. Coordinate covalent bonding may include the alteration of role behaviors on the part of all participants or an alteration in the behavior of one participant followed by an altered response or perception in another. There is a characteristic of reflection or contemplative meditation involved in this type of bonding that is similar to what has been called "double loop learning" (Argyris and Schon, 1974). In this type of bonding, the rules and norms of behaviors are open for reevaluation and transformation. It is therefore particularly suited for democratic microcosms (see below),

Molar/Molecular Characteristics

The molar/molecular concept refers to whole/part relationships, such as that of the group to the member, the subgroup to a person, and the group as a whole to the subgroups. Parts and wholes are complementary entities that are constantly in motion in the course of a group's life, sometimes opposed and at other times in harmony. In order to capture the rich texture of group events, one must understand these part/whole relationships. In essence, person and group are conceptually distinct but phenomenologically interactive elements. In a sense, a staff person is always working with individuals, subgroups, and the group as a whole and must pay attention to all three, as well as to the relationship of the group to other parts of the organization. In other contexts, the term "two-client" system is used to describe these two entities (Shulman, 2001).

Group climates that favor expressive participation may be comfortable for gregarious members and threatening for more meditative or quiet members.

In example C, in the Mount Williams Community Hospital chiefs of service group, the physicians who lead medical departments tend to form a subgroup as well as being participants in the group as a whole. The chiefs of medical departments sit together on one side of the table and direct the majority of their comments to each other, except when crises that affect the entire hospital are being discussed. Dr. Dudley, the chair, has observed that while everyone in the group cares about what the entire group thinks, the opinions of the other medical department heads are particularly important to the physicians in this group. In this example, then, a group climate that favors self-expression is useful for the chiefs of medical departments but not for others, whose private sentiments may be on hold.

In example D, were Mr. Snyder to express his private sentiments, the rest of the group would allow him space and time to do so. One way of understanding this is that Mr. Snyder's personal sentiments and experience constitute a molecular (or person's) part of the group as a whole, regardless of the group's stated purpose at a given meeting. In a sense, the group members who would allow Mr. Snyder "air time" are colluding with him to distort the group's purpose temporarily, for personal motives. Here, a sub-group is exercising membership rights and opportunities within its scope to open a path for a quiet member supportive of its cause.

LEADERSHIP

There are many views of leadership. In general, leadership is a representational concept in that certain members at particular times take on responsibilities that transcend their own personal views or needs. For example, in staff board groups, three simultaneous leadership functions may become evident. Partic-ular board members may represent salient publics in the community, staff members may espouse consumer (client) interests, and the executive may be committed to harnessing both kinds of leadership to the agency's mission. Leadership refers both to major influences within a working group and to influences that a working group may exercise within an organization.

In example B, the executive director of the Avon Friendly Society exer-cises a consistent leadership function within the group by representing the changed needs and desires of the client population. In this way, he acquired legitimacy as a leader because of his representative function. His leadership transcends the competing groups within the board that contend for the ability to determine the agency's direction.

WORK

Work in a group has two components: accomplishing tasks and satisfying members' needs. Work in a group is characterized by expressions of ambiva-lence, trial and error, suggestions, and floundering. Ultimately, the group needs to synthesize disparate elements into an acceptable product or action. Work includes both dependability and uncertainty, consistency and change. Both sets of forces are present in the group's work. Mutually agreed–upon boundaries and shared sentiments keep a group going, enhance communica-tion, and increase the flow and exchange of ideas and feelings. These processes, in turn, produce more differences and occasional retreats into safer and more secure grounds. Groups work by taking some steps forward and some steps backward. Their progress is not linear. The dialectic between change and stability is a permanent force in group dynamics.

In a group, what originally seem to be irreconcilable differences are transformed into subjects for group discussion and decision making. Groups need to develop a commitment to directing their energies toward solving a problem or completing a task. Work includes conscious, deliberate goal seeking and implementation of the group's charge. This rational aspect of work may include routine, stable approaches as well as creative problem solving.

> In example E, the third meeting of the Winterset Advisory Committee was stalled on the question of services to home-bound elderly persons. One part of the group thought that such services were very important. The other was afraid that the entire housing project would get a reputation as a halfway house for frail old people. One group member suggested that perhaps one floor of one of the buildings could be set aside for such residents. This suggestion seemed to have the effect of liberating the group from paralysis. The group moved ahead to suggest some creative ways in which the administration of the project could implement such a plan for a special floor.

In this example, the creative solution may be viewed as the ability to move from polarities (either/or) to paradoxes to be solved. This is an important function incorporated in the maturing process of groups.

LEARNING

Group members learn information and skills in order to accomplish the work of the group. Educational processes in groups may take the form of personal or group insight gained by changing options or feelings or by learning particular information or organizing skills. An example of the last would be the process of learning associated with particular group status such as secretary, treasurer, or chair.

Learning can be vicarious. While one member may be learning how to perform a certain job within the group, the group as a whole is also participating in that learning. Such learning may be very important for the group as a whole as well as for individual members. Group members can learn skills and knowledge that they internalize and then carry into other groups and other aspects of their lives. This kind of learning involves the concept of transfer of learning; viewing the group as a learning laboratory is one of the ways of underscoring the importance of the group as a setting for educational experiences. Learning by doing in groups is a progressive and generative act that operates in two ways: learning to apply a skill to a greater variety of tasks and enhancing the skill so that more complex tasks can be handled with greater ease.

> In example A, Dr. Wiley, as chair of the Mayor's Task Force, will preside over testimony presented by a great variety of people. The task force will generate many written reports and other documents. In effect, Dr. Wiley, together with each member of the task force who participates, will be taking the equivalent of an advanced academic course in the problems, service needs, and demographic characteristics of the frail elderly in the city. This learning is essential for the task force to complete its task. One outcome for the group will be that each member individually will be much better informed than he or she was initially about the problems of the frail elderly. This knowledge will be carried into other groups and other aspects of the members' lives.

DEVELOPMENT

Development implies stages and continuity, beginning and end points. Stages in groups are identifiable aspects of structures and processes that occur at different points along the arc of group development.

In our view, stages in groups take place in two ways. They occur sequentially over time (Garland, Jones, and Kolodny, 1965), or group development can be cyclical. Issues are not resolved for all time at one stage but may well reappear, sometimes in slightly altered form, throughout the life of a group (Balgopal and Vassil, 1983). In other words, stages of group development do not simply take place along a linear continuum, and neither do they recur in random fashion. Stages are maps but not compasses. In addition, subphases may be evident within each of the major phases.

Beginning practitioners with groups sometimes have difficulty discerning group progress. One reason may be that phases of group development are complex. The recurrence of a theme or subphase can easily make a staff person jump to the erroneous conclusion that the group has not made progress, when in fact it is simply consolidating or reworking an issue incompletely addressed previously. It is often useful to allow and help a group to rework a theme rather than to block such reconsideration because the group has been there before. Stages of group development are concepts for group analysis because the concept of stages organizes seemingly disparate events. There is a danger, however, in applying the concept of stages too literally. Doing so can lead to "cookie cutter" perceptions of categories. Stages of group development do not exist in pure forms except for the purposes of analysis and planning.

Furthermore, in many working groups, the first meeting begins a new group only in a manner of speaking. Various group members may be related to each other, have worked together in other groups, gone to school together, or served on boards and commissions together. Most often, a first meeting of a working group is a blending of the old and the new, and thus the process of group formation is uneven. It sometimes happens that a group is able to form more quickly than it would otherwise because of past inter-relationships among the members. This can be a blessing or a curse. Past rela-tionships can be powerfully initiating, or they can be frozen into unresolved conflicts.

At the ninth meeting of the Mount Williams Hospital group of example C, Dr. Dudley became quite irritated with the group's unwillingness to consider changing certain procedures. She suggested, with some anger, that perhaps the group would do better with someone else chairing. This led to a ten-minute discussion of why the group meets weekly in the first place. The group's decision was that Dr. Dudley should continue as chair, but she felt, as she reported to the group, that the air had been cleared and that the group might be ready to consider changing some of the hospital proce-dures in the future. The next two meetings were characterized by a high level of politeness among the members of the group.

THE ORGANIZATIONAL SETTING

Both formal and informal groups in an organization behave differently toward each other and the organization, depending on the missions, goals, size, climate, and auspices of the organization. Small organizations, for exam-ple, are more likely to be informal and open than are large, bureaucratic sys-tems. Small organizations, however, may exist in an atmosphere of uncer-tainty. Large, formal organizations are more predictable and secure, in many ways, for groups within them. Organizations whose technology is relatively routine may provide different climates for working groups than organizations that value creativity and innovation in the services they provide. Organiza-tional characteristics can affect group tasks, composition, boundaries, and innovative possibilities. In addition, organizations vary in the extent to which they value consistency or change within their spheres of interest.

In examples B and E, the Friendly Society of Avon and the Winterset Advisory Committee both function within relatively small organizations. Example C's Mount Williams Community Hospital group is in a large, bureaucratic organization. Each of these organizations will generate different and salient influences and expectations between and among their constituent members.

GROUP TASKS

The specific tasks of a group connect it to its organizational setting. Tasks generate their own requirements for structure and process. Tightly structured agendas require more formality than do meetings that are more loosely structured. Each group task elicits different kinds, numbers, and configurations of member behaviors. Viewed broadly, work in a group can be thought of as a series of clusters of specific activities. Groups that exist over a long period of time often have short-term, intermediate, and long-term objectives. Ad hoc committees will organize themselves differently, depending on their specific tasks.

In example D, the Long-Range Planning Committee came to the conclusion that two particular service areas should be priorities for the federation over the next decade. In order to test this conclusion and to develop a specific plan of action, a subcommittees was appointed for each of the priorities that had been identified. In each subcommittee, members who had been relatively inactive in the larger group assumed leadership roles because of their expertise in the particular service area being discussed. For example, one relatively inactive member of the overall committee was both active and assertive in his participation in the subcommittee on services to the aging. The nature of the task had affected the structure and process of the subcommittee, if not the group as a whole.

THE DEMOCRATIC MICROCOSM

The term "democratic microcosm" attempts to convey the essence of a complete working group, one that is self-regulating and operates under the principle of responsible autonomy. A self-governing group is abundantly able to generate the means and set the limits for its own changes. The group sets its own limits, as well as the processes and methods by which the group can change. There are frequent and open considerations and tradeoffs among the group's personal, interpersonal, organizational, and environmental goals. In order to lead democratic microcosms effectively, the staff needs to sense perceptual and nuanced shifts and influences among these goals in order to anticipate potential crises or to support subtle changes (Weick, 1995).

Self-government in a group means that there is a balance and continuity between legitimated authority, operating within established channels, on the one hand, and spontaneous expressiveness and creative change, on the other. One of the characteristics of a stable, democratic group is that change is not viewed as a threat to the continued existence of the group and therefore proposals for change need not be met with defensiveness. A complete working group capitalizes on controversy and can manufacture the necessary roles to deal with it.

One of the hallmarks of a democratic microcosm is that group members can operate fully and well participating in decisions, contributing to task completion, and dealing with conflict in the group. The establishment of a democratic microcosm is not a luxury to be enjoyed when the group has accomplished its other tasks. Rather, it is often a necessity if a group is to fulfill its charge, and it needs to be supported and exercised in each and every meeting. The culture of a democratic microcosm emphasizes productivity and provides an important linkage with the broader values, ethics, and social goals of the health and social professions.

GROUP COMPOSITION

Group composition is always important. It does not, however, determine exactly what takes place in a group, though it can provide useful guidelines. Because there is a certain consistency over time in how people behave, group composition relates to many of the concepts that have been sketched above. For example, the nature of a group's task and its charge have clear implications for who should be a member of the group. The organizational setting and climate within which a working group operates also affect who should be a member.

There are as many variables to consider in group composition as there are characteristics of human beings. Knowing which variables are important in composing a particular group is a legitimate, professional responsibility. Staff members usually participate in decisions about group composition but may not be able to exercise a veto. Staff should be concerned with who will be a group member and should be comfortable with the idea that their opinions are one of many influences on that decision.

One principle that has stood up well in practice over many years is the "Law of Optimum Distance" (Redl, 1942; supported by Bales, 1983). This law states that it is not a good idea to have just one of anything in a group if that can be avoided. The single member who has a particular characteristic is uniquely situated to be scapegoated, on the one hand, or treated as a token, on the other. It is better to have two members who share any characteristic that is of concern.

Two variables have been highlighted by recent social history: sex and racial/ethnic background. Each of these has been discussed in depth elsewhere as it applies to groups in general (Davis, 1984; Reed and Garvin, 1983). The number of variables to consider in composing an effective working group is so great that one should avoid being too sure or too rigid in approaching questions of gender and racial/ethnic balance. The nature of the group, its task, its setting, the work that will take place within it, the learning expected, and the time frame are some of the other variables that should be taken into account in composing a group.

GROUP CITIZENSHIP AND MEMBERSHIP

Participation in a working group implies members who have been educated, or can be educated, to certain standards of group citizenship. Civility and a commitment to shared values are both important. A working group member needs to be able to express opinions without risking safety and stability within the group. Some predictability of others' responses is essential for this. At the same time, group citizenship requires tolerance of unpredictability and openness to new ideas and new ways of doing things. The group equivalent of a Bill of Rights is essential in order for a group to operate in a productive way. For members' rights to be genuine, all group members need to be committed to them, as well as to the group itself and to the accomplishment of its tasks. This important aspect needs to be one of the key elements in developing a contract. It sets the stage for what is to follow. In other contexts, it has been called anticipatory socialization.

THE GROUP AS A WHOLE

The idea of group wholes or group culture is a key feature of the Bion tradition (Bion, 1961) regarding groups, in which he identified pairing, fight-flight, and dependence as capturing the patterns of unconscious processes in groups. These ideas have been extended and applied to work groups as well

(Stock and Thelen, 1958; Whitaker, 2001) and indeed apply to correlations between subgroups and work itself. The latter point is important because it provided an opportunity for the unconscious group-level processes conceptualized by Bion, drawn from his experiences leading therapy groups to rehabilitate psychologically wounded pilots during WWII, to be effective. These unconscious processes have been extended, applied, and developed into descriptive behaviors characterized as positive, negative, or neutral relating to the work aspect (Stock and Thelen, 1958).

The utility of Bion's concepts applied to individual behavior in small task groups is demonstrated in the examples that follow. The group-as-a-whole concept has been conceptualized as group cultures or ways of behavior, thinking, and feeling in a group, as the group's ethos. To consider a number of individuals as a group is to see them as a single entity for analytical purposes. Our view is that each and every member cannot be assumed to be thinking the same thing at the same time but rather can think and feel independently of the group, although as members they are both responsive to the group's emotional content and able to chart their own courses of feeling and thinking. Members may respond in very different ways to any single phenomenon, whether pairing, dependency, or fight-flight. The group-as-a-whole perspective provides us with order and wholeness out of chaos and fragmentation. We need forms and frames to contain it.

The problem of leadership is to contain within oneself simultaneous foci on the person(s) and the group as a whole. Pieces of oneself are scattered throughout the experience. Members can be drawn to or caught in a particular common theme but react to it individually or idiosyncratically. Consequently, the group leader has to integrate these dynamics of the individual and the dynamics of the group as a whole, together with the elements at both overt and covert levels stemming from various contexts (environment, agency, organization, etc.) in which the group finds itself.

To illustrate the concepts of group culture, we present four examples below. Each is related in an indirect way to the group-derived conceptualization based on variations in leadership style. These can be described as integrative, constrictive, labile, and unstable group cultures (Vassil, 1975).

Integrative Group Culture

In this kind of group, policies are a matter of group discussion and decision, encouraged by the leader's group centeredness; the members feel free to work with whom they choose; and the division of tasks is left up to the group. There are mutual warm feelings and encouragement among members, but this does not restrict them from disagreeing or challenging one another since the idea and practice of open and honest debate is accepted. In addition, members can lean on one another without the expectation that this behavior will retard the expression of individual ideas. Group organization is flexible to the particular demands of the task at hand and is unimpeded by group intimacy. Spontaneity and creativity—based on realistic goals—are accepted patterns of the operating culture.

The group is genuinely activated by member commitment, and members are in tune with their feelings and with each other's. Emotional and intellectual energy is directed and utilized so that it is part and parcel of and contributes to the accomplishment of the work task. A broad range of ideas is generated for problem solving, often accompanied by a high level of imagination. In turn, these are accompanied by an urge to implement group-acceptable ideas into realistic and realizable actions. In substance, satisfaction and understanding of the what and how of their work are more important than agreement for its own sake. A sense of continuity is present in that the group has learned from past mistakes and utilizes this as a resource to solve current problems. Given a lack of resources to solve current problems, the members are able to use the special experience of the leader to help in their problem resolution. The leader tries to be a regular group member in spirit while being careful not to obstruct the members' work and equally careful to perform his or her own specialized tasks. Final responsibility for decisions rests with group members.

In summary, the central governing features of the integrative group are a resonating admixture of the group's basic urges of work and emotions, based on reality, mutual respect, and clear goals.

Constrictive Group Culture

This group sticks obsessively to a work task accompanied by blunted and suppressed emotional sentiments. There is excessive concern with order and form, together with techniques and instructions geared to predetermined outcomes. Emotionality is disciplined or ruled out except for that which supports an operating group culture governed by an authoritative leader. Little differentiation is perceived among members with respect to arrival, task, and departure subgroupings.

The emotional containment produces tensions that find outlets in mechanisms such as rationalization, overintellectualization, displacement, and avoidance. Two group behavior patterns can be identified given this compelling situation. The first is passive, obedient, and compliant; members are secure in the feeling that all is taken care of. The second pattern includes episodic disaffections expressed by members in hostile and aggressive reactions turned against each other. Sometimes these become muted, transformed into humorous asides. These patterns operate against the cultural imperative of task completion and leader-enforced demands.

The leader's personalized praise and criticism of each member's efforts spurs a competitive work ethic that operates to enhance members' self-interests. Each member's finished product is graded and shaped by the leader's exclusive standards. This ritual equilibrium is exaggerated along a single dimension defined by the leader's cognitive, work-oriented perspective. Whatever informal relationships that do exist are fragmented and provide weak interruptions to routine, although they do serve to allay member anxiety and guilt. In this tightly run ship, recognition of original ideas is limited to single members rather than group sponsorship. In summary, the past, present, and future of this group type are inextricably interwoven with the leader's foreknowledge of events, dominated by the essential striving of work at the expense of emotions.

Labile Group Culture

In this group, the ego-concerned emotionalized impulses of group members dominate and disorganize the group's tendencies to cooperate in building a work ethic. The emotionalized expression is out of proportion to the task at hand, and, since the emotions receive full play, their effects are thrown into clear focus. Intellectual imagination may be high among members but lacks implementation into action. Commitment to action occurs when the idea of action provides emotional gratification, and this, in turn, is not systematized enough for reality testing. The worth of an idea, by itself, is generally obscured by its diffuse emotional referents and is consequently separated from action.

Member participation can be widespread, although a great deal of factionalism is present as well as multiple and diffuse goals. Members don't want to look at themselves since that is too anxiety provoking, as are worker intervention and participation. While positive feelings may be engendered among members, they pay little attention to each other's ideas. When a task is presented, each member has his or her own pet solution. Objective control of the activity is sadly lacking, and thus the activity becomes controlled by defensive responses.

The absence of both goal clarity and an internalized, generalized work ethic produces loose group organization with little attention to the interrelatedness of ideas. Attempts by the group to work on tasks result in members reverting to their impulsive, volatile ways since they are more prone to discharge than retain affect. Resources located in the leader are not used, if at all perceived, in this group culture, which exists moment by moment. The group situation is characterized by a sense of irresponsibility, aptly demonstrated in their play, joking, lack of focus, and emotional contagion. In summary, the group operates in a shifting, unstable, widely fluctuating and charged emotional context rooted in the gratification of the immediate.

Unstable Group Culture

This group climate involves a negative, fractured picture of unstable, fluctuating group leadership that alternates between attempts at rigid control and overzealous participation with group members. The members' responses appear to be characterized by dissension and disagreement, often expressed in callous and sarcastic disregard for one another. When they do settle down to routine, it appears to be more out of a need for relief from dominant and conflicted personalities. Breakdown in routine produces individual harassment and blame. The leader attempts to hold the group together by planning and initiating activity. In addition, he or she offers a good deal of personal encouragement and praise in an effort to get members to work together. Inevitably, recalcitrant members find something not to their liking and upset any plans that all the members could participate in together. The members seem incapable of laughing at themselves or joking around. Even this apparently requires more trust than they can spare, and they waste energy arguing, complaining, and demanding. What tasks are followed for any length of time are performed perfunctorily with few creative efforts by individual members. Angry and hostile, the members are unable to work together, unable to follow, and unable to trust one another. They are caught between unsteady group leadership and personal interest, and, except for transitory periods of obedience, both members and leader expend great amounts of energy fighting their time away. This is an unstable culture.[4]

The concept of group culture and the examples we use to illustrate its various forms help define and flesh out the cognitive shorthand group workers often use to describe group activity or way of life. To advance and refine practice, more deliberate and analytical tasks are required to pinpoint specific interventions to move a group, subgroup, or member along. Pregroup planning in the form of preliminary empathy (Schwartz, 1976) and postgroup debriefing and critical incident recording are essential for this task (Cohen and Smith, 1976). No preparatory plan should be set in cement, but one can depend on members (and group) tendencies to repeat, and for this reason preparation is useful.

4

THE DEMOCRATIC MICROCOSM

THE WORK OF MANY health and human service professionals can be divided into two parts. The first is the practice of the profession for which one has been trained, the rendering of services to patients, clients, or consumers. The second part involves leadership and participation in a variety of working groups, such as committees, councils, task forces, subcommittees, and the like. Many curricula of professional education do not emphasize fine work-group participation as a legitimate component of professional practice. Therefore, this work may feel less important than or ancillary to the so-called real work of the professional.

This bifurcation of work is unfortunate, in our view. Work carried on in groups is quite real and is part of the responsibility of everyone who practices in an organizational setting. Programs are planned, begun, or ended; budgets developed or not developed; and decisions made or reversed based on work done in groups. Furthermore, what goes on in groups can be understood and managed, though not always with precision. The study of working groups needs to be approached with the same respect for scientific principles and the same desire for a typology of experiences that one applies to the other aspects of professional practice. It is just as important to understand, for example, the decision-making process in a group as it is to understand the effects of a particular treatment on a hospital patient. This is especially true if the group is a budget committee that is deciding whether to fund the equipment needed for patient treatment. A useful starting point for understanding groups is to focus on groups as democratic microcosms.

The physical and biological sciences have developed a vocabulary of terms that have precisely operationalized technical definitions. This is not the case for most terms that are used to discuss groups. The reason for this is that many of the words we use when discussing groups are common in ordinary conversation. Perhaps it would be helpful to invent a new language so that we could use terms that only have precise and technical meanings when we are talking about groups. On the other hand, it would hardly seem that we need a profusion of new terms to go with the old ones, which are confusing enough. One should remember, however, that the words used to describe group phenomena, though familiar, may have meanings different from their colloquial sense. To illustrate this point, let us begin with the two components of the term "democratic microcosm."

"Democratic" is a word that has various connotations in various contexts. To some, it connotes a sort of anarchy or absence of central authority. To others, it brings to mind a picture of the founding fathers assembled in Philadelphia in 1787, arguing over the clauses and articles of the Constitution. To still others, it represents an ideal of equality that our society has yet to reach. And then there are those for whom it connotes participation on behalf of oneself, responsibility for self and others, shared participation, autonomy, and interdependence. In order to consider the group as a democratic microcosm, these various connotations and meanings all need to be kept in mind.

Democracy also refers to a set of values operationalized within a group through its structure and processes. Some of these values include the worth of each individual group member, active participation by each member, each member's responsibility for actions and behaviors, respect for differences of background, ability, and personal characteristics among the members, and an awareness within each member of responsibility, to some extent, for the entire group.

In a democratic group, leadership is selected by a process that includes the wishes of members and is responsible, to some extent, to the membership of the group. Each member can take the floor—that is, get other members to listen—in accordance with a prescribed procedure, which may be formal or informal. The group has an agreed-upon method for making decisions. Again, this method may be formal or informal. What is important is that it is known to all the members. Finally, each member has agreed to support decisions reached by the group as a whole or to dissent from them in particular ways regardless of original positions, which may or may not have changed in the course of the group's life.

It is important to distinguish a democratically led group from one characterized by laissez-faire or autocratic leadership (Lewin, Lippitt, and White, 1939). Democratic groups operate under a discipline of time, resources, and tasks. The leadership of a democratic group may take an assertive or even a highly structured position as the situation seems to warrant. Democracy should not be confused with the lack of structure or limits. The concepts of process and choice are inherent in the use of the term "democratic." Making choices requires freedom to express preferences, a process of group consideration, a series of tuggings and pullings between and among individuals and groups, and a weighing and balancing of short-term interests.

The term "microcosm" literally means "small world." The reason this term is important is that, in a sense, a mature group does represent a small world. It is an arena encompassing the facts, feelings, aspirations, attractions, repulsions, and accomplishments of its members. Inasmuch as competent adults operate in many small worlds simultaneously, one should not overemphasize the impact of any one group or any particular set of group experiences on an individual. In order for a group to achieve maturity as a democratic microcosm, however, membership needs to become important to some extent in the lives of each member. We shall discuss some issues of commitment later in the book.

MATURITY IN A DEMOCRATIC GROUP

Maturity, in groups as elsewhere, is an abstract idea. Maturity for groups, as for individuals, is a desired end state, probably never fully achieved. Groups that are growing move toward maturity but never fully reach it. Every group that is working for a time at its optimum level of maturity may regress, slip back, have to reform itself, or simply need to rest and recalibrate itself much like a gyroscope. Many groups, however, do reach a level of maturity at which they can be considered fully developed. This meaning of maturity is more useful for our purposes than a static or idealized state.

In groups, as in Jefferson's famous bon mot about society as a whole, "eternal vigilance is the price of liberty." Democracy—that is, full and meaningful participation in determining the direction of a group by all its members—is something that each member needs to work for throughout the group's life. It does not come easily. A system of dominance and submission in interpersonal relationships may come more easily. It is our point of view, together with that of many others (e.g., Zander, 1982; Miles, 1964; Thelen, 1958), that the reasons working groups need to develop as democratic microcosms not esoteric and exclusively philosophical but practical, important to a group's productivity and task accomplishment. Accordingly, the following statements in brief describe the connections between democracy and effectiveness.

1. Working groups that do not operate democratically run the risk of producing less than the best solutions of which they are capable to all but the most routine of problems.

2. Undemocratic groups tend to lose the participation of all but a few of their members.

3. Groupthink (Janis, 1972; there are other more recent references, e.g., regarding the Space Shuttle disaster of 2003) is always a danger in undemocratic groups.

4. As Lewin (1948) pointed out repeatedly, it is difficult to conceive of a democratic society that is not composed of small groups that operate democratically and train people for democratic participation in the broader society.

5. Democratic groups maximize (and undemocratic groups minimize) the salience and depth of meaning of group membership for most of their members (Balgopal and Vassil, 1983).

In sum, then, in addition to its moral appeal, democratic functioning is important for groups in order to maximize their chances of being productive and creative at problem solving, to obtain maximum participation from members, to avoid groupthink, to contribute to the democratization of the broader society, and to get members to take their membership seriously.

Working groups that operate democratically need to develop and maintain climates that include those elements that encourage members to feel safe, valued, and needed. Safety demands basic group rules of civility and orderly procedure, as well as mutual valuation among all members of each other's potential contributions to the group. Sharp and deeply felt disagreements and even expressions of frustration are useful and often necessary (Randel, 2002). Bitter ad hominem attacks, on the other hand, preclude a sense of safety. This fact may be especially important if what is being attacked is the fundamental competence of a member or what entitles a member to hold a job.

Being valued implies that group members have responsibility for each other and deal with each other at a certain level of authenticity. Unquestioning approval is not valuing. To some extent, in fact, it is the opposite. Valuing is based on a perception that the group needs its members—all its members—in order to do its best work. Climates that suggest the group might be better off without some of its members give clear messages to those members to depart or at least to withdraw symbolically. To be a democratic microcosm, a group needs to value all its members as potential contributors to the accomplishment of its goals; this unconditional positive regard is related to the group's goals and purposes. The reciprocal obligation imposed on each member is one of commitment to the group.

Democratic microcosms are not built in one meeting or in two. Indeed, there may be moments or periods of tedium, and, for that reason, groups need continuous attention to the process. Emphasizing democracy requires a moderately long time frame. Because of this, groups that will have very short lives may not, and probably should not, pay too much attention to the development of a democratic microcosm. Groups that will be in existence for a period of several weeks or longer do need to pay considerable attention to this.

CHARACTERISTICS OF A DEMOCRATIC MICROCOSM

In order to understand the essence of a group as a democratic microcosm, it is useful to examine some of the indicators that typify such entities. The democratic microcosm represents a realistic ideal that one can work toward and achieve. A democratic microcosm represents the group as a complete system. To be a complete system, several elements must be present. The group has to be self-sustaining, essentially a striving process, which means that it has the wherewithal to manufacture the roles and behaviors it needs in order to accomplish its tasks. The group as a whole needs an adequate level of self-esteem and sense of its own competence to accomplish its tasks. It also needs to be able to rework and reintegrate insights and data and to be able to use what it learns to guide its operations. These processes encompass both cooperation and controversy. Indeed, a group has to be able to capitalize on differences of opinion or approach and to be able to add these to its data base so as to learn from its own past successes and failures and from its members' past experiences. These experiences are used for purposes of prediction and can contribute much to the group's understanding. Cognition or new information or perceptions can serve the group's purposes as well as members' feelings and emotions (Thelen, 1971, personal communication).

The group needs to be able to give attention in a balanced way to the persons who constitute it, to its own successes as a group, and to the organizational and social environment in which it is located. From the point of view of either a staff member or the chair, one cannot focus either on a member or on the group as a whole. One cannot focus only on the group or only on the organization within which it is embedded. One must focus simultaneously on persons, subgroups that compose the group, the group as a whole, and the organizational environment. If one wishes to further the productive working of a group, one needs ongoing awareness of all four levels of meaning. If one tries to do this and occasionally feels as though one has a stiff neck from trying to look at various angles simultaneously, this must be accepted as one of the real requirements of taking responsibility for a group (Getzels and Thelen, 1960).

In working with groups, there are always two forces at work: those that tend to pull a group apart into its components and those that tend to pull it together into one system. The interaction between these two tendencies, the pushes and pulls, generates dynamic tension and therefore controversy. Personal needs may conflict or compete with each other and frustrate group needs. Individual members may seek to act autonomously at times when the group needs to act in concert for its common purpose. The presence of these oppositional forces is what gives group life its flavor, its excitement, and its complexity. It is one reason that groups often take time to accomplish their tasks. It is natural for members, chair, and staff to wish from time to time that groups were less complex and therefore could accomplish tasks more rapidly. But when a group does not go through a series of processes over time in order to accomplish its tasks, it is not behaving truly as a group. Some organizations, paradoxically, form groups in order to have them solve problems and then operate in such a way as to prevent those very groups from ever forming in any genuine sense.

From a systems framework, stability and change are permanent aspects of groups, providing the dynamic and dialectical tension associated with social systems. Stability derives from cohesion or safety; conflict derives from change. In unequal ways, the closer members get, the more possibilities there are for annoyance that produces disconfirmations and a retreat to safety, at which point recalibrations occur and the group moves to another level of function. The more annoyances, the more retreat to safety, and from there the cycle continues to the movement from safety to conflict. Disconfirmations are easy to produce; understanding and transformation to new products are much more difficult (Glidewell, 1972).

One of the places where oppositional pulls can often be noted is in the definition of a group's charge or, more precisely, in a group's redefinition of its charge. Commonly, working groups will take a formal charge and discuss it in considerable depth so as to try to get agreement among the members, in operational terms, about how to proceed.

In example A, Dr. Wiley, the mayor's selection as chair of the task force on the frail elderly, defined "old age" as sixty-two years and older. The group as a whole, as it turned out, was primarily concerned with the so-called old-old, those aged seventy-five and over. Tension created by this problem of definition spurred the group to a detailed discussion of their charge and how they would go about fulfilling that charge as a task force. The staff person, Ms. O'Brian, several times underscored the importance of the group's resolving this issue operationally so that it could lay out its own work plan; at the same time, she scrupulously avoided imposing her own point of view about the group's charge. This example demonstrates succinctly the three leadership skills of focusing, recasting, and containing (self-limitation) supporting group abilities.

FOSTERING A DEMOCRATIC MICROCOSM

It may be useful at this point to reflect on the reasons why working groups are created. Groups are formed for one of two broad classes of reasons. It may be thought that a group will be better able than an individual to solve a particular problem, fulfill a particular function for an organization, or synthesize data from various sources. Or it may be thought that a working group will be an effective way of both receiving input and disseminating outputs to a variety of relevant publics. In either case, it is thought that a group will accomplish a particular purpose better than an individual would.

Strangely enough, one needs to be reminded of this fairly consistently in order to avoid the thinking trap that the staff member, or the chair, or a particular member knows better than the group as a whole (see the example above). If, indeed, one knows better, then one does not need a working group but an audience to whom one can convey one's superior knowledge. If, however, one really needs a working group, either for problem solving or for developing a joint decision to which each of the members feels a commitment, then one needs to remember not to stand in the way of the formation or operation of that group. Some people verbalize a commitment to group process but then proceed to behave in such a way as to make it clear that, deep down, they believe they as individuals know better than the group. One needs to guard against these behaviors because they result in shooting one's self in the foot, as it were. At the risk of belaboring the point, if one needs a group, one needs a real group; if one doesn't, then why have one at all?

Several behaviors flow from this principle, and these behaviors are applicable, in different ways and at different rates, whether one is staff, chair, or group member. First, in order to help a group to form and operate, one needs to allow it the physical space in which to do so. That is, a group needs to meet under the kinds of physical conditions that allow members to devote attention to its operation. Groups need quiet space, an appropriate temperature, and chairs that are comfortable to sit on. They also need minutes of previous meetings, copies of relevant data being discussed, and other materials. Second, groups need time in which to meet: not an excessive amount but enough so that group members do not feel that they're always acting under the gun. Perhaps even more important, groups need emotional space in which to operate. Workers as well as chairs should avoid monopolizing the floor. As a rule of thumb, if either a worker or a chair is talking more than 20 percent of the time at the initial meeting or more than 10 percent of the time at subsequent meetings, the reasons for this should be examined carefully. Workers and chairs should avoid strong emotional overreactions to statements by group members, since these may have the effect of chilling the willingness of others to risk their points of view and their questions. Careful follow-through on decisions made during meetings and on promises to furnish members with particular information is important for fostering a sense of importance and self-esteem in the group's members (Tropman, 1980).

Both chair and staff need to adopt a nurturing point of view toward the group, especially in its early phases. Like a farmer with a new crop, staff members need to foster the growth of what is at first a relatively fragile entity. A group that has been in existence for a long time or one that has achieved maturity of functioning will be much less fragile, of course. Even such groups, however, will benefit from an approach that values and sustains its processes and its accomplishments.

We shall discuss stages and phases of group development in greater detail in chapter 9. The trajectory or arc of group development needs to be kept in mind. Many things that happen in groups can be understood developmentally, that is, as reflecting the struggles of a group to form, to engage with topics, and to develop worthwhile products. Such a developmental perspective is useful, because it prevents both staff and members from overreacting to particular events or a particular phenomena in the group. The developmental perspective has many uses as a guide, but it is not prescriptive.

A working group that is moving toward becoming a democratic microcosm should be "our" group. It is never "their" or "your" group. By these labels, we mean that each member of the group carries some responsibility for the totality of the group's functioning. Everything the group does is the business of every member. All suggestions should be welcomed, even those that cause problems for the group's leadership, because they represent an expression of concern and an input of energy from the member or subgroup offering the suggestions. Each member's suggestion is representative of the group, as well as becoming the property of the group.

One approach that has proven its merit in nurturing groups in the early stages is to focus on small successes. Groups, like people, build their sense of competence and esteem as a result of progressing from small successes to grappling with larger and more difficult issues. For this reason, it is important that the first meeting or two of a group demonstrate to the members their beginning capacity for decision making. Such decision making may be restricted at first to setting an agenda, or to structuring the group internally, or to reaching decisions about time, place, and frequency of meeting. Nonetheless, they are important as building blocks for the group's growing capacity to deal with more and more complex and difficult issues.

It would be nice if groups experienced only successes. Unfortunately, such is the case only rarely. One of the objectives of both staff and chair, especially in the early stages, thus needs to be to help the group to integrate failures without feeling its existence or worth challenged or becoming overly defensive. Some problems are too complex for a group to deal with, whether in its early stages or even at all. Maintaining a sense of perspective—keeping the ledger in balance, as it were—is an important contribution that a staff person can make to a group throughout its life.

One way to think of this balance is to focus on the need for groups to develop and maintain equanimity (Thelen, 1981). That is, the experience of a staff person can be very useful in helping a group not to overreact, despite the vicissitudes of successes and failures. Another way to accomplish the same end is to focus on the importance of the group's task. In the five examples presented in chapter 2, it is clear that the purposes for which each group exists are, in fact, important. They affect meaningfully the lives of a significant number of people. They are not tasks that should be undertaken lightly, and neither should they be sloughed off as incidental.

Emphasizing equanimity helps a group learn to refocus and recenter itself. It dampens oscillations that go too far in either direction from the center of the group's purposes and capacities. At the same time, the concept of equanimity is important for staff, chair, and members as people. It is all too easy to overreact to what happens in a particular group at a particular time at a particular stage. Groups can experience wide mood swings as a result of good and bad meetings. Any working group that is in existence for a significant period of time will experience both good and bad days, easier and more difficult meetings, more and less skillful dealings with conflicts and problems.

The role of the staff—and, to a considerable extent, of the chair—should be to maintain a focus on the central purposes and thrust of group life. Such a focus can enrich the processes of a microcosm over time. Maintaining focus is sometimes not easy. It helps to have had experience in a variety of working groups and to be able to draw on such experience. Belief in the natural tendencies of groups and group members to move toward health and accomplishment is also helpful. Finally, one cannot overestimate the effects of simple patience.

A Closing Note: "Trusting the Process"

It is natural for all of us to prefer smoothness in group life. A common experience in life in general is that one feels one has sufficient stress not to need to seek more as a result of involvement with working groups. At the same time, it is a truism of group life that when things are going smoothly and seem to be going well, not much may be happening. Conversely, when group meetings are full of tensions, disagreements, and conflicts, these may be precisely the times at which groups are operating at their highest and most productive level. One needs to learn to discern the differences between destructive processes and constructive growth processes that are simply messy. Most productive groups are at their best when their processes are somewhat messy, occasionally loud, and particularly fraught with conflicts and disagreements. (J. Lipman-Blumen and H. J. Leavitt's work *Hot Groups* (1999) is devoted to this dynamic.)

An important proviso is that, despite these conflicts, a climate of safety for the groups' members is always a requirement. The process of gaining skill with working groups, which we shall address specifically in chapter 13, is in large part a process of learning to substitute recognition of growth and task accomplishment for the desire for smoothness and meaningless politeness in groups. Trusting a group's process does not mean losing a focus on time constraints, resource constraints, or deadlines. It does mean reminding oneself at each step along the way of the reasons that a particular group was formed and of its purposes. We turn next to a specific consideration of group processes within the context of group structure.

5

LEADERSHIP THEORY:
BENCHMARKS AND GUIDEPOSTS

GOFFEE AND JONES (2002) trace the history of leadership theory
through the ages, revealing in the process strengths and weaknesses, cul-
minating in their view of the importance of context theory. The time line
sketched below describes the significant milestones. The authors state that the
rationalist model followed in the Enlightenment stressed the use of reason
alone as the essential element in solving problems. This optimistic viewpoint
was challenged by two powerful ideas: the unconscious as source point of
behavior posed by Freud and the limit of reason found in the dehumanizing
associated with the efficient aspects of bureaucracy as noted by Weber. By the
twentieth century, the response to reason and continuity was skepticism, thus
foreshadowing interest in leadership. Trait theory was unable to show conclu-
sively common characteristics of effective leaders. Style theory, characterized
by openness and meritocracy, falls short when confronted with conflict and
warrior mentality. The next step, contingency theory, correlated leadership to
a specific situation, though one is hard-pressed to capture the many life situations one encounters. From their analysis, the authors conclude the following:

> We ransacked all the leadership theories to come up with the four
> essential leadership qualities. Like Weber, we look at leadership that is
> primarily antibureaucratic and charismatic. From trait theory, we
> derived the qualities of weakness and differences. Unlike the original
> trait theorists, however, we do not believe that all leaders have the same
> weaknesses; our research only showed that all leaders expose some flaws.
> Tough empathy grew out of style theory, which looked at different
> kinds of relationships between leaders and their followers. Finally, con-
> text theory set the stage for needing to know what skills to use in vari-
> ous circumstances. (65)

Like other authors (e.g., Weick, 1995), Goffee and Jones (2002) find other characteristics to be important to leadership in addition to such elements as expertise, strategy, energy, vision, and authority. They describe four other qualities, each with both a positive and potentially negative outcome. They also attach caveats to each of the qualities described—namely, sensing, revealing weaknesses, tough empathy, and differentiation—that are meant to cluster in various ways and degrees depending on the context. For this reason, the term "context" is used to denote the next stage in leadership theory.

"Sensing" refers to the use of one's capacities finely tuned to interpret soft data. Certain leaders are able to "read" or pick up the meaning in situations with relatively few cues. To avoid the error of overprojection, common in the intuitive process, leadership information gained through sensing has to be reality tested with close associates or with group members. This process is ongoing in group work.

"Revealing weaknesses" refers to small weaknesses that may be invisible to many. These allow the leader to humanize him- or herself, thus affirming a degree of credibility. An example would be a group leader who talks a bit too much. Large weaknesses, such as dismissive attitudes toward certain members, are counterproductive. Another example of a large weakness would be a leader who shares high discomfort in the group, with possibly devastating contagious effects.

"Tough empathy" involves providing staff members not what they want but what they need to develop. A demand for education and work that allow members and staff to move on is one example. Pointing out obstacles (Shulman, 2001) is another. Feeding dependency, on the other hand, is counterproductive.

The fourth characteristic, "differentiation," relates to the ability to distance oneself from others. This is important because a measured distancing from fellow members or colleagues is one way to demonstrate the skills germane to the task. This suggests the parallel process between the group leader and members (Schwartz, 1976). Each has a task to perform. Another example would be handling conflict by moving it from a polarity to a paradox, from destructive to constructive possibilities. The ability to remain calm in the face of aggressive and demanding members is yet another example of differentiation. On the other side of the equation, overdifferentiation can result in losing contact with and perhaps respect from some group members. Finally, leaders who exhibit and demonstrate imagination, and nerve, sometimes in nonverbal ways—through facial expression or mannerisms, for example—also establish differentiation and uniqueness.

Gender and ethnic characteristics can influence the leadership role in many ways. Self-image as a leader at whatever organizational level influences behaviors. Some may choose to disguise their needs through defensive behavior. This overemphasizes collegiality. In addition, any formal or informal scenario may model negative stereotypes that can interfere with leadership execution and development. In a review and summary of a contemporary point of view regarding leadership function, Hartsock (1997:32) noted that managing a group process leading to greater understanding among members is more important than the use of personal influence to achieve goals. Two distinct characteristics that can be identified as "transactional" and "transformational" address the point. Transactional leaders engage in exchanges between themselves and followers. Presenting and implementing a vision or mission and developing solid bonds with members is an essential ingredient of this type of leadership, which typically will raise aspirations among group members. Transformation, the second aspect, implies that leaders assist others to lead themselves. Thus leadership is not only concerned with task accomplishment but with the development of morale and a climate for change that encourages members to assume roles for self-empowerment.

LEADERSHIP IN THE EARLY TWENTY-FIRST CENTURY

At the beginning of the twenty-first century, a group of scholars and applied social scientists attempted to take a look at leadership in relation to societal needs, development, technology, and related features (Bennis, Spreitzer, and Cummings, 2001). They were concerned with organizations of all sorts, and the points they raised, some to be addressed in succeeding chapters and some for the reader to think about, are worth reviewing. The various thoughts are summarized below under the names of the authors.

Warren Bennis entitles his observations "The Future Has No Shelf Life." He asks, what will the world be like in 2010 (3–13)? Who will be its leaders? More directly, what about the future of "high involvement," or innovations? What about the implications for democracy of superior and inferior talent? Should we be worried about the increasing huge gap between the top and bottom of our society? And, finally, he asks two questions that should concern anyone who works with working groups. What about "great groups," groups of outstanding accomplishment in whatever realm they work? Have we learned anything about how to produce such groups? Second, what about a balance between work and personal life, an issue that confronts people in highly developed, postindustrial societies to a much greater extent than is generally realized? How does one find this balance, and how does leadership of an organization involve addressing this issue?

Edward E. Lawler III states that "the era of human capital has finally arrived" (14). Major sources that can combine to produce winning organizations are human capital, organizational capabilities, and core competencies. Democracy is inevitable, even in the workplace (16). Winning organizations will have "flat, agile structures and systems that create knowledgeable employees throughout the organization. . . . We need to move to an era in which leadership is an organizational capability and not just an individual characteristic that a few individuals at the top of an organization have" (24).

Charles Handy raises an issue under the heading "A World of Fleas and Elephants." Elephants are the large organizations of business and government. Fleas are technological start-ups, small consultancies and professional firms, self-employed experts, and specialty suppliers. Elephants get all the attention; but most people work in fleas. Fleas provide new challenges for leadership. Founders have passion for them. Cores are tiny. True fleas survive without being bought up or combining with other organizations. "Perhaps the time is right to discover the merits of what the French call *formation* and the British call 'professional development'" (40).

Thomas H. Davenport writes about "Knowledge, Work and the Future of Management." As more and more work becomes knowledge work, management will change

- from overseeing work to doing;
- from organizing hierarchies to organizing communities;
- from imposing work designs and methods to understanding them;
- from hiring and firing workers to recruiting and retaining them;
- from building manual skills to building knowledge skills;
- from evaluating visible job performance to assessing invisible knowledge achievements;
- from ignoring culture to building a knowledge-friendly culture; and
- from supporting the bureaucracy to fending it off.

Thomas A. Stewart, in "Trust Me on This," suggests that networks are essentially an alternative to hierarchies. "Flatter hierarchies and network relationships change the sources and uses of power" (69). "Trust's first crutch is competence. . . . Trust needs a second crutch: community. . . . Trust depends on the degree to which people are willing to support the organization's purposes. . . . Trust of course depends on communications, which can be its best friend or its worse enemy . . . A revolutionary way to build trust: tell the truth" (70–76).

James M. Kouzes and Barry Z. Posner, in their article "Bringing Leadership Lessons From the Past into the Future," point out that "leadership isn't a place, it's a process." "It's far healthier and more productive to start with the assumption that it's possible for everyone to lead." "Leadership is a relationship." "Leadership starts with action." "Leadership development is self-development" (82–86).

Karl E. Weick says in his article "Leadership as the Legitimization of Doubt," "the effective leader is someone who searches for the better question, accepts inexperience, stays in motion, channels decisions to those with the best knowledge of the matter at hand, crafts good stories, is obsessed with updating, encourages improvisation and is deeply aware of personal ignorance" (94).

Philip Slater, in "Leading Yourself," states, "People don't need to be controlled and manipulated to commit themselves to a heartfelt vision, and being controlled and manipulated tends to destroy that commitment. Those trained to a mechanistic worldview often find it difficult to learn this. But it becomes almost impossible if you've never learned it in relation to your own organization" (115).

The reader will notice a common theme that runs through these observations by an outstanding list of authorities. What they seem to have in common is an interest in developing the kind of organization in which people at various levels have a mission orientation to the work of the entire organization. Some might refer to this as a culture of mutuality, that is, a focus on mutual obligation, responsibility, and work rather then the pattern of reward and punishment that have traditionally been associated with enforcement on the part of an organization.

These observations have particular relevance and force for working groups in the human services for similar reasons. We have for many years been struck by the dissonance—the lack of fit—between the instructions that human service organizations give to their staffs on how they should deal with clients or patients and the way the same organizations deal with their own staffs (see Ephross, 1983). It seems to us as though a well-known principle of parenting needs to be applied to the job of leadership in working groups. In each case, the instruction "Don't do as I do, do as I say!" is ineffective. Leadership in an organization involves a responsibility to demonstrate by one's own actions the ways in which members of the organization are expected to behave. Staff will tend to treat clients or client systems as they themselves are treated.

This implies no less accountability to the organization, no less emphasis on high standards of performance, and no less emphasis on setting standards (of which the most difficult to set is always the one between minimally acceptable and minimally unacceptable). It does mean, however, that leadership consists of mobilizing the talents, capacities, motivation, ambition, and self-referential behaviors of staff and participants. It should be noted that volunteers, citizens, and representatives of various organizations need the same kind of leadership as paid and professional staff do.

WORK

Bion theorized about the connection between work and emotions in groups, and Thelen and his colleagues at the University of Chicago further developed and refined his conclusions (Stock and Thelen, 1958). Jaques explored the process of ambivalence applicable to tension between public and private domains between and among persons, subjects, and groups. (Jaques, 1970). Within the interpersonal domain of members and groups, emotional states and the consciously formed reality of the task, essentially cognitive, are inseparable but not equal. Recent studies on leadership emphasize the influence of emotions on both the person and the group (Goleman, 2000; Druskat and Wolff, 2001). Both overt and covert aspects at individual and group levels may appear as needs for domination, competition, avoidance, anger, aloofness, and so forth.

Jaques addressed the dynamics of the work process from a psychoanalytic perspective, offering an analytic interpretation of processes involved in the capacity for work. He focused on processes leading to and through ambivalence to a final decision, starting with energy, focus, hunches that may or may not recycle, and a certain amount of letting go of preconceived notions. The group perseveres through uncertainty to a resynthesis of different ideas. The process dictates that members will flow back and forth between previously held ideas and potentially disturbing beliefs and their public display experienced personally or vicariously. Exploration, assessment, and reassessment of the pros and cons of an issue—primarily the staff person's responsibility—are continuously faced. At a deeper level, Jaques considered the psychological processes of dealing with loss or control as potential emotional barriers to change.

The public and private aspects of interpersonal relations and their relevance have been the subject of interest and concern to many authors (Stock and Thelen, 1958; Zaleznik and Moment, 1964; Goleman, 2000; Druskat and Wolff, 2001). Sometimes, hidden agendas, group or individual, get in the way of constructive work. Instances are needs to be perfect, the inability to control anxiety, envy of a colleague with one whom may experience as a rival, competitive feelings of omnipotence that take the form of "I'll show you!" and milder forms such as set ideas, indecisiveness, ruminations, or regrets ("If I only had done more," "If I only had done such and such"). At the group level, apathy, avoidance, competition with a leader, and excessive small talk can compound the work with a group as a group.

On Learning

Empathy is related to a theory of learning that describes it as single loop versus double loop (Argyris and Schon, 1974).

Single loop learning can be likened to a climate control system that adjusts the temperature in a room. The thermostat receives information from the room, checks it against the set figure—say, 72 degrees—and then turns the heat on or leaves it off, depending on whether there is a deviation. Some might argue that keeping a group on course is good leadership and therefore the single loop function is important. We submit that this is but one function and that more should be considered.

In double loop learning, the thermostat assesses the degree to which there is deviation in terms of the temperature but goes one step further, evaluating whether the set room temperature is a reasonable goal (let us assume a system can do this). In terms of group leadership, double loop behavior within a group requires the entire context within which the group functions be taken into consideration. Evaluations must be continuously made and fed back regarding the variety of alternative goals and means to achieve these goals, attendant consequences of the goals, the relationship of goals to values and members' behavior, and so on.

Double loop learning involves an emphasis on the present and attention to a number of variables, part-whole relationships that include the staff member, that one must take into account. The staff person's use of empathy and detachment permits him or her to develop and assess the state of the members and the group at a particular point in time and, from there, to generate certain types of interventions. Double loop learning, since it includes the presence of the group worker and the context of the group, also requires a continuous reevaluation of the group worker's sensitivities. We believe, therefore, that double loop learning is more appropriate for group work and, furthermore, that it is more attuned to the meaning that members develop and accrue in the context of the group itself.

CASE STUDY: A COMMUNITY ORGANIZATION RECORD IN WORKING WITH GROUPS

This is the first meeting of a tenants' group. The day has been marred by a steady downpour of rain. I had been unable to arrange for the flyers concerning tonight's scheduled meeting to be distributed. An hour after lunch, it was still raining, and there was no sign that it was going to stop. My very recent bout with the flu was giving me still another cause for concern. I must admit that my own interest in attending a meeting that night was rather low. Any uncertainty voiced by the group could have caused a postponement.[1]

When I arrived at Mrs. Green's apartment, she was busy talking with Mrs. Brody, who was fixing her hair in the bedroom. Mrs. Green. asked her son John to tell me that she would be out soon. John, who was studying for some of his vocational high school courses, indicated his feeling that the meeting tonight was long overdue. He chatted back and forth to his mother and the other woman, "Some of these folks are afraid of Mr. Smith. I'm not; tonight we're going to fix him." I asked John if he would help tonight. I explained that, since there were no flyers, it might be helpful if someone contacted the other residents to remind them of the meeting. He was more than enthusiastic about the prospect.

Mrs. Green. and Mrs. Brody. came out and discussed arrangements for the meeting. I was surprised that Mrs. B. had changed her "I'll be at the wrestling matches" attitude and was taking an active part.

I brought in the forty-two-cup coffeemaker, made arrangements to pick up a box of cookies and some hot-drink cups, and stopped to see a bachelor tenant on the second floor, who was, once again, not at home. Mr. Harris, the projected leader, had moved his family to another address during the past weekend when a home had become available to them.

I came back to Mrs. Green's apartment and found that things were starting to move. The coffee was brewing, and John was contacting residents. It was 7:20 when Mr. Dietz, a construction worker, and Mr. Carter, a waiter, came upstairs. There was no cream for the coffee. Mr. Dietz and I went to get some as the store in the Whitelock business district. I had not previously talked with him. I learned he was interested in youth activities and that he was a veteran, presently unemployed. He was from Salisbury, Maryland, and previously was involved in an urban renewal project in D.C. Mr. Dietz stated his concern was with his rent being so high and said that somebody had to do something.

After we returned, Mr. Carter, Mrs. Green, Mr. Dietz, and I spent fifteen minutes discussing the possible outcome of the Job Corps. Mrs. Green left to contact several others who had not yet come, and in walked Mr. Leonard Barts, an individual I had contacted previously. He remembered me. He stated that John had told him of the meeting. Mr. Barts explained that his apartment was one of five owned by Mr. Smith at 2246 Front, directly next door. All five apartments were in "deplorable condition," he said. I learned that 2304 was also owned by Mr. Smith; it had approximately eight units and was also in very poor condition. I asked John if he might contact someone there, and he said he already had.

At 8:05, there were thirteen people in the apartment. Because of the heat, the door was left open. Others were scheduled to come, and, as I began an introduction, Mrs. Barts arrived. The group appointed Mr. Carter to take minutes.

I opened the meeting by stating that, during the past two weeks, I had contacted residents in the building, and it has become evident that there were many problems common to them all. I then stated my position as a part-time community organization adviser who was interested in trying to help them work together on some of the problems they shared. I advised them that, whatever action they, as a group, took, I would offer help as an advisor. I emphasized that the strength of the group was dependent on the individual members.

I then asked if each person in the room would introduce him- or herself. Mrs. Mitchell (who earlier in the evening had admitted that, until that night, she had gone by her maiden name or "Mrs. Gates") was very hesitant. The majority of the group seemed to agree that, since I knew who they all were, I should introduce them. I explained that there couldn't be much of a group without participation and observed that introducing oneself was a form of participating. I asked for introductions again and again but met with hesitation. For a long fifteen seconds, I paused. Finally, Mrs. Mitchell introduced herself; at the prompting of several others, so did Mrs. Sheldon, then Mrs. Miller, Mrs. Winningham, Mrs. Martin, Mrs. Ashley, Mr. Mason, Mr. and Mrs. Barts, John, Mr. and Mrs. Brody, Mrs. Houston, Mr. Dietz, Mr. Carter, and a resident from 2204, who came late with Mrs. Mitchell's husband. The introductions seemed to break the ice.

As Mr. Ashley, the caretaker, began the discussion, Mrs. G. poured coffee and passed it to members. Mr. Ashley was quick to note that as caretaker, he had to represent both himself and the landlord. The group agreed that his name should not be mentioned in any communications. Mr. Ashley voiced his concern that the lack of a lock on the front door was causing excessive work for him. Mrs. Winningham volunteered that her apartment had been broken into several years before, that she had paid for a "jimmy-proof" lock on her door; but that she was still afraid because of people coming in. I asked if any others felt this way. One at a time, the group voiced concern over strangers coming into the hallway. A discussion of a possible door lock at the main entrance followed. I asked the caretaker to explain the landlord's position concerning his reasons for not giving a key to the mailman. Mr. Mason explained his feeling that the landlord was lying, that the mailman could have a key. Mrs. Brody asked me if it were illegal. I advised that I would find this information for them by contacting the postmaster's office.

Mr. Brody expressed his concerns that the children in the building might not be able to use a key and might get locked out. Mrs. Miller and Mrs. Martin took offense at the statement, and Mr. Brody seemed to apologize. I asked if his suggestion was not something to consider. Mr. Dietz and Mr. Mason agreed with Mr. Brody. Mr. Brody pointed out that already we were experiencing difficulties in reaching agreement, and he stressed the need to have alternatives. He considered where the group would be if the landlord confronted them with such a question when they were not in agreement.

Mrs. Winningham and Mrs. Martin brought up the lack of a laundry room even though it was advertised. Several in the group implied that, with a lock on the door, there would have been no need to close the facility several years before.

Mr. Mason complained about the lack of a fire escape for the third floor. Mr. Dietz implied that he had heard the basement did not count as a floor and that the third floor was the second. This meant no fire escape is necessary. Mrs. Carter asked me if I could check this regulation; I said yes.

After the group aired several other complaints, I asked if they felt a need to unite. The feeling was unanimous. Everyone had been heard but Mrs. Houston. I asked if she had anything to say. She expressed her feelings that the people in the development needed a door lock, paint, and several small items but that Mr. Smith gave them service if they asked. On the other hand, she complained that, where she lived, there were large violations, such as rats

and roaches, and Mr. Smith refused to help. She said that, had she known
about the meeting, she could have brought others. Mr. Carter told her to be
sure to bring them to the next meeting. Mrs. Barts described developments
at 2246, stating that some tenants there were "impossible." She commented
that one apartment was ruining everything she tried to do. I reinforced the
group by explaining the purpose and goal of a strong tenant union. With
strength, they could have a voice in whom the landlord rents to.

Mr. Brody showed leadership. He stated that he was interested in helping the other two buildings, too. He explained his feelings about helping
his race. A discussion of rent strikes and the need for unanimous participation in the same ensued.

The group declined to select even a temporary leader, but several names
for the group were suggested: (1) The Unknowns; (2) The Well-Doers, and
(3) The Congressional Society for Rehabilitation. Mrs. Winningham asked
me to supply a name. I explained that this was their group, that the names
suggested thus far were good. Mr. Barts implied that a name was not so
important, that there would be time to think it over, but he expressed his
feelings that the group should name itself.

Mr. Carter talked about the importance of getting a letter to the landlord immediately to let him know of the group. Mr. Dietz implied that we
should not do this for some time, that the people at the meeting did not
represent everyone in all three buildings. He suggested that no action be
taken until everyone was contacted and agreed. I helped these two and the
group see the validity of both views. Mr. Brody was selected to contact
everyone in 2300, Mrs. Houston volunteered to do the same in 2304, Mrs.
Barts in 2246. The three would discuss a possible meeting on Wednesday,
April 23. Mr. Carter then restated his opinion that the group at that time
should form and begin to take action. It was suggested that I contact Mrs.
Barts the next day to examine the "unbelievable" conditions in the building at 2246, and I agreed.

I briefly summarized the meeting and placed emphasis on the fact that
they were getting to know each other and seemed interested in the possibility of organizing as a group to work on some of their common problems related to the landlord and the housing conditions. I pointed out that
although they discussed a number of problems, it would be helpful if they
began to consider priorities at the next meeting. Mr. Dietz asked if we
could get flyers for the next meeting. The majority of the group stayed for
another half hour, until ten, for more coffee from the second pot. Seventy-
six-year-old Mr. Mason summed things up: "After four years here, I have

talked for the first time to people I've seen everyday." Judging by the group's caution in not saying they represented everyone and by their immediate willingness to expand, they should become able to handle other areas. Mr. Carter, Mr. Brody, Mr. Barts, and Mrs. Winningham were the leaders so far, along with Mr. Dietz, who seemed to be very eager to involve others. The dynamics of urban renewal planning were discussed briefly over coffee.

Case Analysis

There is much to be learned from examining the leadership role in this case study. The staff person had conducted preliminary research for the assignment by interviewing a number of residents in several buildings of the housing development. The purpose was to find out present concerns affecting living conditions. She may have gotten information through other agencies, key informants, media, formal and informal contacts with organizations who have a stake in the problems, and so forth.

In the beginning of the role-induction phase, which here consists of the participants moving from neighbors to group members, the staff person gained information and experiences by way of individual interviews, using knowledge gained from previous interviews as a pathway for both validating and enriching data in succeeding interviews. At the initial stage and continuing through several meetings, this worker was the central person through which the hopes, doubts, and concerns became articulated. In many of the dyadic interactions that followed, each of the parties was assessing and testing the boundaries and scope of the beginning relationship. Judgments made in the first few minutes can be critical in maintaining and defining future work. Experience in these matters shows that factors such as abilities to relate, commitment, patience, and articulateness also figure in the assessment process. Apart from the influence of content, particular emphasis needs to be placed on the manner in which content is displayed or communicated and on nonverbal cues such as body language, dress, facial mannerisms, and the like.

Many experienced practitioners can identify with the negative feelings and motivations expressed by the staff person; a combination of nasty weather and recovering from the flu is sufficient cause to look for a postponement. But true to a professional's attitude—and to her credit—she persevered. This is particularly crucial when working with populations for whom attending a meeting is considered a chore.

The worker performed a number of actions at this initial meeting of what appears to be a grassroots neighborhood group intended to work toward improved living conditions for concerned tenants. She was constantly in motion from the time she arrived at Mrs. Green's apartment. She involved John, an adolescent, who had negative sentiments toward the landlord, to help distribute flyers to notify neighbors of the meeting, thus converting negative energy to a positive outcome. In addition, John's comments, though perhaps intensified by adolescent sentiment, provided her with clues to the neighbors' fearful perception of the landlord, a significant dynamic on its own. Mrs. Barts's choice to take an active part rather than attend a wrestling match, as she had previously stated, offered another indication of the seriousness of the meeting and the potential for participation. Ambivalent tenant-landlord relationships are hardly new ground, especially when owners are perceived as uncaring, demanding, and perhaps callous.

Typical of neighborhood meetings, the staff person made arrangements for some sort of refreshment. Staying in motion, she stopped to contact a bachelor tenant, not at home. In the process, and through pregroup work, she learned that Mr. Harris, previously projected as a leader, had moved, thereby validating the information she had gained in the role-induction phase.

The worker returned to the apartment prearranged as a meeting place, a strategic choice not only for purposes of safety but as a symbol: a centerpiece of representing interests of other neighbors. This strategy is essential for instilling conditions for bonding.

Having discovered that there was no cream, the worker recruited Mr. Dietz, a member, to go purchase the item, and together she and Mr. Dietz did so. At the same time, the worker added to her assessment of Mr. Dietz, which could be utilized later as various members' roles developed.

Like many meetings, this one started off slowly, with participants trickling in. During these moments of formation, additional content and informal discussions between the worker and others took place. Even in these brief episodes, assessment on both sides continued, and the staff person was working.

The learning process about conditions and concerns continued for some time, and at 8:05 P.M. thirteen neighbors were present in the apartment. Inclement weather notwithstanding, the apartment is hot, requiring that the door be left open. While it is not clear how Mr. Carter was chosen to take minutes, this indicates the presence of some dynamics in operation already. In the process of a two-week interview schedule before the meeting, the staff person, operating at both cognitive and affective levels, had succeeded in inspiring sufficient trust to cause a significant number of tenants to appear. Clearly, the worker had had to communicate an understanding of the issues and the deep meaning they held for the tenants and had succeeded in doing so.

The beginnings of meetings are crucial because whatever has been communicated in private interviews regarding concerns, roles, ways of thinking, and possibilities needs to be reframed again in the group context. In this case, the worker stated her interests, work, title, and role as advisor and at the same time emphasized the source of strength represented in the group through the membership. Significantly, two events took place at this juncture. The staff person asked the members to introduce themselves rather than doing it herself and resisted the invitation to do so. The first step to commitment was implied in encouraging the members to introduce themselves. The fifteen-second delay before anyone complied revealed participants' apprehensions concerning the landlord, as did their preference for having someone else perform the introductions. But the demand for work that the staff person's insistence that participants introduce themselves suggested was important (Shulman, 2001). Once a member started, the others continued. Breaking the ice was a large step, perhaps assisted by informal discussions as members trickled in. Issues and concerns began to emerge. Mr. Ashley, a tenant caretaker and employee of the landlord, fearful that his role would be compromised, was supported by the group when they agreed not to identify him in the minutes.

There is clearly a sense of the group as a group. Various issues were raised, such as front-door locks, apartment break-ins, strangers in the hallway, and the landlord's resistance to granting mailbox keys to the tenants and giving the mailman one for the front door. In this last case, there was a question of legality, and the worker assumed responsibility for checking it out. The worker was establishing early on her special role in the group.

Differences arose among several members about whether children could use front-door keys, views that could have produced simmering negative feelings. The worker handled this admirably by suggesting both points of view could be considered. Other issues of concern included lack of a laundry room, which had been closed several years before because of safety concerns. The lack of a fire escape added to a full agenda for the group to consider.

The worker volunteered to assume responsibility for checking the necessity of a fire escape by reviewing building specifications. Slowly but surely, the viability of a group appeared to be becoming promising.

To check progress as a group at this point, the staff person asked if there was a need for the group to unite, to which she received a positive response. Attempts to name the group were put on hold, however, since that seemed premature, though it was recognized as a reasonable next step. Not only would it firmly establish the identity of the group as a group, it would gain recognition from those outside the group, thus affirming the beginning of authority.

Whether a letter should be sent to the landlord regarding concerns was postponed until all three buildings could be contacted, thus extending the scope of the group. The timing and content of the letter needed further discussion since there was not unanimity on either of those questions. A subgroup was formed to contact members in other buildings as well as to assign a date for the next meeting, which signified authority, subdivision of tasks and responsibilities, and group development.

At the end, the staff person summarized the actions taken by the group. She had done her job well, from start to finish, defining her role in helping the group establish a beginning identity. In addition, plans for next steps were articulated, and a subcommittee authorized to pursue several issues. The need to prioritize was firmly established. After the meeting, about half the members stayed behind to engage in informal discussions, quite likely evaluating their experiences, among them, the dynamics of urban renewal. The information was important because issues were reinforced and concerns unstated at the meeting raised. In some ways, the informal discussions increased safety, bonding concerns and laying groundwork for the next meeting. For the worker, as part of the continuing assessment, the pool of potential leaders was clarified and needs for affiliation met.

In summary, this case study documents a creditable job by a worker who, though fretful at the start, competently guided the process of group formation and planning. In addition to developing affective (interpersonal) boundaries, she was able to exercise the demand for work as well. To increase the group's sense of itself, she sidestepped potential conflicts; took on responsibilities as her domain, and cemented her role, identifying next steps and being patient about group development. Her high level of activity is characteristic of work with grassroots citizens' groups in their beginning stage.

6

LEADERSHIP IN WORKING GROUPS

A s WE POINTED OUT in chapter 5, there exists a considerable amount of literature dealing with leadership, of which we review only a very small portion. Leadership has been divided into subconcepts such as trait-based, situation-based, and structurally based leadership, leading to recent thinking about context, among other subjects. In this chapter we offer some comments that flow from our consideration of leadership phenomena, in the hope that they will prove useful both to professional practitioners and to chairs and group members, whether paid or volunteer. In our view, skill in filling the role of staff, chair, or member of a working group includes a flexible and comfortable ability to assume leadership roles and to cast them off, using conscious judgments of the needs of the group and the needs of the group's task as guides. Being frozen into a need always to function in a leadership capacity or, conversely, never to do so is not helpful for group practitioners and members.

LEADERSHIP AS REPRESENTATIVE AND DISTRIBUTIVE FUNCTIONS

Leadership as a representative function means leadership status obtained within the group by representatives of particular publics or influential bodies or by individuals who are powerful either inside or outside the group. The legitimacy of such leadership, whether for individuals or subgroups, derives from their positions, their abilities, or their backgrounds, acquired elsewhere and carried into the group. Leadership as a distributive function means the readiness of individuals within the group to assume leadership at various points in the group's life, depending on their own expertise, the nature of the group's task, the group's stage of development, or pressures and turbulence in the group's external environment.

At its best, there is a fit, or dialectic, between these two types of leadership that in mature working groups produces productivity and a readiness on the part of individual group members to meet the group's needs. At its worst, there is a lack of fit between these two, which results in unfulfilled desires for leadership positions on the part of group members and unfilled leadership roles within the group when it needs these roles to be filled for its own productivity and success. These concepts grow out of the early work of Redl (1942), who identified a series of ten "central persons" for groups, each reflecting a response to a need within the group's membership at a particular time. The concepts were further developed by Thelen (1958), who demonstrated empirically that leadership and membership may be further divided into positive, negative, and neutral categories in dimensions such as fight, flight, dependency, counterdependency, and pairing, all based on Bion's theoretical formulations (1961).

The Personality Strand

People in positions of group leadership carry, to a greater or lesser extent, fears of exposure and fears of being negatively evaluated.[1] Fears of negative evaluation may stem from early socialization experiences. Sticking out in a crowd can mean taking a chance of being knocked down. Yet, in order to be effective and to be perceived as legitimate in a leadership position, one must find sufficient security to act decisively. How this security is found is a somewhat mysterious process, but some are able to find it sooner and more easily than others, and most learn to find it better given successful experience. For example, a staff person who works with a board of directors has to be able to set aside the fact that the board collectively controls his employment if he is to work effectively. How does one do this?

Group members may or may not carry a moral presence into small groups. Such presence has something to do with but is not the same as competence. It seems to be linked to a normative perception by group members that a particular individual is able to balance caring about the group's success, respect for the contribution of group members, and knowledge and skill at group processes, as well as possessing the ability to help the group work within an atmosphere of "equanimity" (Thelen, 1981). This is what prevents a group from going off track and/or helps bring the group back from such excursions. Moral presence also reflects a perception of others that a member's own needs are sufficiently under control that they will not overwhelm the prospects of the group's success.

To occupy a leadership position, one need not be exceptional, but one does need to be able to behave in specific patterns in a disciplined way. These patterns should cause the group as a whole to view the leader as a helping person rather than as someone who operates out of biases or a desire to satisfy his or her own needs. Later in the chapter, we will list helpful and destructive role behaviors in groups, which may help to give shape to this point.

The messages that come from an effective leader need to communicate the energy and commitment to follow decisions through and implement them. A certain resilience is also needed, so that the leader is not perceived as fragile and unable to handle the overt expression of intense feelings. If a leader is so perceived, this will inhibit the expression of strong feelings within the group and may limit the amount of genuine investment that group members feel they can make.

A sense of perspective, including identity with the historic mission of the organization and the part that the group plays in this history, is important. What is needed here is not only knowledge about the past but also a sense of historic patterning. Work groups often seek and feel rewarded by a sense that what they do is contributing to an organization's mission over time. Sometimes, especially in fiduciary groups, this perspective extends over decades or even generations. It is perhaps for this reason that service on building committees is often viewed as desirable for someone who aspires to leadership. Building committees produce something that is tangible and generally lasts for a long time. A sense of participating in a long-lasting and significant work can give meaning to groups and to their members.

Social/Organizational Strands

During times when conservative ideologies are ascendant, whether in the broader political sphere or within a particular organization, there is often a sense that resources are limited or even decreasing. These times tend to reward leadership that is viewed as oriented toward organizational survival and established ways of behaving and linking with other groups. On the other hand, in times when progressive ideologies hold sway and resources are perceived as increasing or as relatively unlimited, exactly the opposite types of leadership may be rewarded. In either case, one of the demands of leadership is a dual regard for a sense of history and continuity within the group and within the larger organization.

In the Winterset Advisory Committee of example E, controversy arose when a group of conscientious objectors and draft resisters wanted to use the neighborhood house in order to propound their points of view. Though several staff members were individually in sympathy with the purposes of the new group, their perception of the community was that it prided itself on having sent heroes to virtually all the wars of American history. The controversy about the group's proposal needed to include the members' sense of the community's history and self-perception.

Variables of gender, class, race, ethnicity, and age affect small group processes and the nature of leadership in groups in several ways. The variables may mediate perceptions and norms within groups and thus may affect the standards against which leadership behavior is judged. They may influence perceptions of "us" and "them," provide frameworks for infusing both words and actions with meaning, and determine in part the group's sense of proprieties.

Status positions in the outside world have a way of being reflected in a group, especially when these positions are widely known within the community of reference. In a sense, working groups can fall victim to a "halo effect." One way this can happen is in the selection of formal leadership, such as group officers. Unexamined and unaware status transfer can be destructive. Picking an unusually successful businessperson as chair, for example, because of his or her status in the community can be destructive to the group and its task accomplishment if this person is unprepared to assume formal leadership of the group.

The location of a group within an organization needs to be taken into account. Where a group falls within an organizational hierarchy, to whom it reports, and at what levels are examples of organizational location issues. It seems to us that this factor mostly works indirectly, through an intervening variable of group self-esteem. These strands will be discussed in greater depth in chapter 9.

The status of a leader within the total organization is a factor within a working group. A considerable body of research demonstrates that job satisfaction is partially a function of one's superior's perceived status in the organization (Harris, 1976). Indications that a leader is or is not in favor in an organization's hierarchy affect group members' perceptions not only of the leader but also of themselves.

The higher a group is within the organization—that is, the closer the group comes to having major policy or fiduciary responsibility for an organization—the more concerned, we hypothesize, that group is likely to be about the organization as a whole and the interorganizational world. This is not to say that such groups or their leadership will have less concern with the substance of group task. Rather, their frame of reference or field of vision is likely to be significantly broader, and thus their concern with the interorganizational field of action greater. At the same time, we hypothesize that the higher a group is in the organizational structure, the less free it is likely to feel to attempt innovative solutions or seek creative new directions in its own group life.

The clientele served by an organization is an important component of the way working groups within that organization will operate. The term "criminal lawyer," though the adjective refers to the attorney's clients and not the attorney, is widely viewed as a term of opprobrium. The folklore of guilt by association affects not only attorneys but also organizations that deliver health or human services to deprived populations and those who are associated with those organizations. Conversely, some organizations may be elevated in others' and their own views, particularly in the views of those whom they serve. Characteristics of clients/patients can serve as markers for prestige or stigma for staff and members of working groups within organizations. Each group, together with its staff leadership, engages in a self-definition process based on its task, its membership, the nature of the organization of which it is part, and those whom it serves.

Health and human service organizations by definition serve people who need services. Various myths of our society stress self-reliance. Thus a person in need of help as well as the organization that seeks to help that person both may start out with a deficit in symbolic self-definition. The stigmatizing process seems to operate more directly with regard to organizations that serve the poor than with regard to organizations that serve the sick. Perhaps this is because our society has learned that sickness is not the result of moral deficit, while parts of our society still believe that poverty is. In any case, the stigma or lack of prestige that attaches to an organization, while deplorable, can be a fact of life for the working groups within it.

One's authority in a service delivery organization stems largely from one's bureaucratic position. Organizational authority is real but evanescent and temporary. Authority in a bureaucratic system is vested in an office and not in a person (Weber, 1947). This is a significant fact for leadership in groups. Effective leadership requires comfort with the nature of organizational authority; neither a refusal to assume it nor a self-important confusion of person with office.

The extent to which group leadership can obtain access to the appropriate organizational resources plays an important part not only in the group's but also in the leader's self-perception. Effective leadership requires both access to resources and a clear sense of boundaries between the group's resources and those that are not under its control. This is not to preclude conflict and rearrangement of resources. Rather, the organization's resources are defined by the successful group leader as assets rather than as magic, unreachable keys to success.

The Citizenship Strand

Ephross (1983) has pointed out the negative consequences of ignoring staff members' needs for personal satisfaction through their work. There is no contradiction between meeting a staff's interpersonal needs and those of clients/patients. These two processes are intertwined parts of a productive organizational orientation. This is especially the case for staff who work with working groups. The sensitivities required in working groups are often experienced as intense and personal, so the behavior of an individual leader is important both in and of itself and because the leadership role is likely as a magnet for responses from group members. The behavior of a leader can exacerbate, enhance, neutralize, or energize various behaviors among other group members. All leaders attract some hostility, for example. Some leaders, however, exacerbate this hostility through their behavior and self-presentations. Others tend to minimize hostility; as a result, negative feelings are not expressed in such a way as to prevent the group from operating.

In keeping with the general theme of this book, we do not regard leadership talent as something inherent at birth or developed for all time. Many leadership skills—like many other kinds of group skills—can be practiced and learned. At any given point, however, it is important for any leader in any group to understand one's personal strengths and weaknesses and to work consistently to maximize the positive aspects of his leadership behaviors, as well as to pursue the use of language and interpersonal communications that can facilitate group success and minimize group failures.

THE PROACTIVE LEADER

The group is an arena for action. Group leadership is a proactive concept. In order to lead, one must do some things in order to bring about other things. Even sitting quietly and reflectively in a group is an action: leaders do not need to talk all the time or to engage in any other particular kinds of behaviors. We do suggest, however, that passivity is an inappropriate stance for a leader in a working group.[2]

In example A, the Mayor's Task Force, Dr. Wiley became noted for his characteristic reaction when someone suggested "the group will work it out." Dr.

Wiley would respond, "The group will work it out if we help them to frame the problem, present alternative solutions, and help them to work it out." Dr. Wiley was expressing his understanding of the principle just named. Leadership needs to lead. A passive dependence on group process, in his view as in ours, does not lead to the successful accomplishment of group goals.

One cannot lead a working group and be liked, admired, or approved of at all times. This is not to say that leadership does not carry with it affective rewards. Often, groups give their leadership approval and emotional rewards, but this takes place over the long haul. At any given moment, leadership may be resisted, met with hostility or anger, or invested by the group with strong feelings that come from other experiences and other groups. Leaders in working groups, in our view, need to avoid the trap of being "love junkies." Insofar as one emotionally needs approval and "love" from a group at all times, one is incapacitating oneself for effective group leadership.

LEADERSHIP AND REFLECTION

Bales (1970) noted that we seek to understand each other through empathic identification. In order to understand what is going on in a group, a leader has to be able to intuit relevant parts of in the cognitions and feelings of others. This ability to sense, feel, synthesize, and reproduce selective aspects of the behavior of another person is called empathy. One cannot restrict one's empathy to one person or one subgroup that holds one view. The route to empathy is self-understanding through meditative reflection or meditative reflection shared with another. In other words, in order to be an effective leader, one has to be able to empathize with others, including individuals and subgroups with whom one may or may not agree (Goleman, 2000).

A leader needs to be able to scan and comprehend both the internal group environment and the external organizational environment to avoid getting stuck in any one orientation. Detachment and empathy are two parts of highly synthesized processes called understanding and assessment. In this context, sense making, or mindfulness, particularly in fluid situations, is useful (Weick, 2001). One needs to be able to consider the group part to part, part to whole, and as a whole in a relatively rapid and systematic rotating fashion. This is a skill that can be learned; once learned, it seems to become second nature.

In trying to understand a group's needs for leadership, it is important to be as empathic and imaginative as possible through the full use of one's abilities and sensitivities. This means that one has to be able to act on one's hunches as well as on the basis of available data. Often, the most useful thing a leader can do in a group is to share a feeling. We suggest a very simple formula: "I am getting the feeling that ... ," or, "The discussion that has just taken place leaves me with the feeling that. . . . " A group leader is a learner as well, and phrases like these help one to learn.

Group leaders as well as group members tend to block things that are not well understood. Isolated and sometimes paradoxical facts that are not understood can constitute excellent points of entry into improved understanding. An ability to withstand unpleasant facts can be a great help to understanding. (This last is a sentence that most leaders of working groups would do well to reread periodically.)

It is difficult to gain genuine understanding of a person, a subgroup, or a whole group all at once. Being open to acquiring new information and examining it for its implications is essential. One needs to gain new insights from various sources continuously and to search constantly for indicators of impending changes in the group. The processes of change in a member or group need to be monitored by constantly gathering new information. A function of leadership in a group is to help the group to be able to monitor or track such indicators.

To understand group behavior, one must look for patterns in order to formulate generalizations. One does well to open one's mind to new perceptions and combinations; it is hungry for information and enjoys combining, synthesizing, and achieving new insights. Changed circumstances can serve as a starting point for new syntheses. Bales (1970) points out that most of the basic difficulty in studying and working with groups comes from the complexity of their internal and external environments. Viewing what's going on in a group simply, one is probably misperceiving it: groups are hardly simple.

To be able to engage reflectively with the situation is the hallmark of professional leadership. Argyris and Schon (1974) and Schon (1983) have stressed the role of theory-in-use in explaining a great deal of human behavior. Members have their own theories, and leaders need to help create a group culture within which there is opportunity for each member to test out theories and their utility for the group. Intuition is also important for leaders; one intuits and feels things going on within the group's life. It is important to think about one's intuitions before translating them into action.

SOCIAL WORK PRACTICE

In social work with groups, practitioners oftentimes find themselves dealing with an array of competing demands between and among individual members, the group, and the organization. Problem solving in this context posses considerable challenges to assessment and intervention, and it is not possible to have sufficient and complete knowledge of the person-in-situation, given that the windows for assessment can vary among the personal, interpersonal, and organizational domains.

In general, social work practitioners cannot approach a task as a fixed reality but have to deal with problems and possibilities in a time-limited, task-specific world. In this regard, worker activities require a broad range of knowledge, which includes abilities to recognize and prioritize problems, search for pertinent data, set forth directions, work with people, reach decisions under the pressure of time, and control and evaluate performance. Qualities such as imagination, flexibility, and fortitude are necessities. The process of sensing is quite relevant here.

Schon's (1983) work on professional practice is instructive in developing a framework for practice. The question he raises and addresses is, to put it simply, "rigor or relevance"? Rigor addresses the technical rationality or grounded specificity one sees in formulaic problem solving. Relevance refers to the expertise needed to deal with or manage the diversities demonstrated or exercised by divergent and possibly competing interests.

Three processes are conceptualized in encompassing professional practice.

1. Knowing-in-action: This refers to intellectual intuition or common sense that results in a spontaneous, skillful behavior.
2. Reflecting-in-action: This denotes thinking on one's feet, demonstrated by thinking about what one is doing in the act of doing it. Schon calls it learning while doing and doing while learning.
3. Reflecting-in-practice: This aspect broadens reflecting-in-action from a situation to a professional arena in which one repeatedly reflects on the work at hand. It is manifested in spontaneous pauses to think through a situation or a mood. It can be likened to the use of solitude, idle speculation, or the exercise of preliminary empathy.

The practice approach encourages on-the-spot decision making in the context of repetitions and variations commonly found in direct practice. There is honest respect for both the unencumbered moment for theorizing as well as the formulas developed empirically.

We visualize a leader at this point reflecting as follows: What's being discussed is real. But does it correspond to the reality that I experience in trying to lead working groups? In my work, I experience deadlines, budget demands, pulls and tugs from various parts of the organization and various group members. How am I to make use of this comforting but somewhat abstract discussion? How do I know when to reflect and analyze and when to respond and take decisive action?

We suggest as a guide here the principle of the "middle range," also known as "moderation," also known as the "comfort zone." Infinite reflection leads to paralysis and inaction. On the other hand, "shooting from the hip," or behaving in unexamined ways in groups, rarely leads to success. What is needed is a middle range, a balance, between reflection, on the one hand, and willingness to risk by taking action, on the other; between intuitive responsiveness, on the one hand, and an awareness of external constraints and limits, on the other. Effective group leaders are able both to engage in the world of internal reflection and "process" and respond to the constraints and opportunities set by the external environment, the charge of the group, and the structure of the organization. Perhaps most important, effective leaders in working groups are able to help groups alternate between reflection and action without excessive fear, guilt, or internal senses of conflict.

A final reminder is that leaders have a right to fail. In fact, groups have a right to fail. It is from examining these failures that groups and leaders can learn for the future. A fear of failure can inhibit looking at what has happened in a group. Groups that are afraid to fail generally do.

SUMMARY AND CAUTION

Leadership in groups can be compared to conducting an orchestra. What does a conductor do? A simple answer is wave one's arms. Surely, however, this does not describe adequately the function or the role behavior of a conductor. A better answer might be that a conductor hears inwardly what the notes on the printed page can sound like and then proceeds to share this hearing with the members of the orchestra. Were this not so, each conductor would produce an identical rendition of the same piece, which is certainly not what happens.

A leader—whether staff, chair, or member—similarly needs to be able to "hear," which translates in groups into creative anticipation. Once group patterns are beginning to be set, leadership moves between these patterns with increasing precision and understands the likelihood of variability. Great conductors, for example, can hold an entire score in their heads (though they may refer to the music now and then), and an effective group leader needs to be able to do the equivalent.

One of the responsibilities of a leader, then, is to maintain a sense of balance and perspective and to transmit this sense to group members. The ability to frame and reframe what is going on in a group and the group's charge are important skills in this regard.

In example B, a consistent contribution from the executive director of the Avon Friendly Society was his ability to reframe issues in such a way that the group could understand that what was going on in Avon was related to—though possibly not identical with—what was going on across the country in a variety of traditional family service agencies. Each time he reminded the group of this fact, there was a perceptible lightening of the atmosphere within the group. The guilt that members were experiencing about how they had succumbed to a particular problem was dissipated as members realized that they were engaging in a process related to major changes within the broader society. Instead of being defined as failures of the board, the situations were experienced more and more often as chances for creative planning and responses to changing social circumstances and needs on the part of the population being served.

Leadership and Authority

There are several kinds of authority in a working group. The first, and perhaps the most obvious, is that which derives from the status of leader, whether staff or chair. Leaders begin, in most groups, with a sort of initial capital of authority. All other things being equal, groups tend to respond to leaders as legitimate rather than the opposite. (Note that this is the case even within groups that define themselves as alternative, antiestablishment, or radical.) Leaders generally begin with authority capital on the positive side of the ledger.

A second kind of authority derives from the performance of leaders in their role. Leaders build credibility through successful and appropriate performance; when they have helped the group to deal with one situation, there is an increased faith within the group that they will help it deal with subsequent situations. In this way, a small success leads to greater success. The converse is also true, if one bears in mind the fact that a leadership failure is not the same thing as an unsuccessful piece of work by the group. A leader may have been successful in that she was able to help a group survive failure and derive the maximum learning from that the experience. Failure in a leadership role, however, erodes the capital of authority.

A third kind of authority derives from the authority of the group. Successful groups build self-esteem, and that self-esteem generalizes to those who occupy leadership positions within the group. Individual members, with their personal and organizational backgrounds, aid in this process.

A fourth kind of authority can be called "the authority of salient publics". This kind of authority is especially noteworthy in groups that are coalitions, councils, or representative in some formal way (Ephross and Weiss, 1985). Each of the members has authority that derives from his place in the public he represents; group leaders enjoy the total of this authority.

Leaders also carry personal, "moral" authority. Leaders in working groups need to develop self-concepts based on their own competence, ability to work within an ethical framework, and ability to influence others. Some people develop this kind of authority from early childhood, while others learn it slowly and painfully as adults. The wise group, and the wise staff member in such groups, will maximize the use in leadership positions of group members who carry a high degree of personal moral authority (Bums, 1980).

Finally, there is a form of authority in groups that derives from the method of free inquiry, which is often expressed as "doing one's homework." This authority, the authority of knowledge, derives from a full, open, and clear consideration of the issues, including the political issues that surround a particular problem or task. This done, there is a feeling of certainty that allows a leader as well as a group as a whole to feel comfortable with their own processes, products, and decisions.

A new element in organizational power that has been developing over the past several decades accelerated its growth around 1990. This is the authority that comes from expertise in the use of technology to create, analyze, and report data. Computerization serves as a label for this process, though in fact its influence goes far beyond actual computer equipment to encompass the entire field of information technology. Health and human service organizations are major users of new technologies, and this use can be expected to increase in tandem with greater demands for the production of data for purposes of gaining support, accounting to the public and to funding sources, and improving both tracking and the ability to analyze data regarding both the quantity and quality of services.

It is only recently that the professional education of health care and human service personnel has begun to include information technology expertise. More and more students, it is true, are coming to their professional educations with previous experience in the use of computers, email, the World Wide Web, distance learning sources, computerized literature searches, and other applications of technology to gain access to good and services. Long-distance courses of professional education and consultations-at-a-distance proliferate, as does the use of both audio and video recording in professional education, continuing education, meetings of professional societies, and committee meetings by conference telephone and video.

Our aim is not only to note the growth in the use of technology but to examine the influence of this growth on the processes of working groups within organizational settings and, indeed, on organizations themselves, as well as to look at the implications for group and organizational leadership. It is a cliché to observe that, in an organization, knowledge is power. In the past, this comment has been made about both intra- and extraorganizational knowledge, and the principle remains true, in our opinion.

What is new, however, is both the achieved and ascribed power that accrue to people within an organization who are, or are viewed as, experts on technology. They may be experts in the entire field or have more limited expertise in the use, strengths, and weakness of a brand of hardware, a particular piece of software, or a given system of word processing or statistical analysis. The power of such experts (or, sometimes, self-declared experts), can take one or more of several forms, for example:

- influencing or determining which data are collected;
- developing instruments to collect data, especially evaluative data, on organizations, people served, outcomes, and so on;
- making judgments, often forcefully expressed, on the validity,. feasibility, value, or potential findings of particular administrative and research programs, protocols, and designs;
- accessing the Internet, with its huge supply of findings, which range from the most questionable to the most highly supported;
- interpreting ethical and other requirements insofar as it is proposed to implement them, analyze them, or perform comparative studies of their effects on clients/patients, often those of the most intense need; and
- influencing the use of resources, both human and material.

The power that can accrue to technology experts is generated largely outside of the usual bureaucratic or other organizational trappings of power. This authority can accumulate unchallenged and out of synchrony with the structure and operation of the organization. In some circumstances, relatively junior staff members can, with the aid of their technological sophistication, find ways to involve themselves in organizational decision making that would otherwise be dealt with at a level some echelons above their own.

Understanding the uses and pitfalls of technological sophistication and working effectively with technology experts are major tasks for organizational leaders at all levels that have only rarely been mentioned in past programs of professional education.

Leadership Roles: Facilitative and Inhibitive

For leaders as for members, particular role behaviors can at different times be constructive, destructive, or both. What makes the difference is not the behavior but the needs of a group and its members at the time and the motivation and emotional connotations that surround the behavior at a particular time. The extent to which a leader is open to receiving feedback from a group that may modify his or her behavior also contributes to the constructive potential of particular behaviors.

Table 6.1, taken from Underwood (1977), is a useful summary of the ways in which particular behaviors can be facilitative, provided that they are carried on within a middle range and that the leader is open to group feedback. Extremes of behavior can be inhibitive—that is, destructive—to the group.

What we have argued throughout this chapter is that leadership is a transactional phenomenon. It is related to everything else that goes on within a group. If we have slighted the task-specific aspects of leadership, it is because we will cover these in succeeding chapters. For review, we close this discussion of leadership with an ad hoc list of danger signals leaders should watch for in themselves that may be useful for quick reference.

LEADER DANGER SIGNALS
1. Postmeeting depression.
2. Not understanding what's going on.
3. Making remarks that are too smooth or too crude.
4. Attempting consistently to impress client (members).
5. Obtaining a lot of satisfaction from others' praise and becoming dependent on it.
6. Wanting an intervention to lead to a terrific success.
7. Focusing only on one subsystem.
8. Creating change overload or swamping the system.
9. Inappropriate attachment to the group: getting too close, or too distant, or too angry.

TABLE 6.1 *Ways in Which Particular Behaviors Can Be Facilitative or Inhibitive*

INHIBITIVE	FACILITATIVE	INHIBITIVE
Task-Oriented Roles		
Initiating New Ideas		
Not initiating ideas when needed.	Suggesting or proposing new things to do or changes in doing something	Initiating ideas of changes when not needed.
Seeking Information		
Allowing issues to bog down when new information is needed	Asking for clarification of additional facts	Seeking information when enough is already present.
Seeking Opinions		
Not asking others for opinions when they might be helpful.	Asking not for facts but for the opinions or values pertinent to issues.	Seeking opinions when facts are relevant.
Giving Information		
Withholding information when it is needed.	Offering facts or generalizations about issues or relating own pertinent experience.	Clouding the issue by supplying more information than is needed.
Elaborating		
Withholding sufficient elaboration.	Developing a clearer or additional meaning or providing reasons or deduction	Providing elaboration when issue is already clear.
Coordinating		
Not providing coordination when needed.	Showing relationships between ideas and events. Pulling ideas, suggestions, and activities together.	Forcing relationships between the ideas or events.

TABLE 6.1   *Ways in Which Particular Behaviors Can Be Facilitative or Inhibitive* (continued)

INHIBITIVE	FACILITATIVE	INHIBITIVE
Task-Oriented Roles		
Orienting		
Failing to supply needed orientation.	Defining the position of a goal with respect to its start and conclusion. Showing deviation from appropriate direction	Orienting that is overdeterminative and restrictive.
Evaluating		
Evaluating too little or no at all	Supplying standards of accomplishment and subjecting group progress to measure	Too much or unrealistic evaluating.
Stimulating		
Accepting lethargy or apathy.	Prodding the group to greater on-target action. Arousing greater or higher-quality activity.	Overstimulating resulting in non-productive activity.
Maintenance-Oriented Roles Encouraging		
Failing to encourage others or deflating them.	Commending, complimenting, supporting the contributions of others. Indicating under-standing, interests, and acceptance of others.	Shallow encouraging.
Harmonizing		
Not acting to reduce stifling conflict.	Mediating differences between others. Endeavoring to reconcile disagreements.	Preventing needed conflict from occurring or surfacing.

INHIBITIVE	FACILITATIVE	INHIBITIVE
Task-Oriented Roles		
Compromising		
Refusing to yield or give in.	Yielding own position, admitting error, or "coming half way" when involved in disagreement or conflict.	Yielding too soon or too far.
Open Communication		
Undertalking or not trying to encourage or control others.	Keeping channels open. Assuring that those who want to contribute feel comfortable doing so. Limiting overtalkative members, soliciting information from nontalkative members.	Overtalking or controlling others.
Evaluating Process		
Not paying attention to or ignoring process problems	Calling attention to group needs. Offering observations about group functioning problems. Encouraging members to work on process needs.	Overfocusing on process or creating pseudo-issues.
Accepting		
Engaging in too little accepting and interested listening.	Going along with group movement. Serving as interested audience.	Being too passive and not contributing.

ROLES NORMALLY DESTRUCTIVE TO BOTH ACCOMPLISHMENT AND GROUP MAINTENANCE

Aggressing

Withholding aggressive behavior.

Deflating others. Expressing disapproval of ideas, opinions, feelings of others. Degrading members of group

Expressing aggression in a constructive way

Blocking

Withholding blocking behavior.

Being negativistic, stubbornly resistant. Maintaining or returning to issues the group has rejected. Disagreeing or opposing beyond reason. Being caustic, cynical.

Admitting blocking tendencies and asking for help dealing with these tendencies.

Dominating

Withholding dominating behavior.

Trying to exert authority in manipulating the group or certain members. Using flattery. Directing, demanding.

Channeling dominating tendencies into constructive help for the group.

Seeking Recognition

Shifting recognition to others

Maintaining a central position or the center of attention. Overtalking, being boastful, or seemingly humble.

Entering central position for specific purpose then leaving it.

Playing

Inhibiting low-involvement behavior cues.

Maintaining and displaying lack of involvement. Using nonchalance, joking, raising off-target or mundane issues.

Using levity to relieve tension for constructive purposes

TABLE 6.1 *Ways in Which Particular Behaviors Can Be Facilitative or Inhibitive* (continued)

ROLES NORMALLY DESTRUCTIVE TO BOTH ACCOMPLISHMENT AND GROUP MAINTENANCE

Pleading Special Interests

Resisting pleading special interests when not constructive to the group.

Using the group to satisfy personal interests only. Standing on stereotypic principles to the detriment of the group.

Expressing only those personal interests that are helpful to the group.

Sympathizing

Withholding expression of self-pity.

Endeavoring to elicit sympathy responses from whole group or certain members. Depreciating self beyond reason. Self-pitying.

Honestly expressing feelings when useful to the group.

7

LEADERSHIP AND CONTEXTS

SLOWLY AND STEADILY, a new paradigm has been developing and gaining momentum on the American landscape. Paradigms are models or patterns meant to represent a worldview. A paradigm contains within its scope the most basic beliefs about the human condition. According to Patton (1975), a paradigm is "a world view, a general perspective, a way of breaking down the complexity of the real world. As such, paradigms are deeply embedded in the socialization of adherents and practitioners telling them what is important, what is legitimate, what is reasonable. Paradigms are normative; they tell the practitioner what to do without the necessity of long existential or epistemological considerations" (29). At any given time, there may be many paradigms, each relating to something different, for example, the Olympic Games, directions for social work practice, ideas about good and bad, and other issues.

Central to paradigms are beliefs. In an era of transition, the old stories of how we envision the world give way to new narratives not yet quite in place. Peter Schwartz and James Ogilvy (Schwartz and Ogilvy, 1979: 14; quoted in Lincoln, 1985:32–33), at the Stanford Research Institute, have tracked the emergence of a new paradigm through years of exploring how and in what ways formal disciplines are changing in fields as diverse as physics, religious studies, chemistry, the arts, and so forth. The authors note the following changes:

1. From a simple probabilistic world toward a diverse and complex new society.
2. From a hierarchical system to a belief that there are several, or a plurality of orders.
3. From a mechanistic view to one of organic development, including constant interaction and differentiation.

4. From a determinate to an indeterminate social world, simply not controllable or predictable.
5. From causal (if ... then) thinking to a recognition of the importance of visuality and symbiosis.
6. Morphogenesis—creation of new parts and combinations without predicting on the basis of knowing individual pieces.
7. Multiple views of the same phenomenon in multiple realities and multiple forms.

Broadly speaking, in this view, every unit contains within it enough information to represent the whole. Therefore, viewing any one entity has the possibility of leading to other entities, large or small.

In terms of organization, the new paradigm is a direct contrast to Weberian thinking. Weber, a paradigm builder, described an organization in its pure form: concepts such as efficiency, division of labor, official functions and rules, authority traveling downward, regulations of conduct, disciplines, and legal authority, conducted through offices or bureaus for a rational and calculable unit in which standards ruled the day. The essential assumptions of Weber still govern popular conceptions of organizations (policies, rules, organizational charts, etc.), plans, projections, personal evaluations, and so forth. Against this, organizations responsive to the new paradigm tend to focus on diversity, the development of networks, loose coupling arrangements and subunits, creative ambiguity in smaller stable units whereby greater skills are developed. The simple, stable configurations of teams are a response to complex states. The orderliness is present between and among linkages in the small units. In simpler terms, organizations may be viewed as an association of small groups. Not only are small groups essential to expediting, redefining, and implementing policies, but the linkages between and among these small groups are imperative for defining what the organization will or will not do, as well as in terms of the growth of the members.

Glidewell's view is instructive in relating small groups to organizational structure. He states that "the actions of larger forces in the community act through resources interchanged among small face-to-face groups—dyads, triads, families, neighborhoods and work groups. Decisions are not sufficient unless they are reinforced by the actions of many of the small face-to-face groups which are the basic implementing social component of the community—families, neighborhoods, classroom, work groups, church groups, recreational groups (1972:216).

One begins to see a picture emerging of an organization in which leadership becomes central, if for no other reason than the emphasis on small units. The leadership model has to be built into the system's culture and practices inherent in the structure. The social, emotional, interpersonal aspects of human capital that will drive the organization become important benchmarks for consideration. There may be less emphasis on coordination, direction, and control in favor of trust, permeable boundaries, and mutual support. To the extent that leadership is spread around, it becomes a source of creativity and intelligence, necessary in a changing world, not only within the organization but external to it as well. In this view, the organization goes through a process of confronting and exercising democracy with its varieties of types of leadership necessary for difference kinds of contexts.

Karl Weick states that issues of meaning, direction, and sense making occupy a central role in leadership. In contexts that are loose, one can expect ambiguity, which in turn can determine structure as well as open up opportunities. Rationality, he argues, reduces intuition, group responses, and openness to trial and error, all valuable tools when risk taking is increased. Arguing for patience, Weick makes the point that looking backward (retrospection) is a poor guide for prospective action; staying in motion, improvising, continually reworking ideas with new information will be the cornerstone of future leaders. In Weick's view, the map is not the territory it represents, which can become knowable only by using a compass. Thus, for Weick, a leadership act could be one where "I don't know" is the starting point, followed by exploring and reviewing situations at first unknowable, where it is not always possible to predict the effects of an action, where remaining silent is not an option. Weick makes a case for sense making or mindfulness, whereby one searches for a better question, accepts inexperience, stays in motion, and channels decisions with the best information available at the moment. For Weick, this legitimates doubt as a reasonable starting point for growth (Weick, 2001). This view of leadership is responsive to fluid, diverse, organizational focusing in stable small units and loosely linked systems.

In simple terms, the leader is one who can or will be able to find meaningful patterns when confronted with data that can be characterized as imprecise. Connectedness to other relevant units will be available, and, given the information, they can be moved into action. In the process, effective interpersonal skills will be at a premium

LEADERSHIP STYLES

Leadership and groups' organizational climates, synonymous with group cultures, have been examined most recently by Goleman, who argues that variations in leadership style produce different corresponding climates that expand the Lippitt and White formulations of autocratic, democratic, and laissez-faire (Lewin, Lippitt, and White, 1939).

Goleman (2000) states the following based on extensive research with various leaders in companies national and global. First, he believes that emotional intelligence is a prime mover of leadership. This is not to dismiss innate competence or managerial skill, but mood is extremely important in leadership, which in turn affects the organizational climate. Unlike perception, which rests at the top of personality, mood is a much more enduring quality of the person.

While Goleman focuses on both large and small start-up companies, his work is applicable to leadership of any kind in any organization, given that we view organizations, as mentioned before, as associations of small groups. The most salient elements of emotional leadership are self-awareness, self-regulation, motivation, empathy, and social skills (see table 7.1). In addition, Goleman argues that emotional intelligence isn't entirely an innate talent but measurable, teachable, and capable of being developed. Innate factors are altered through experience.

Goleman makes the point that the leader's moods and attendant behaviors set off a chain reaction affecting the behaviors and moods of everybody else. Cranky and unfeeling bosses create toxic responses that produce fear and anxiety. Where the climate is endowed with trust, sharing, risk taking, and learning, the dynamic interplay produces a high-level work culture. In trying to ascertain the way emotional intelligence drives performance from leader to member, Goleman suggests that the leader's actions and presence spread through a system like an electric current. An upbeat environment fosters finely tuned mental achievement and the expression of mood in both verbal and nonverbal ways. Laughter and humor, for example, when they resonate with the reality of a situation, have been found to enhance the group's work.

Using the five aspects of emotional intelligence, Goleman's research derived six leadership styles from various combinations of emotional intelligence. He designated these styles "coercive," "authoritative," "affiliative," "dem-

TABLE 7.1 *The Five Components of Emotional Intelligence at Work*

	DEFINITION	HALLMARKS
Self-Awareness	The ability to recognize and understand one's moods, emotions, and drives, as well as their effect on others	Self-confidence Realistic self-assessment Self-deprecating sense of humor
Self-Regulation	The ability to control or redirect disruptive impulses and moods. The propensity to suspend judgment, to think before acting	Trustworthiness and integrity Comfort with ambiguity Openness to change
Motivation	A passion to work for reasons that go beyond money or status. A propensity to pursue goals with energy and persistence	Strong drive to achieve Optimism, even in the face of failure Organizational commitment
Empathy	The ability to understand the emotional makeup of other people. Skill in treating people according to their emotional reactions	Expertise in building and retaining talent Cross-cultural sensitivity Service to clients and customers
Social Skills	Proficiency in managing relationships and building networks An ability to find common ground and build rapport	Effectiveness in leading change Persuasiveness Expertise in building and leading teams

ocratic," "pacesetting," and "coaching." Next, he correlated these styles to six key factors that influence an organization's working environment or culture, such as flexibility, responsibility, standards, rewards, clarity, and commitment. Of the six styles, summarized in table 7.2, only four had a positive impact on climate, though the other two may be useful in certain circumstances.

Coercive

Bullying and demeaning subordinates are key features of this style. Top-down decision making stops the production of new ideas. Self-initiative and pride in one's performance become devalued, and consequently whatever tools for motivation are available do not apply. While it seems reasonable to write off this approach. Goleman notes in a few specialized cases it may be advisable, such when there is a need for quick change in an organization or group frozen in self-destructive ineptitude.

Authoritative

Boldness and a clear vision characterize the authoritative style, which is often associated with new missions. In his research, Goleman states that this style is the most effective, benefiting every aspect of climate (83). Members are well informed as to their specific roles and goals. Clear standards, steady feedback, both positive and negative, and abundant leeway for members to innovate and take risks are important characteristics of this style. This style, however, is less effective when working with a group of experts (team members) and has a tendency to be overbearing, which will trigger resistance.

Affiliative

This style focuses on individuals and their emotions ranked higher than tasks or goals. It can foster fierce loyalty, flexibility, trust, and risk taking because it provides a protective envelope. Positive feedback spurs performance. Celebrations and informal personal meetings enhance group identity and feelings of belonging.

This style is particularly useful for building morale and improving communication. It is not unusual for the leader to be fairly open and above board about his or her own emotional states. One criticism, however, is that the affiliative style may produce mediocrity. It is not terribly useful when clear directives are needed to navigate through complicated scenarios and may lead to group failure.

Democratic

Leaders adopting this style spend time inviting input from fellow members, which helps build trust and commitment. Flexibility and responsibility are key by-products of this process, as well as a sense of realistic expectations. The democratic leader has a keen ability to listen and to exercise empathy such that group members can get involved in their own individualistic ways.

Sometimes this approach can produce many more meetings than are necessary. Progress can be slow, and specific decisions and deadlines often suffer. To gain consensus, necessary in any group session, a leader has to be skilled and sensitive to framing responses focused on the immediate goal, talents that may not be in the democratic leader's repertoire. Also, without a minimum level of competence among members, the democratic process may be weakened. but when fresh ideas are needed and there is uncertainty about next steps, the democratic style can be advantageous.

TABLE 7.2 *The Six Leadership Styles*

	COERCIVE	AUTHORITATIVE	AFFILIATIVE	DEMOCRATIC	PACESETTING	COACHING
The leader's modus operandi	Demands immediate compliance	Mobilizes people toward a vision	Creates harmony and builds emotional bonds	Forges consensus through participation	Sets high standards for performance	Develops people for the future
The style in a phase	"Do what I tell you."	"Come with me."	"People come first."	"What do you think?"	"Do as I do, now."	"Try this."
Underlying emotional intelligence competencies	Drive to achieve, initiative, self-control	Self-confidence, empathy, change catalyst	Empathy, building relationships, communication	Collaboration, team leadership, communication	Conscientious, drive to achieve, initiative	Developing others, empathy, self-awareness
When the style works best	In a crisis, to jump-start a turnaround, or to deal with problem employees	When changes require a new vision or where a clear direction is needed	To heal rifts in a team or to motivate people during stressful circumstances	To build buy-in or consensus or to get input from valuable employees	To get quick results from a highly motivated and competent team	To help employees improve performance or develop long-term strengths
Overall impact on climate	Negative	Most strongly positive	Positive	Positive	Negative	Positive

Source: Based on Goleman (2000).

Pacesetting

Demanding excellence and using him- or herself as an example, the pace-setter wants results and is always striving to do better. Weak performances draw negative feedback quickly and, if not rectified soon, likely call for replacement. Such a leader sets extremely high, perhaps unrealistic, standards, which can demoralize constituents. Criteria for excellence are likely only known to the leader, causing confusion and second-guessing. The single-mindedness of the chief fosters neither trust nor loyalty, but when members are highly motivated, competent, and less likely to need confirmation, results can be excellent and quick. Except in those situations, pacesetting should not be used by itself.

Coaching

A leader using the coaching style is like a counselor listening, building relationships and trust, and laying out in small realistic steps a pathway to competence and reward. In the process, strengths and weaknesses are identified and integrated with immediate and long-term goals of individuals. Instruction, feedback, quasi-educational plans, and booster shots of morale and support are the norm, even in the face of short-term set backs. Goleman reports that this style is used less frequently despite its potential usefulness because the process is so time-consuming and tedious. While coaching focuses on personal improvements, when lined up with other complementary roles in the group (such as ad hoc, time-limited assignments), its relation to the group task can be powerful. For members who feel insecure, shy, or reticent, coaching may be the method of choice. It can be especially useful when used with role playing designed to explore and reform troublesome barriers, identified or not, to the group task. Coaching can also be used to clarify anticipated responses to proposals or actions in the wider sphere.

In summary, leaders need to employ many styles, and it is unusual to expect even great leaders to be adept at them all. We describe the various styles with the hope that, when stuck, group leaders will stop to review and reassess events, trying a new tack when this seems appropriate. This means taking risks and courting failure; so be it. Success is often built on the back of educative failures, and sensitivity to their impact on others and skill in assessing group cultures, members' roles, and personalities can prepare the ground for trying something different. These are skills that can be learned, a requirement for effective leadership.

Leadership and Civility

Stephen L. Carter's work on civility supports and in some ways extends the foregoing comments. In a thoughtful summary, Carter states a set of rules or guidelines for constructing civility that are applicable to the democratic microcosm. He argues that civility does not require likability, and its essential elements are generosity and trust, valid for social relationships in general and work in particular. Differences and criticisms, sometimes in the form of resistance, are acceptable and are faced head on. Indeed, the openness required of civility may reveal that the leader's ideas might be wrong and those of others right. In summary, civility values diversity, disagreement, and the possibility of resistance (Carter, 1998).

These ideas are hardly new to the social work profession, and for social workers, the exercise of civility is a powerful tool, especially in situations of sharp disagreement. The concept of civility has to do with politeness, courtesy, a sense of decency and regard, and forbearance of rudeness. It carries a polish and delicacy of action that initiate and perhaps maintain the kinds of relationships among colleagues that every organization needs to flourish and even to survive. Beyond legal requirements and absolute personal freedom, which can keep people apart, there has to be civility: the art of creating bonds of support delivered quietly, without fanfare, of trust, of manners and morals, including good will to worthy adversaries. It has to do with rules of conduct or action lying between pure regulations and personal freedom. It is, in the words of the distinguished English jurist Lord Moulton, "obedience to the unenforceable." When done well, it is inconspicuous. Its expression is as seamless as a string of soft phrases (Silber, 1995).

Essential Elements in the Leadership Function

Benne (1976) has concisely and thoughtfully described three essential elements to the leadership function. Leadership, he argues, incorporates its values from the orientation of science, from democracy as a process, and from pedagogy as a method. Science is a process of inquiry that is marked by conflicting knowledge claims by various stakeholders. The value of science is in the method of inquiry through which clusters of claims are transformed into verified knowledge.

Democracy is a process by which persons and groups with different interests seek, through deliberation, opinion exchange and joint investigative action. The uncovered biases are the bases of a common public life. The group must be committed to becoming aware of and responsible for the effects of its actions on the life and growth of the people affected by it. In this context, and in addition to active leadership, democracy does not mean each and every person is equal in talent. Indeed, different levels are likely to produce mistakes, surprises, and unanticipated consequences that will be subject to and often the product of open communication and full participation.

Pedagogy refers to the art of teaching, which can incorporate the process of mutual aid involving empathy, reciprocity, a positive attitude, and a culture that promotes giving and taking. Given this pedagogy, we could expect authority to be built and rebuilt in relation to changing situations, the full use of resources both factual and subjective, processes of self-evaluation and correction, focus on tasks at hand, and collaboration guided by the experimental method. The job of leadership is to develop conditions in a group culture for these processes to take place. Why the staff person does something, and how, is based on evidence of effectiveness. The essential elements are theory (why?), practice (what?), and empiricism (does it work?).

8

PROBLEM SOLVING AND
DECISION MAKING

IN WORKING WITH GROUPS, there is a constant interplay between an emphasis on the group's work production at its many levels, on the one hand, and members' feelings, emotions, and interpersonal relationships, on the other. A group has to manage itself in both realms. What needs to be done in both realms is sometimes harmonious and sometimes not. At times, a group can pay attention to both work and relationships simultaneously. Sometimes, a group needs to direct its attentions more to one or the other, and there are occasions in which a group has to choose between getting its work done and keeping its members happy. Problems can occur at personal, group, or organizational levels and can be overt or covert in both work and social realms. Groups thus need to develop a capacity to solve many different kinds of problems.

Figure 8.1 shows the conjunction or influence of a number of intersecting windows within an organization. At both public (overt) and private (covert) levels, at any one point in time, the correlations between and among person, group, and organization are in motion, each and every one able to exert influences and directions.

Two powerful forces are continually being played out in a small group, which is, in our way of thinking, a mediating unit between centripetal (external) and centrifugal (internal) demands. We suggest that an organization can be viewed as an association or network of small groups, sometimes overlapping, other times quasi-independent. The term used to describe the external or centripetal is "nomothetic," and the personal has been named "ideographic" by Getzels and Thelen (1960). Both ideographic and nomothetic dimensions are embedded in a system of beliefs and way of life, which we call the cultural dimension. The normative or institutional/organizational dimension refers to recognized and established traditions. These include goals, select persons who are employed with respect to completing those goals, and rules and procedures

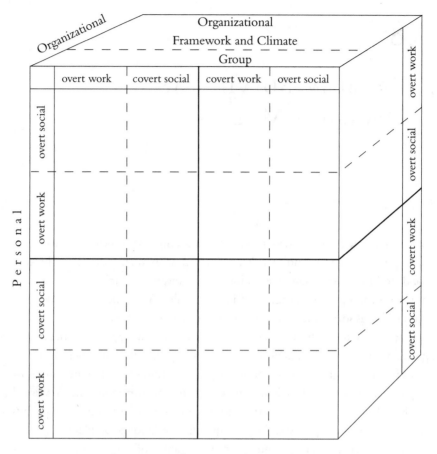

FIGURE 8.1 *Organizational, Group, and Personal Attention Foci*

about what and how the parts (or roles) might be related. In addition, there are specific tasks for achieving the goals and each has specific expectations accompanied by sanctions to ensure compliance. The span of behavior over each of the positions may lie along a continuum from required to prohibited. To summarize, organizations have rules, procedures, and expectations located in specific person behaviors (roles) that are clear and sanctioned.

The personal ideographic emphasizes the individuality of the person, and, even within two key specific role requirements or jobs, no two persons are exactly alike in their performance. In terms of personality, each person incorporates a stable set of characteristics and tendencies that govern similarities and differences in psychological behavior. By the latter, we mean thoughts, feelings, and actions that encompass capacities designated as internal (cognitive, perceptual, affective), interpersonal (empathy, competence), and social (role stability, role adaptability, integration, and differentiation) (Balgopal and Vassil, 1983). An extensive list of capacities can be found in Balgopal and Vassil, as well as in table 14.1. In general, these needs (drives, urges, and attitudes, conscious and unconscious) can be exercised in a variety of ways and can be viewed as real or imagined. These tendencies can be further conceptualized as needs for dominance, rebellion, dependency, and so forth, in each instance influencing the role. Hence, a variety of need dispositions may find outlets in a range of ways, producing a wealth of consistent dynamic tendencies, all of which one can find, observe, and must deal with in leader-group interactions.

As we stated, both personal and external aspects are located within the small group, representing the interpersonal window. Groups have their own variety of forms, such as supportive, resistive, dependent, engaging, and so forth, providing the arena within which needs to belong, participate, compare oneself, anchor identity, and so on mesh. In addition, there are a variety of groups, such as task groups, committees, boards of directors, friendship cliques, activities, and the like, in which these events take place. As a unit, each group will be guided by norms and a way of life that one can classify as cultures, and these are defined by certain sets of intentions or expectations that in turn regularly promote certain types of group-relevant behavior.

This brief overview of analytic schemes sketches various assessment points in our work with groups and organizations; whether loosely centered small private agencies or highly organized bureaucratic constellations. All the designations we mention may influence behavior and purpose in different ways, such that the empathic and sensing skills of leaders will surely be tested and developed, especially since leadership activity must constantly shift among the three windows. Developing, reconfiguring, and altering schemes of action are inherent in the democratic process.

As part of its evolution, each group needs to develop and test methods for solving various kinds of problems, methods that are in keeping with the goals, composition, and climate of the group (Thelen, 1958). How a group solves problems may be as important as reaching a particular solution. For us, there are clear advantages to using the "method of inquiry" in a democratic microcosm. The method of inquiry requires that each group member is free to contribute to, and indeed responsible for contributing to, the consideration of a problem and steps toward solution. It also requires that the group's processes of problem solving be valued by the group and its members. We shall discuss the method of inquiry in more detail later in this chapter.

Decision making is a more circumscribed process, in our view, than is problem solving. In fact, making decisions is a type of problem-solving activity. Problem solving and effective decision making require commitment by the group's members. Commitment in turn has two parts: safety and risk. As a group forms and develops, members feel an increasing commitment to it. They feel an increasing commitment, as well, to engaging in group processes and taking responsibility for the group's solutions and decisions. In a mature group, members' commitment to the group's solutions outweighs their commitments to their own personal points of view. Further, members support group business even when they themselves were not active in the decision-making process.

One should not exaggerate these commitments. A minority view, especially one strongly held, will still be held after a majority decision has prevailed. In a mature working group, however, members feel a greater commitment to the group as a whole and to its decision-making processes than they do to a particular decision or solution. In fact, how members commit themselves to group problems can be used as a rough guide for judging the stage of development of a group. When a decision becomes "ours," one that "we" made, even when "I" was not in agreement with the group's ultimate decision, then the group is functioning at a level of maturity, or differentiation— in other words, as a group should. A way of restating this principle is to say that a mature group is one that can do work at the same time that it is experiencing internal tensions among different points of view. A mature group need not be in a state of consensus in order to be productive.

The best group judgments are made under conditions in which members have a substantive, sometimes strong, but moderated investment in their own particular points of view. Too little investment in a particular point of view leads to detachment and makes problem solving and decision making merely intellectual exercises. Too great an investment in a particular point of view leads to a situation in which a particular solution or decision is valued more than the processes of the group and its integrity. Groups sometimes respond to such situations by inviting members who are committed ideologues to leave them. It may be for this reason that groups whose members are strongly ideological tend to split with such regularity.

Sometimes, when it looks as though problem-solving and decision-making processes are working well, they really are not. Such is the case when a group's assent is sought as though the group were merely a rubber stamp, when no real discussion is called for and decisions are virtually already made. Sometimes, however, a rubber-stamp process masquerades as a true exercise in decision making, a confusion that leads to disillusionment, regarding not only the particular issue at stake but the worth of the group as a whole.

In the Avon Friendly Society of example B, a great variety of committee reports were presented, at the rate of four or five per board meeting. The vast majority of these were presented for board ratification rather than for discussion and possible revision. In effect, the board was being asked to ratify work that had already been done by its various committees with the aid of staff. New board members often objected to this process because it denied them an opportunity to influence committee decisions. They needed to learn that the way to influence committee decisions was to participate in the work of the committee. The board ratification was a necessary legalism, but little work could be accomplished if each of the issues decided by a committee were to be rehashed by the entire board.

This case illustrates the "illusion of work" (Shulman, 2001), which is essentially a process of avoiding the real effort required. A group where this occurs needs to be confronted by someone, preferably the leaders.

Problem Solving as a Process

In general, we believe that the quality of a group's problem solution will be determined by the extent to which the group is successful at making the best use of its own resources in the course of solving the problem. One traditional way of thinking about the process of group problem solving is to divide it into phases, as was suggested many years ago. Bales and Strodtbeck (1956) conceptualized three phases of problem solving, which they called, respectively, orientation, evaluation, and control. These three phases may take place within a particular meeting or over a longer period of time; in either case, groups may go through each phase with regard to each problem. Orientation includes generating ideas or brainstorming in some form, assimilating data relevant to the problem, and working at defining the problem. In the evaluation stage, the group is involved in thinking about some of the pieces of the problem-solving process, proposing alternative solutions in part or in whole, discussing the pros and cons of each part of the solution, and testing these by playing out alternative consequences of alternative actions. The testing can be done by the entire group, by subgroups, or by individual members. The control phase include the actual decision making and the implementation of the decision, often reinforced by a discussion and justification of the decision just made.

These phases overlap in real groups. Part of the group may be engaged in orientation while another part is ready to enter evaluation. Similarly, one member may be at a different stage from others. Nevertheless, visualizing the problem-solving process as including these three phases can be useful for practitioners, because it helps them anticipate the complexity of the process. Inhibitors and facilitators of effective problem solving have been studied over a long period of years by Goffman (1961) and Maier (1963, 1971). Among the inhibitors that tend to have a negative effect on creative aspects of group problem solving, the following have been drawn from their work:

1. High-status members or members who use their authority are more likely to have undue influence over decision-making processes and also to inhibit free expression of ideas by lower-status members.

2. A member who talks more is more likely to have his suggested solutions accepted by the group than a member who talks very little, even if the one who talks very little has a better solution. This finding has implications for what a chair or staff member does in relation to quiet members. It is worth remembering that quiet people can also make thoughtful contributions and that they may have more time to think because they are quiet.

3. There is a tendency for individual members to move toward the point of view held by the majority of the group. That is, the majority seems to have the ability to influence the minority toward conformity. Minority points of view tend to be particularly inhibited when unanimity is required.

4. Friendships among members can either facilitate or inhibit problem solving. They can facilitate by reducing barriers to communication, but they can inhibit by interfering with group productivity. The latter can take place when friendship outweighs the honest expression of opinions.

The same influences—for example, heterogeneity, homogeneity, pressures toward unanimity, the use of brainstorming techniques, the open discussion of conflicting ideas—can be facilitating or inhibiting to group problem solving depending on the particulars of a situation. The job of the staff person is to support these influences when they are facilitating and to attempt to neutralize or convert them when they inhibit effective group problem solving. The staff person is a group member, a "person" in the terms used by Maier (1963, 1971). The first task is thus to guard against the possibility of acting in ways that inhibit the group's ability to solve problems. Past this, it is the job of the staff person, and the chair of a working group, to enhance the group's problem-solving efforts.

Why should decisions be made and problems be solved in a group in the first place? Maier (1971) has given an economical and useful series of answers. Groups have assets for solving problems that individuals don't have. There is a greater total of knowledge and information in a group than in any of its individual members. A group can consider more alternative approaches to a problem than can an individual. The more group participation there is in problem solving, the greater the likelihood that the solution ultimately arrived at will be understood, accepted, and implemented by the entire group. According to Maier, however, groups face some liabilities as problems are solved. Social pressure may make for conformity. There may be a tendency for the group to move prematurely to an agreement on a solution whether or not it is the best. It is possible that an individual will dominate the problem-solving process. Finally, there may exist in a group what Maier has called "conflicting secondary goal(s)," or the desire simply to win the argument, which takes precedence over responsible participation in group problem solving.

DECISION MAKING

There are several ways to think of the stages that groups go through in decision making. According to Lewin (1951), the change process can be described as "refreezing" or "relaxing" and then reviewing previous standards and processes related to decisions. Jaques (1970) describes the change process in more detail, citing the following as a possible series of steps over time: (1) engagement at thought and feeling levels, brought on by a felt need for a decision; (2) some allocation of mental energy to the decision-making process by the group; (3) the organization of the search for solutions around some hunches or hypotheses; (4) a willingness to engage, followed by struggling and floundering, unfreezing, fragmenting and splitting, uncertainty, and risk taking; (5) a recentering of the problem, involving crystallizing or synthesizing the various, heretofore uncrystallized, fragments; (6) consideration of alternative solutions and consequences; (7) the actual decision and the commitment of resources to its implementation; and (8) evaluation of the decision and its outcomes. In summary, this is similar to the method of inquiry referred to above.

Another point needs to be made about decision making. Not to decide is to decide. To avoid making a decision means, in effect, maintaining the status quo. It also means that a judgment has been made that the group is not willing, or not able, or not ready to change the status quo. As is true for all behaviors in groups, the effects of not deciding can be positive or negative. Thoughtful change on the part of a working group often involves expenses of time, energy, and resources in implementing that change. Maintaining the status quo may serve as a way of maintaining an area of safety and comfort for a group and its members until such time as the group is willing to make an investment in implementing a change. In any case, maintaining the status quo ought to be done as a conscious decision rather than as a defense against considering alternatives.

These facts are very important in health and human service delivery organizations. Like all organizations, these may have policies, practices, and procedures whose justification is that they are traditional. Examples can be drawn from a variety of sources. One is the use of elaborate and time-consuming forms, which are never actually reviewed by anyone, for recording data about clients or patients. Another has to do with intake procedures for patients that may have become ritualized over time. A third example can be drawn from the way in which staffing patterns are developed based on presumed rather than tested notions of efficiency. In each of these instances, a decision not to reexamine ways of operating is a decision to maintain the status quo, whether for positive reasons of self-preservation or for negative reasons of resistance to change.

Factors that Affect the Quality of Decision Making in Groups

Janis and Mann (1977) have abstracted from a variety of sources "seven 'ideal' procedural criteria" regarding individual decision making. With two additions, to be indicated below, we think that these apply to groups as well.

> The decision-maker, to the best of his ability, and within his information-processing capabilities, 1) thoroughly canvasses a wide range of alternative courses of action; 2) surveys the full range of objectives to be fulfilled and the value implicated by the choice; 3) carefully weighs whatever he knows about the costs and risks of negative consequences, as well as the positive consequences, that could flow from each alternative; 4) intensively searches for new information relevant to further evaluation of the alternatives; 5) correctly assimilates and takes account of any new information or expert judgment to which he is

exposed, even when the information or judgment does not support the course of action he initially prefers; 6) reexamines the positive and negative consequences of all known alternatives, including those originally regarded as unacceptable, before making a final choice; 7) makes detailed provisions for implementing or executing the chosen course of action with special attention to contingency plans that might be required if various known risks were to materialize. (11)

To this list we would add, in the case of groups: (8) makes decisions within the time frame that is required in order for those decisions to have an impact on the subject; and (9) makes decisions with due regard for their implications for group structure and for the organization of which the group is part. One implication of this list is that, to the extent that a group is able to avoid the creation of taboos or forbidden subjects and is able to consider alternatives that were thought to be unacceptable a priori, its decision-making capacity will be enhanced.

The completion of every step on this list may strike any one member, whether consciously or not, as a formidable task. Indeed, there is a risk of paralysis by analysis. These procedural statements can best be used as guidelines by the group leader, a map toward solid decisions. It is not likely that they will emerge in a linear form. The give and take of group process as members pitch in with their own comments is at best uneven. Therefore the leader's work, much like all group leadership work, will include assessing, member roles, benefiting from the clarity provided by this assessment, and merging ideas and interests by synthesizing single ideas to major themes, corroborated by members' feedback. This process will take time, possibly the creation of subcommittees, the use of "what ifs," or suppositions, to test and target specific solutions with consequences.

Based on his earlier work, Janis has identified a phenomenon called "groupthink." Groupthink results in groups making bad decisions—as Janis noted often in historically significant situations—because of distortions of the decision making within the group:

> Eight major symptoms characterize the groupthink or concurrence-seeking tendency. . . . Each symptom can be identified by a variety of indicators. . . . The eight symptoms of groupthink are: 1) an illusion of invulnerability shared by all or most of the members, which creates excessive optimism . . . 2) collective efforts to rationalize in order to discount warnings which might lead the members to reconsider their

assumptions . . . 3) an unquestioned belief in the group's inherent morality, inclining the members to ignore the ethical or moral consequences
of their decisions . . . 4) stereotyped views of rivals and enemies as too
evil to warrant genuine attempts to negotiate, or as too weak or stupid
. . . 5) direct pressure on any member who expresses strong arguments
against any of the group's stereotypes, illusions, or commitments, making clear that such dissent is contrary to what is expected of all loyal
members . . . 6) self-censorship of deviations from the apparent group
consensus . . . 7) a shared illusion of unanimity, partly resulting from this
self-censorship and augmented by the false assumption that silence
implies consent . . . 8) the emergence of self-appointed "mind guards"—
members who protect the group from adverse information that might
shatter their shared complacency about the effectiveness and morality of
their decisions.   (Janis and Mann, 1977:130–131)

What circumstances would lead working groups in health and human
service agencies to become victims of groupthink? Here are several hypothetical examples:

In example C, the Mount Williams Community Hospital group had a high
level of shared, unexpressed resentment over Dr. Dudley's assumption of
the chair. On one occasion, a majority of the members of the group sat
thinking to themselves, "She's going to go down the drain on this decision—I think I'll let her make it, and that's one way to get rid of her."

The staff person here might have sensed the negativity, and it needed to be
confronted. One way would be to explain issues and potential biases early on.

In example A, one of the members of the Mayor's Task Force was the assistant director of the city's Department of Human Services. Newly
appointed to that position and not sure of her acceptance by the group, she
was worried about challenging the prestigious chair by pointing out that
a plan he was advocating was clearly unworkable, given the current structure of the various city departments. She contained herself, did not express
her opinion, and in so doing let the group adopt a clearly unworkable plan
for services to the frail elderly.

Confrontation is called for here as well. This member could have recounted
some of her experiences and suggested alternatives. The group leader would

have been wise to support this by asking for viewpoints from new members, who bring with them different and valuable perspectives.

In example D, members of the Jewish Federation's Long-Range Planning Committee were sharply aware of changes in government policies that would shortly involve the Jewish Federation in taking much greater responsibility for providing health care services. When this message reached the upper echelons of the federation, a message was returned to the group saying that the fiscal implications of such a point of view were absolutely unacceptable given the current state of the organization's resources. The members of the committee understood the message to mean that they should stop considering the implications of changes in governing policies. As a result, the plan the committee finally presented omitted essential consideration of changes in health services delivery to significant populations within the community.

The minimum interventions called for here would involve the committee's reviewing its mission, taking a stand, and considering the consequences of not omitting relevant information. This example also raises the question of linkages between and among significant groups in an agency. The group leader's task is to keep track of linkages and select key personnel who can be moderate and influential if these are the critical connecting roles. Issue are not always dichotomous. Linking mechanisms provide a broader information base on which to build, and group leaders' provision of such information to their committees is an important function, mandated or not by the members. Working in the interfaces between and among members is critical in these efforts.

In example A, two members of the Mayor's Task Force became exclusively identified with fostering a positive alliance with the services of the city's Department of Health. They only participated in discussions when this department was involved and otherwise tended to withdraw. At one point, as the group was nearing consensus on a massive, multimedia publicity campaign, these two members devoted themselves to shooting down the plan because they did not view its adoption as furthering public regard for the Department of Health.

There are powerful implications here. The Department of Health's resistance could have negative effects on the merger and raise more objections by other parties with a stake in the problem. Since the group is nearing consensus, however, there is still time to check out the possible miscalculations being raised by the Department of Health members.

This situation also might lead to negative fallout in the wider public sphere of activity, including the political. Having considered this, the group leader would be wise to slow down the proceedings and explore (unpack) the elements of resistance to open up the parameters of the final decision. This might take up more then one meeting, and it would be advisable, if resistance were heated, to ask a small subcommittee to explore possibilities, including asking Department of Health members to speculate on possible outcomes, both positive and negative. It would be critical to view the resistance as positive and to consider that the model adopted to achieve resolution could well be incorporated into the group's overall decision-making process.

Another factor can produce groupthink or, perhaps more aptly, group non-think. This is exclusive self-concern on the part of a particular group member or a subgroup. One situation in which this can be observed may be set into motion by one group member's imminent retirement. Preoccupied with calculating the future benefits of his or her pension, a group member may simply not invest in the group's problem-solving process. One indicator of such a situation could be a member's statement to the effect that he will not be around when the implications of a decision come about. Further, a particular group member, a subgroup, or the group as a whole may be under overt instruction not to consider a particular solution. If it is covert, this instruction may inhibit the group's ability to make decisions.

There are several typologies of group decision-making processes. All of them tend to include the following, among others: subjugation, elimination, and the absence of decision making; compromise, which is usually presented as having both positive and negative aspects; and a preferred method, called integration, presented as having no winners or losers but instead melding aspects of several different proposed solutions into one positive solution. No doubt, many groups can arrive at integrative decisions so that there are no winners and losers. In most decisions in most groups, however, there are winners and losers, at least comparatively speaking. Many groups vote, and many decisions are reached by relatively small majorities. We believe that great care should be taken to preserve minority opinions. Often this can be done through minority reports attached to the majority reports. Still, many decisions involve one point of view winning and another one losing.

made. Also, good groups do make mistakes. There is little point in attacking those who shepherded the previous decision. In all likelihood, they did so in good faith and with at least the tacit support of the rest of the group. The process of reconsidering or undoing a previous decision needs to parallel the original decision-making process, with the exception that the time involved may be shorter because the group is now in possession of the data it assembled for the original process. And there is nothing wrong in stating that a decision has more negatives than positives and needs to be reworked in order to achieve the desired outcome. If this is a legitimate group sentiment, it should be stated.

There is a natural letdown after a decision has been made, and the letdown may recur or be intensified when the decision needs to be reconsidered. There are two ways for groups to frame such reconsideration. One is to blame itself for having made the wrong decision. The other is to congratulate itself for having the flexibility and data-processing capacity to recognize that a decision needs to be remade. In our view, if reconsiderations are framed in the latter manner, the review of a decision has the same learning potential as does all decision making. It is an opportunity for the group to act effectively and to increase its own supply of self-esteem and sense of competence. A sense of humor may be useful at this point, as at various others, in the decision-making process. "Here we go again," said with a smile, can help tension dissipate, The same comment, expressed with anger and intensity, only exacerbates negative feelings.

Finally, damage control is an idea worth considering. Who was hurt by the previous decision? Are there actions that the group, or parts of the group, need to take in order to neutralize the effects of such damage? Does the original press release, for example, need to be contradicted, and what are the least harmful ways to do this? How can the group best demonstrate that, though it acknowledges an earlier mistake, it has lost neither its nerve nor its conviction about the importance of its mission? One way to do this is through the tone of its communication to its organization and to the outside world. Dealing with bad decisions is arduous, often consumes a good deal of energy, and may not be pleasant. But it should not be avoided.

In our view, such outcomes of decisions are perfectly legitim
tive members of working groups need to be prepared for these p
and to face them with equanimity, whether they are on the winni
ing side. Graceless winning and losing have no place in a mature
group. "I told you so" and "I knew it all the time" are signs of withdr
group participation rather than investment in it. The concept of a d
microcosm, like the concept of a larger democracy, includes a willi
accept losing without packing up one's emotional marbles and goin

Members who find themselves continuously on the losing side i
to reexamine the positions they take and/or the way they express th
tions in the group. It is also true that groups sometimes run roughs
their minorities, only later to recognize the wisdom of the minority's
view. In general, however, a commitment to democratic group life ii
commitment to being a gracious loser or winner. Winning and losing
be feared; they are part of the day-to-day realities of group decision
Adopting any strategy means not adopting its alternatives. Deciding to
a given direction means deciding not to move in alternative direction:

PROBLEM SOLVING, DECISION MAKING, AND PRAC

Sometimes, groups become aware that they have made unfortunate de
This may lead to a judgment that a previous decision must be reversed
diately or disaster will result, on the one hand, or merely produce a
sense that something that was decided needs to be reconsidered. In c
emergency, of course, groups may need to be prepared to cast procedur
to the wind. An emergency is an emergency and needs to be dealt v
such. Groups may respond with special sessions, emergency me
marathon weekend sessions, or the like. Executive committees may con
special session and take it upon themselves to reverse a group's dec
Groups should be careful, however, when they define situations as eme
cies. Overuse of this frame of reference is a classical means of subverting
ocratic processes.

Most situations are not emergencies. Groups receive data from o
more sources that indicate they need to change a decision. How should
go about this, and how should a staff person help in this process? First, th
uation should be framed as a need to rethink an issue rather than as an a
on the validity or competence of the group or its members. The proce
decision making may have been excellent; simply, a wrong judgment

9

STAGES/PHASES OF
GROUP DEVELOPMENT

O VER THE PAST FIFTY YEARS or so, a series of formulations of stages
of group development have appeared. Early social and behavioral formulations included those of Bennis and Shepard (1956), Bales and Strodtbeck
(1956), and a variety of others, which have been summarized well by Tuckman (1965). Within social work, there have been several influential formulations, among them, those of Garland, Jones, and Kolodny (1965), Sarri and
Galinsky (1967), Northen (1969), and Hartford (1972). Among social psy-
chologists, stages have been conceptualized by Mann (1967), Mills (1984), and
Glidewell (1975). Table 9.1 summarizes the various formulations. The similarities are striking. Each of the frameworks posits a sequential series of stages,
or phases. The specific stages vary somewhat, in that the number of specific
stages and the titles assigned to them differ. Thus Garland, Jones, and Kolodny
posit five stages. Tuckman's previous four-stage model may be extended to a
five stages by including termination as a phase. Sarri and Galinsky listed seven
stages; Hartford five, and so on.

A number of authors have suggested, at first indirectly and later directly,
that women's groups, groups exclusively made up of women or groups that
are staffed by women, particularly groups of a therapeutic purpose, may go
through different stages or a different progression of stages from either mixed
groups or groups that are composed of men. Among these writers are Reed
and Garvin (1996), Schiller (1995), and Garvin (1997).

The best developed of these stage theories is Schiller's, which suggests
normative differences for feminist groups and for women in groups. While
accepting the first and last stages of the Boston model (Garland, Jones, and
Kolodny, 1965), she suggests that stages 2 through 4 for women in groups are:
(2) the establishment of a relational base; (3) mutuality and interpersonal
empathy; and (4) challenge and change.

TABLE 9.1   *Models of Group Development: Equivalent Stages*

GARLAND, JONES, KOLODNY (1965)	SARRI AND GALINSKY (1967)	HARTFORD (1972)	NORTHEN (1969)	TUCKMAN (1965)	MILLS (1984)	MANN (1967)	GLIDEWELL (1975)
Preaffiliation	Origin formative	Pregroup formation	Orientation	Forming	Encounter, testing boundaries, and modeling roles	Initial complaining, premature enactment	Prudent exploration, involvement
Power and control	Intermediate I, revision	Integration, disintegration, and reintegration	Exploration and testing	Storming	Negotiating an indigenous normative system	Confrontation	Conflict
Intimacy	Intermediate II		Problem solving	Norming			
Differentiation	Maturation	Group functioning and maintenance	Problem solving	Performing	Production	Internalization	Solidarity Work
Separation	Termination	Termination	Termination	Adjourning (Tuckman and Jensen, 1977)	Separation	Separation	

Source: Balgopal and Vassil, 1983:*167*.

An unfortunate lack in the literature on working groups is to be found in the area of gender diversity. Insofar as attention has been paid to this subject, we find this has been part of a general concern with the inclusion of women, women's issues, and women's ways of learning, acting, and functioning in groups. We have included Schiller's suggested stage models among those we present and discuss in this chapter.

Each of the stage theories can be useful in two ways. First, they remind us that group life takes place over time and that each group goes through a process of birth, life, and dissolution. Second, the stage theories enable one to prepare for transitions in the texture of group life. Which particular formulation will be most useful is a matter of individual choice. Several aspects of one or the other formulation, however, appeal to us because of their clarity and because they correspond to our experiences in working groups. For example, Hartford's (1972) description of the "pregroup phase" is a major contribution to clarifying the beginnings of groups. Garland, Jones, and Kolodny's (1965) definition of the framework of the "power and control" phase has been particularly useful for us. Both Sarri and Galinsky (1967) and Hartford (1972) visualize a developmental crisis and reformulation at a relatively early point in group life, which is congruent with our own experiences. Northen (1969) and, more recently, Northen and Kurland (2001) advance the idea of a cyclical aspect to the group's working phase, while also emphasizing cultural aspects of the meanings of various stages to members of various identities. We find both of these to be helpful concepts. Each of the models talks about termination, a phase discussed most thoroughly and perceptively by Shulman (1984, 2001). Thus there is a richness of theoretical material on which a practitioner with groups can draw.

Stages, in our view, are not distinct or discontinuous one from the other. Concerns at one stage often reappear later in the group's life, in major or lesser ways.[1] Stages refer to major emphases, themes, or tones of group life. In working groups in particular, group task and time frame tend to blur, to some extent, some of the clarity of stages that one may be able to observe in other kinds of groups.

Within the patterns of phases or stages, various subcycles may recur over and over again in any given group. These cycles will be triggered by particular issues that may remain the same in any given group or vary over the life of the group. As Bales and Strodtbeck originally pointed out (1956), the two major problem-solving activities facing groups at each and every stage are those related to accomplishing a task and those related to group maintenance. Included in the latter is the task of maintaining appropriate levels of feeling and relationship among the members of the group. Our view is that working on the tasks of the group and working on group maintenance are inextricably intertwined. One affects the other. Each of these areas of attention, the task and the interpersonal, has its own particular dynamics, and each affects the other as well as affecting each group member.

Beginnings, middles, and ends are important in groups. This observation applies not only to the overall life of the group but also to each group meeting. This point has been made by many and diverse writers (Bales and Strodtbeck, 1956; Tropman, 1980; Schwartz, 1994; Shulman, 1984, 2001).

A caution may be in order. The fact that group life goes through stages does not mean that groups are predictable in terms of particular behaviors. Planning and designs are relevant, but the immediacy of practice dictates the action. Even so, preliminary planning, or what some have called creative anticipation, is a good training discipline for a practitioner as a source from which expectations may be drawn. Similarly, knowing that a group is in the first stage of group development, to be outlined below, can frame a set of expectations about the issues that may arise and the meaning these issues may have in a group. Other factors that can provide more specific expectations include the type of group, the characteristics of a specified group, and the organizational framework within which it lives. The formal and informal characteristics of small and large organizations are likely to affect groups in different ways. In other words, one forms the most general set of expectations based on the stage of group development, and this corresponds to ways in which a particular group is like all other groups. Next, one forms a set of expectations based on the specific charge, task, and composition of the group, as well as on the other variables listed in chapter 3. This provides a frame for expectations in relation to ways in which a particular group is like some other groups. Finally, one frames a set of expectations based on the characteristics of a particular group. This corresponds to ways in which a particular group is different from all other groups. Each of these three levels of expectations is important for the practitioner, chair, and member. In effect, each must ask:

1. What do I know about groups in general that leads me to expect certain things to happen in this particular group?
2. What do I know about groups of this type that leads me to expect certain things about this particular group?
3. What do I know about this particular group that leads me to hold particular expectations for this group?

All three questions are useful, and form a grid for the kinds of thinking that a professional practitioner should do before, during, and after each group meeting. Answering these questions will not, by any means, enable total accuracy and prediction to take place. It will, however, help to move group behaviors from the realm of the unknown and the mysterious to the realm of the comprehensible and manageable.

The Pregroup Stage

The pregroup stage encompasses all the activities that lead to a first meeting.[2] This preparatory stage lays the necessary groundwork for group life. Goals, objectives, contracts, expectations, and the meanings of membership can be explored. There is evidence to suggest that the better the preparation of its members, the clearer its goals, and the clearer the contract between its leader and sponsor, the more productive a group will be (Hartford, 1972; Shulman, 2001). The pregroup stage ordinarily includes choosing members and having members agree to join, formulating group purposes, outlining the group's charge, and clarifying the expectations of members, staff, and organization. It is also the stage that requires a staff member to make a first effort at tuning into the members' predispositions, skills, strengths, and interests and to make an educated guess as to what contributions each member will be able to make to the group both at the beginning and over the long run.

It is at this stage that the first contacts with members are made, after a pool of members has been developed through organizational sources, private contacts, volunteering, or other means. One should certainly not expect congruence among the parties; the nature of beginnings and the natural hesitancies that prospective members have will be most obvious at this stage of an agreed-upon contract. Beginning understandings will need to be reworked repeatedly as the group develops. The mandate for whatever occurs over the life of the group starts with the pregroup phase, however, and a considerable part of the group's life is shaped in this beginning phase.

A caveat is in order at this point. The goals of both staff member and chair will be somewhat different in the pregroup phase simply because a group has yet to be developed. The priorities and behaviors are required in order to form a group are different from those that will reign once the group is under way. In other words, one set of staff priorities at the beginning may well be simply to get people together at the same time and place, so that the group may begin its life. At this point, the leaders need to visualize what the group might look like. Bales's (1983) prescriptions are worth reviewing. Essentially, the leader is a central person who becomes the object of cognitive, affective, and behavioral sentiments projected, evaluated, and responded to in the initial interviews. Also, in a serial way, each interview not only sets the stage for each succeeding interview but begins to lay foundation of the group symbolically and realistically.

While it is always preferable to complete the desired tasks in the pregroup interview, sometimes leaders are asked to take over a group already in process or become coleaders assisting someone else. Both of these options have their own demands. For those walking into a group without some group experience, the process of assessment and relationship—for both leader and group members—begins in the first meeting. Thus some intuitive projections are in order, each with a plan of action, held in abeyance until its appropriate moment in the group. The processes of introduction, defining purpose, goal setting, feedback (as a corrective), contracting, and problem or idea swapping by members, followed by helping the group unpack, thematize, partialize, and identify next steps, constitute the essential tasks in the beginning phase.

Where coleadership is indicated or required, it is desirable for coleaders to get together to exchange particular views, processes, and experiences before the group meets (ideally, the week before, the members having been broached with the idea), as well as to discuss the next steps, such as introductory processes, including what questions members may have. Group rules and history are essential where there are precedents (Weiss, 1998).

Among the most important tasks of this stage is the exploration of the potential benefits of membership in the group. Specific statements outlining the values of the group, its potential rewards to members, and the potential contributions of its work need to be shared with prospective members. Individual pregroup interviews, whether by staff member or by chair, in person or by telephone, are very helpful and sometimes essential. The purpose of these interviews is to ascertain and delineate members' characteristics, interests, and talents that may be called upon by the group.

Formation: Preaffiliation, Exploration, and Involvement

Preaffiliation refers to the beginning of the process by which members are introduced and the composition of the group begins to determine itself. The next phase, the true beginning of the group, can be divided into two subphases that we have labeled for convenience "exploration" and "involvement" (Glidewell, 1975). These two subphases can be seen in the first several meetings, assuming that a group is starting from scratch. It should be kept in mind that often working groups are composed of fragments and subgroups of other working groups. For example, three members of a given committee may have worked together in another group, and thus their relationships with each other are not at a beginning phase, though their engagement with the other members of the current group is. Such phenomena make for uneven starting points and often explain the fragmented feelings of members of some working groups during their first few meetings. Some groups are composed of several such fragments. Subgrouping may have to do with other factors besides previous group membership, such as family relationships among members of a group.

Exploration corresponds to what others have labeled "preaffiliation" (Garland, Jones, and Kolodny, 1965). The major themes here are the approach/avoidance issue, which involves a tug-of-war between wanting to belong and wanting to remain independent, and a group context that is not intimate. Themes of exploration, orientation, inclusion, and preliminary questioning of the group's mission and charge are characteristic of groups at this stage. Members ask, what is our task? How much cooperation does it require? What do I need to know? How much time and investment will this group expect of me?

At the interpersonal level, one would expect to see at this stage psyching-out behaviors, hesitant participation, and some silent and active testing of other group members. In general, one expects to see members operating within stereotypical roles they have practiced and learned in other groups throughout their lives. In effect, one might call this each member's "committee of internal activity" at work. Individual members may seek to present themselves in favorable lights in order to project their best images. While members are sizing each other up, they may be thinking to themselves: What have I gotten myself into? Or, more bluntly, Are other members more powerful or competent than I? Are other members likely to be hurtful to me? What will happen to me in this group? Will others listen to me?

It is not unusual for a group to deal with such private processes by behaving in stereotypical ways, exchanging courtesies and diffusing conversations in order to mask the self-comparisons that are going on. Conversations and questions may be directed to the group leadership, whether chair or staff member, rather than toward each other. Members tend to seek safety rather than to take chances.

Approaches to the group's tasks at this phase also tend to be stereotypical and may reflect a confidence that members do not really feel. Both tasks and affective (feeling) aspects of member roles manifest themselves very early in the life of a group. It is often a mistake to take what is said in the first few meetings too literally. What members are saying may be as much a reflection of their inner states as the expression of mature or considered judgments.

As always, one's expectations at this early stage need to be affected by the particular realities of a group. Thus, for example, a group that will only be in existence for a relatively short time will seek to telescope these early processes in two ways. One is by accelerating the processes of group formation such that a group may, for instance, seek to take care of all its initial housekeeping in the first ten minutes of its existence. The other way, as has been suggested in chapter 3, is by limiting the depth to which members invest themselves in the group. This latter can be viewed as an attempt to save time at the expense of depth. Often such attempts are successful and adaptive and help a short-term group to complete work quickly. Sometimes, however, such processes reveal a lack of genuine task accomplishment. Groups that telescope this stage risk incomplete formation, and task accomplishment, done under the pressure of time, may be inadequate.

The second subphase within the beginning phase has been called "preliminary involvement" and incorporates a phenomenon that may be called "the risky shift" (Glidewell, 1975). Members are influenced by a general set of cultural and personal values regarding risks and cautions. Each tends to rank him- or herself as a greater risk taker or as more cautious than others. When members begin to discover that they are more like others than they are different from them, some members take the next step. They take chances and stick their necks out and, in so doing, receive some support from others for what they are saying. (One example of support at this phase is careful listening by others.) A demonstration that one is not really hurt in the process of exposing one's ideas, and in fact that one may gain attention from leaders or other members, often leads others to follow and begin to express their ideas. Once members begin to realize that no one will be demolished because of participation, the outlines of a group begin to emerge. The dynamics of risk tends to overtake the dynamics of caution, though the latter remains present. This cycle leads to genuine group formation and moves a group ahead rapidly.

If, on the other hand, one learns from taking an initial risk that one is in danger, the group is at an impasse. It is probably for this reason that ad hominem attacks on individual members are to be avoided almost at all costs during the initial phase. Bernstein (1965) has pointed out a kind of behavior that looks on the surface as though it is taking risks but in fact is an expression of caution. It consists of oversharing or seemingly overrisking in the initial phase, though the apparent sharing and risk taking both seem to be and are defenses against real involvement. For example, a member, because of anxiety or some other reason, may give a long speech testifying to his investment in the group at the initial meeting. This may turn other members off rather than on, be perceived by them as a maneuver on the part of the individual, and retard rather than aid the process of group formation. Both staff and chair should not hesitate, in our view, to cut short such inappropriate self-revelations, not because they lack sympathy with the group member involved but because they are aware of the potentially destructive effects of such behavior on the group as a whole.

One way to help members put aside some of their initial anxieties is through an early attempt to structure the group's tasks. Agendas, background information about the group's task, organizational charts that locate a group within a broader structure, and brief historical introductions are ways of doing this. Such aids are particularly appropriate during the first meeting or two and need to be understood both for their realistic value in relation to group tasks and for their symbolic meanings in relation to group formation.

The Mayor's Task Force of example A began its first meeting with two kinds of introductions. First, each person introduced him/herself in terms of background, profession, neighborhood, and so on. Then, the chair distributed a one-page chronology that the staff person had been developed. This chronology listed seven significant dates that had to do with the formation of the task force and ended with a brief quotation from the mayor's executive order. When the group had gone through both of these introductory processes, it entered a beginning stage of readiness to the group's charge and the purpose for which everyone had assembled.

Endings of meetings carry a specific significance. The ending phase (lasting ten or fifteen minutes) involves at least four separate but interrelated steps. The first is to summarize where the group is, which should be handled by either leader or member(s). Feedback to confirm the content of the summary is required and should lead to the next step: identifying what should happen after the meeting, including specific tasks to be performed by the worker, such as gathering information, checking legal issues, preparing to engage other members, and so forth. The third step that has proved valuable is a brief summary from the leader of what the group has accomplished as a group, that is, process characteristics, decisions broached, differences of opinion honored, commitment to a long-term view, and a sense of civility. Finally, in most meetings, it has been our experience, one or more members always wish to hang around and talk. This is an important moment because the discussion may reveal individual needs for psychological support, provide clarifying comments on members' positions, and furnish useful information on other issues germane to the group but not necessarily raised during the meeting. At the psychological level, some have framed this activity as "door knob therapy" (Shulman, 2001).

The Middle Phase(s): Integration / Disintegration / Reintegration; or, From Power and Control to Problem Solving

Once a group gets past the beginning stage, it moves into the middle phase, which we think of in terms of three subphases. The first has been called "power and control" (Garland, Jones, and Kolodny, 1965), "storming" (Tuckman, 1965), "integration, disintegration, and reintegration" (Hartford, 1972), and "uncertainty—exploration"(Northen and Kurland, 2001). The second one has been called "intimacy" (Garland, Jones, and Kolodny, 1965), "norming" (Tuckman, 1965), and "solidarity" (Glidewell, 1975). The third, most enduring subphase has variously been labeled "problem solving" (Northen, 1969), "mutuality and goal achievement" (Northen and Kurland, 2001), "group functioning and maintenance" (Hartford, 1972), "differentiation" (Garland, Jones, and Kolodny, 1965), or a "system in mutual aid" (Schwartz, 1994). Whether one regards these three subphases as separate or as interrelated aspects of the same phase is a question only of semantics. Each of the processes represented by these subphases represents a focus for a developing group during the middle of its existence.

Some view the first subphase as the second stage of group development. In this phase, issues that may be expected to include competition for power among and between members, chair, and staff; conflict about who is to lead the group; issues of authority, dependency, and counterdependency in general; and, more broadly, themes of ambivalence about the group and with respect to members' relationships with each other and toward the group leadership. There may also be ambivalence about the group's tasks. In fact, if ambivalence is not expressed at this phase, one should be somewhat suspicious, since this may mean that the ambivalence issue is being hidden or suppressed in some way and will only emerge later in the group's development, when it may be less appropriate. What we are arguing is that power and control is a theme, a sort of leitmotif which carries the other themes of the group with it.

It is common for group members and staff to experience struggles over power and control as negative. This is understandable, because few of us are socialized to regard conflict or even competition positively. Most of us have think and feel that when things go smoothly they are going well and that the reverse is true when things are not going smoothly. In fact, this is not the case in groups, particularly at this phase. If a group is working at resolving the issues listed above, the chances are that members are experiencing growth and progress. If all is smooth, it is possible that nothing is happening in the group and that the surface smoothness conceals a sort of group-process emptiness that bodes ill for the future of the group. In many ways, differences or disconfirmations between individuals and even at the group level provide a significant amount of energy for work.

In the power and control phase, there is often a feeling of an authority vacuum. The group has to come to terms with the fact that it belongs to its members and that they have to exercise energetic participation and take responsibility for moving the group along. The group leadership—and this is often divided between the elected or appointed chair and the staff person—represents expertise and is supposed to supply clear instructions, answers, and expectations. On the other hand, if the group leadership lets itself be seduced into taking the entire responsibility for the group's progress, other members may withdraw from the group.

In this phase, the contract among the group members is both like and unlike the more general social contracts in society. The group's leadership is expected to give clear answers with regard to reality issues such as meeting times and places, the group's position in the organizational system, the resources available to the group, and the like. Unlike the situation in the outside world, however, the leadership should not—indeed, often cannot—provide clear and simple answers about the ways in which the group should proceed. To do so would be to interfere with the responsibility of the group's members. This paradox often constitutes a strain on the group's leadership, since the pressure to do the group's work for it may be strong. In fact, there may be occasions when the time frame within which a group is operating makes it essential for the group's leadership to abridge the processes that need to be accomplished at this phase. This should never be done, however, without a clear sense of what is being lost. To shortcut group development and to do a group's work for it interferes with the deepening of members' investment in the group and the group's building a sense of its own capacity and problem-solving ability.

During the power and control phase, old alliances shift, and new alliances in the form of subgroups develop within the group. Petty annoyances may develop among members and may loom unusually large. Bennis and Shepard (1956) suggest that three kinds of subgroups typically emerge at this phase: (1) subgroups composed of members who are still dependent on the leadership and prefer to wait for instructions; (2) those who are counterdependent, who begin to assume direction in the group by giving opinions or suggesting topics in an authoritative and controlling way; and (3) subgroups that begin to act productively and appropriately and move the group along by generating ideas and evaluating others' opinions. At the task level, one may see members developing group rules, engaging in parliamentary bickering, questioning the limits of their own and others' authority, and engaging in similar kinds of interactions.

> In example A, the second meeting of the Mayor's Task Force began with two of the members alternating questions about how much power the group really had. Speaking in tones of disillusionment, these two members questioned seriously whether the mayor or anybody else really wanted changes to come about, whether the group was expected to act as a rubber stamp, and so on. These represented themes that had not been mentioned at all during the first meeting. Explanations of these issues becomes the immediate order of business for the leaders.

The next subphase in this general middle phase is what one may call "solidarity" (Glidewell, 1975). It is comparable to the phase that Garland, Jones, and Kolodny have referred to as "intimacy" (1965). The group's major focus in this subphase really is on cohesion, on the sense of attachment members feel for each other, and on their sense of pride and investment in the group and the particular tasks for which the group has been assembled. One may observe at this phase a "we" feeling that reflects cooperation, support, and reassurance. Where the power and control phase may be marked by questioning and disillusionment, the solidarity phase may bring a marked degree of enthusiasm and excitement about the power of participation and the momentum of the activities. What these messages begin to signal is evidence that participation in the group has developed positive meanings for the members.

The developing cohesiveness may also produce a concerted effort to collect, share, and analyze information. There seems to be a greater degree of involvement regarding the task at hand. Feelings among group members such as interdependency and closeness, involvement, a beginning sense of the group's authority as a group, and even a sort of institutionalized happiness and togetherness may be apparent. With regard to working on tasks, one may expect to see more opinions expressed by the membership and more of a focus on problem solving and carrying out plans. The group is able to make decisions and to evaluate possible consequences of its activities, though there may still be a need for consensus and not hurting each others' feelings.

Not all of what happens during this subphase should be expected to be pleasant or benign, though in general this is an easier phase for chair, members, and staff than the previous subphase. Greater cohesion often brings greater personal honesty both about the task at hand and about the contributions of others. There may be some disenchantment as these more honest feelings, some of them negative, are expressed. Alternative interpretations of data may emerge at this phase. Particularly in planning groups, these alternative interpretations may be an important contribution. It is at this phase that some groups begin to develop majority and minority views of problems, solutions, and plans. It is critical that the group culture developed by the leader provides sufficient safety so that members can retreat, regroup and continue with the task. This is important for work and support, twin ingredients necessary for movement to occur at process and content levels.

This subphase often sees the reappearance of issues that were raised in earlier phases. On a subjective level, issues feel more "real," that is, opinions and perceptions seem more rooted in an appropriate investment by the member or members who are expressing them than was previously the case. As groups move through this phase, one often notices a marked decrease in defensiveness and an increased willingness to listen to other opinions and perceptions. Gradually, the membership begins to realize that disagreement does not threaten one's acceptance in the group. In fact, open and serious disagreement may enhance members' positions. Members' statements are more likely to be seen as contributions to a discussion rather than as blocking maneuvers, as may have been the case in earlier phases. The shift from "I" to "we" is a very important step in the development of a working group. This shift is genuine, of course, when it reflects the cognitive map of the group member, not merely a ritual use of the right words.

The major tendencies in the third subphase of the middle stage include free expression, mutual support, few power problems, high levels of communication, and, most important, a sense on the part of the group that it has become its own frame of reference and is able to learn from itself. At the task level, one is likely to see comfortably divergent thinking and actions, an efficient interchange of ideas, and exchanges of membership between and among subgroups. Differently stated, the ability of members to ally themselves with one subgroup on one issue and with another on another issue without incurring charges of disloyalty is a rule-of-thumb indicator of the stage of differentiation.

Differentiation takes place in another sense as well. It has become acceptable for "our" group to do things differently from other groups without a need for defensiveness or excuses. The shared sense that "we" know what we are doing, have developed appropriate mechanisms for doing it, and are proceeding on schedule with our tasks is a hallmark of this stage. There is more freedom to express different ideas, behaviors, and emotions. The opportunity for discovery and autonomy is high, as is the authenticity of the relationships among members, and members are exerting their best efforts. The group has taken on the essence of an internal reference group and sounding board.

Differences within the group are valid and are used to spur work. In addition, cycles of success and productivity replace cycles of ambiguity, indecision, and frustration, though the last may return in smaller and smaller cycles. In short, the democratic microcosm (see chapter 4) has become as much of a reality as it ever will be in this group. The group's ability to process data has reached its peak. Members participate in the group without fear and without a sense of anyone's looking over their shoulders.

No group ever achieves fully the somewhat idealized picture just given. Defensiveness, rankings, insecurities, inhibitions, and other mechanisms make most groups stop short of the ideal. This phase is the closest approximation to desirable group characteristics of which a particular group is capable.

In a mature group, the membership views the leadership as contributing to moving the group along rather than as monopolizing social power. There is a sense of gratitude toward those who perform important instrumental functions for the group, rather than jealousy and petty competition. Often, a staff member will have less to do during this phase than previously. The group has more self-direction, and the expertise of the staff member may be a resource for the group only at particular times. This may be experienced by a staff member—or by a chair—as a failure when in fact it represents a high degree of success. When a group functions in a largely self-directing manner, consciously turning to its leadership and its resource person for help only as needed, the leadership has helped the group to advance to a point of maturity. As one gains experience with working groups, one needs to train oneself to recognize this phase as a success, rather than to sit through meetings suffering from a sense of not being needed, appreciated, or wanted.

> In example D, the Long-Range Planning Committee of the Jewish Federation of Metropolitan Avon devoted its entire fourteenth meeting to a consideration of two draft statements that the two subcommittees had prepared on long-range priorities. The staff person sat through the entire meeting without saying anything; judging that the group was doing an excellent job of reviewing both the text and the more covert meanings of the two drafts. Discussion was free, fluent, and sophisticated. When the staff member said at the very end of the meeting that the next one was sched-

uled for two weeks from that day at 8 A.M., for breakfast, it was with an awareness of not having said anything since the outset of the meeting. The staff person left the meeting with a sense of real accomplishment and joy at how far the group had come but also a sense of frustration and some regret at not being needed by the group.

Termination

More attention has been paid in the study of groups to beginnings than to endings. However, endings are particularly important in groups for two reasons. In working groups, endings include a delivery of a product, that is, a report of the extent to which a group has been able to fulfill its tasks or charge. Also, in working groups as in other groups, one needs to be aware of an element of what may be called transfer of learning. Individual group members may leave one working group only to become part of another. What they have learned, both in relation to the task and in relation to the skills of working in groups, can be considered as outputs of groups just as much as the group's more formal products. Therefore, one of the purposes of working with groups in the ending phase should be to help members consolidate, become aware of, and be able to transfer what they have learned to other groups.

The themes of the ending phase tend to center around demoralization, ambivalence, and evaluating, of both the good times and the bad times the group has gone through. A feeling of pride in the group's accomplishment is important in order to enable the experience to be viewed as positive and productive. Sufficient attention needs to be paid to the possible consequences of the actions that the group has taken and the positions or solutions that its particular product embodies. It seems to be characteristic of many groups that some form of ceremony, celebration, or ritual is desirable to mark the ending of the group. Often, groups have a party or some form of social get-together at the end. This is one way of dealing with feelings of loss and regrets over the breaking of old ties, emotions that are frequently evoked when groups end.

It has long been observed that groups tend to end through the inverse of the processes by which they form (Schutz, 1956). In the processes of termination, one may need to guard against a tendency to become maudlin. Or, in order to deal with feelings of loss, there may be a withdrawal from the meaning that the group has had for its members. This withdrawal should be understood as a maneuver intended to help members deal with their feelings and should not be taken too seriously. The group's leadership needs to guard against being convinced by this withdrawal during the course of termination that members did not value the group experience. On the other hand, it is often true that the more powerful the influence of the group has had on members, the more emotional the statements will be at the end of the group. Helping members focus on the future and on the contributions they will be able to make individually to this and other organizations is a useful way of channeling energy.

One needs to recognize that having made difficult decisions is the hallmark of a "good" or "successful" group. A rule of thumb here may be that the extent to which members can identify themselves with all the group's decisions and products, including those they individually opposed, is a mark of maturity for the group as a whole. Old groups should neither die nor fade away. Instead, they should continue to live in the gains and learning that members take with them into other group situations as well as in the group's accomplishments.

QUADRIFOCAL VISION

Throughout the process of group development that has been traced in this chapter, it is essential for the staff member at all times, the chair and the membership of the group as it becomes able to do so to maintain a quadrifocal vision, simultaneously focusing on individual group members, on subgroups, on the group as a whole, and on the place of the group in the organization of which it is part. To neglect any one of these is to court failure in group development and task accomplishment. At any given time, one may be directing one's attention more toward one or more of these four levels. For example, during a period of intense struggle over group norms, a member whose deviant behavior seems set on destroying the group's progress may monopolize attention and may for a short period of time obscure broader organizational concerns. Conversely, during a time when the group is having difficulty fitting its plan for procedure into the charge given it by the organization, the group and organizational levels of analysis may monopolize attention. Particularly in a small organization, attention may need to be devoted directly to issues dealing with the external environment, even going beyond the organization itself. We suggest a crude rule for staff of working groups and their chairs: if within the course of any given meeting, conscious thought, however brief, has not been given to each of these levels—to the meaning of what's going on in the group for individuals, for subgroups, for the group as a whole, and for the group and its relationship with its organizational and external environment—one should feel some discomfort and ask oneself why.

10

Teams and Team Building

Emotional Intelligence and Groups

The connection between emotional intelligence and groups is discussed by Druskat and Wolff (2001), who note that much of the important work in organizations is done in small working collectives. In this regard, they agree with Glidewell's 1975 position on the same issue. Glidewell goes on to suggest that small temporary systems are major methods by which policies get enacted and implemented in small groups. Druskat and Wolff argue further that equally important to teams is emotional intelligence, which goes beyond individual competency. Three factors are central to a group's effectiveness: "trust among members, a sense of group identity, and a sense of group efficacy" (Druskat and Wolff, 2001:82) A basic requirement for these to exist is a group atmosphere underpinned by expectations of emotional capacity. While personal and social competence are critical to individual emotional intelligence, a group must be mindful of individual members' emotions, group emotions, and emotions of other groups/individuals outside of but connected to the group's boundaries. They, in a sense, represent the external world.

Druskat and Wolff's summary of the connections among individual members, group processes, and external group relationships are presented in table 10.1. The table clarifies and reinforces several important attributes of leadership, including attention to individual members, group members, and the organization in which the group is embedded. This is critical for analysis and change. The specific items (norms) depicting the three domains can be used as specific benchmarks to serve as guides for intervention schemes.

Working with individuals' emotions means being empathic or aware of the behavior or posture of members. In this regard, a norm of interpersonal understanding would encourage sensitivity to each and every member to the

TABLE 10.1 *Building Norms for Three Levels of Group Emotional Intelligence*

INDIVIDUAL	GROUP	CROSS-BOUNDARY
Norms That Create Awareness of Emotions		
Interpersonal Understanding	*Team Self-Evaluation*	*Organizational Understanding*
1. Take time away from group tasks to get to know one another.	1. Schedule time to examine team effectiveness.	1. Find out the concerns and needs of others in the organization.
2. Have a check-in at the beginning of the meeting, that is, ask how everyone is doing.	2. Create measurable task and process objectives and then measure them.	2. Consider who can influence the team's ability to accomplish its goals.
3. Assume that undesirable behavior takes place for a reason. Find out what that reason is. Ask questions and listen. Avoid negative attributions	3. Acknowledge and discuss group moods.	3. Discuss the culture and politics in the organization
	4. Communicate your sense of what is transpiring in the team.	4. Ask whether proposed team actions are congruent with the organization's culture and policies.
	5. Allow members to call a "process check." (For instance, a team might say, "Wouldn't a process check be the most effective use of our time right now?")	
Perspective Taking	*Seeking Feedback*	
1. Ask whether everyone agrees with a decision.	1. Ask your "customers" how you are doing.	
2. Ask quiet members what they think	2. Post your work and invite comments	
3. Question decisions that come too quickly.	3. Benchmark your processes	
4. Appoint a devil's advocate		
Norms That Help Regulate Emotions		
Confronting	*Create Resources for Working with Emotion*	*Building External Relationships*
1. Set ground rules and use them to point out errant behavior.	1. Make time to discuss difficult issues and address the emotions that surround them.	1. Create opportunities for networking and interaction

TABLE 10.1   *Building Norms for Three Levels of Group Emotional Intelligence* (continued)

2. Call members on errant behavior.
3. Create playful devices for pointing out such behavior. These often emerge from the group spontaneously. Reinforce them.

Caring

1. Support members: volunteer to help them if they need it, be flexible, and provide emotional support.
2. Validate members' contributions. Let members know they are valued.
3. Protect members from attack.
4. Respect individuality and differences in perspectives. Listen.
5. Never be derogatory or demeaning.

2. Find creative shorthand ways to acknowledge and express the emotion in the group.
3. Create fun ways to acknowledge and relieve stress and tension.
4. Express acceptance of members' emotions.

Creating an Affirmative Environment

1. Reinforce that the team can meet a challenge. Be optimistic. For example, say things like, "We can get through this" or "Nothing will stop us"
2. Focus on what you can control.
3. Remind members of the group's important and positive mission.
4. Remind the group how it solved a similar problem before.
5. Focus on problem solving, not blaming.

Solving Problems Proactively

1. Anticipate problems and address them before they happen.
2. Take the initiative to understand and get what you need to be effective.
3. Do it yourself if others aren't responding. Rely on yourself, not others.

2. Ask about the needs of other teams
3. Provide support for other teams
4. Invite others to team meetings if they might have a stake in what you are doing.

point of soliciting feedback—positive or negative—with respect to the issues at hand. Beyond soliciting individuals' perspectives, emotional intelligence requires recognizing the collective personal and interpersonal struggles members may have in presenting their points of view. In a small way, it often calls for a minibiography of the person to be shared. For this to happen, groups need to consider, absorb, and act on expectations regarding conflict and support. As we have mentioned before, the dialectic between these two powerful sentiments is critical to developing a group culture that fosters trust and group identity as well as work. Confrontation as a tactic may divert the group from its task to responding instead to the confrontation and its effects on group members. So, in effect, confrontation can have a paradoxical effect. Though it seems to try to focus the group by addressing issues directly, it may instead divert the group from accomplishing its work. On the other hand, confrontation may extend the group boundaries or expectations that define the scope of acceptable behavior. Thus a latecomer needs to be confronted, as does someone who continually clogs group progress with negatives about why each and every idea is incomplete. While individualism is to be supported in the work of the group, the effort of the whole assumes greater priority; in a metaphoric sense, it is first among equals.

Druskat and Wolff define group self-awareness as comprising "emotional states, strengths and weaknesses, modes of interaction and task processes" and go on to say that "self evaluation and soliciting feedback from others are critical to this aspect" (2001:84). One way to clarify and direct group emotions could be the use of humor to point out a reflective process comment.

Regulating group emotions is a goal that can be reached through activities developing team spirit. Ad hoc lunches, surprise gifts, competitions, and at-large pronouncements, such as assembly meetings or creative problem solving in response to crises. Clearly, in the presence of a negative cycling of complaints and pessimism, activities and energy need to be focused on a "can do" positivistic outlook. Sometimes, timeouts can be helpful, as can be the use of one-time-only outside consultants whose backgrounds may be entirely different from those of the group.

Relationships outside the group are relevant as well. Developing pathways to other stakeholders through informal meetings is one way to foster such relationships. There is no substitute for developing workable relationships with other invested parties, and this task can fall to the team leader or perhaps to other members. Noting good performance through letters to superiors and informal praise through organizational networks enhances organizational networks that may be essential to a team task.

Another important factor has to do with what may be called "movability" on the part of the group leader. This refers to work outside the specific group meeting to include contacts in "corridor committees," during water cooler conversations, at lunch, and at other specific points or places where valuable information is exchanged. Besides liaison contacts, we believe that staff persons may profit from having one or more "shadow" consultants whose purpose is to provide honest and reliable feedback. For the chief executive of an organization, the board of directors is one such sounding board. One has to be careful of confidentiality, but there is great value to this practice. Finally, it is useful to review and advance the idea of temporary systems (Miles, 1964), which can serve as valuable guides in leading and understanding the time-limited groups likely to be prevalent in the "new" and changing organizational environment.

Balgopal and Vassil describe temporary systems as follows: "Temporary Systems. Among the most salient characteristics of agencies in the innovative mode are (1) capacities for being in touch with a wide variety of other systems including relevant constituencies external to the organization; (2) a sense of venturesomeness and comfort with occasional marginal roles with respect to significant others; and (3) an ability to manufacture and act upon different roles that are required in different circumstances" (1983:107). The recurrent features in temporary systems, as we have already noted, include novelty, newness, experimentation, egalitarianism, present-centeredness, authenticity, and task focus. These attributes, together with judicious application of the method of inquiry as a problem-solving methodology, make up the rules of the game, as it were. The authority for change is group-inspired rather than deriving from the personal charisma of any one individual. In addition, temporary systems are defined as oriented toward changed individuals, programs, or organizational structures. Small face-to-face groups are a special case of temporary systems, for example, when they are used with traditional classrooms.

Certain phenomena characterize groups designed for change induction purposes. Miles (1964) noted

> increased energy devoted to the accomplishment of novel, significant, focused, internalized, shared goals, effective, controllable procedures for achieving the goals, esprit de corps, group support, and mutual identification with peers; high autonomy and spontaneity, with freedom for creative experimentation, along with norms actively supporting change itself; higher-quality problem solving via increased communication

among participants and fuller use of member resources, active meeting of members' needs for autonomy, achievement, order, succorance [*sic*], and nurturance; high involvement and commitment to decisions, followed by group support for implementation after the termination of the temporary group's life.   (655–656).

TEAMS

Brills (1995) has summarized many of the central issues regarding teams. Knowing that there is no one ultimate model of team building, flexibility, open-mindedness, and adaptability are key. Greater expertise and a wide problem scope are qualities that together generate special group processes or context, such as Miles (1964) designates as characteristics of temporary systems, that can produce creative ideas. Differing frames of reference provide and enhance divergent and convergent modes of problem solving. These assets need to be considered against other features that are liabilities, such as slowness, role conflicts, and tensions, both cognitive and emotional, arising from competition related to status differences.

For the group worker, satisfaction has to be secondary to the greater need of group achievement. There is likely to be no one right way, and collegiality may indeed increase tensions and anxiety. Different standards of evaluation may compromise the authority of group or individual decisions. With luck, however, collaboration will not submerge innovation and creativity.

In reviewing the history of social work and its relevance to teamwork in an early study conducted by the University of Chicago, Margaret West concluded: "The efficiency and effectiveness of service improve more with the team approach then with a conventional case method of service" (169). She went on to note that, in the development of the profession, workers had a tendency to participate in two types of teams: interdisciplinary teams composed of other professionals and teams of nonprofessional workers and volunteers to extend and enhance agency function. Among problems common to teams are professional rivalries, role blurring, stereotypical views of colleagues, and members' allegiances being split between their own particular agency authority and the authority of the group.

Kanter (1986) makes the persuasive point, based on a wealth of experiences observing and working with various leaders, that strong leaders and strong teams can coexist. Power can grow by being shared, and a skillful leader mobilizes others to assume almost equal ownership in bringing an idea to life. These leaders Kanter has named "change masters." In initiating and dealing with change, considerable political skills are manifested in team building with an emphasis on collaboration. Among some of the skills she notes are valuing member differences, crafting coalitions, encouraging individuals, gathering information to articulate a point of view, singularizing individual responsibility, and opening new sources for expertise and experience. Prepackaged expert solutions are not effective. Friendships tend to block honest team or personal evaluations. This does mean that sidebar conversations inside or outside the group should be discouraged. Indeed, these can contribute to bonding and the clarification of issues. The ability to articulate opinions and develop arguments is an important skill to nurture, thereby defining teams as educative vehicles. Certainly, inequalities exist. For example, groups develop their own language, signs, symbols, and rituals, which may intimidate new members. An exclusionary cycle may develop, where the most active members almost form a dominant monopoly. A family-type hierarchy instituted by a power-driven boss tends to reduce peer competitors and meetings of such groups are among the most complex. Kanter summarizes her work in the following way:

> But each person has to be invited to participate in their expertise; for example, sense of humor, analytic ability, strategic intuitions, etc. It is clear to me that managing team work is always a balancing act between a leader's control and team opportunities; between getting the work done quickly and giving people a chance to learn; between seeking volunteers and pushing people into it; between too little team spirit and too much team spirit. As individuals in an entrepreneurial vent find the power tools to initiate innovation, they create and work through particular teams. And those teams make it possible for other potential entrepreneurs to step forward with useful ideas.
>
> Groups neither automatically submerge individuals nor automatically give everyone in the group equal opportunity. Leaders must nurture carefully the teams they rely on to implement their vision, and understand that the best team work acknowledges individual differences. Ironically, teams only work if the individuals in them are strong. The individuals get stronger because they are supported by committed teams. (5)

As an example of a good meeting, we offer the brief description below:

Their appointment as committee chairman takes people in different ways. Some seize the opportunity to impose their will on a group that they see themselves licensed to dominate. Others are more like scoutmasters, for whom the collective activity of the group is satisfaction enough, with no need for achievement. And there are the insecure or lazy chairmen who look to the meeting for reassurance and support in their ineffectiveness and inactivity, so that they can spread the responsibility for their indecisiveness among the whole group.

But even the large majority who do not go to those extremes still feel a pleasurable tumescence of the ego when they take their place at the head of the table for the first time. The feeling is no sin: The sin is to indulge it or to assume that the pleasure is shared by the other members of the meeting.

It is the chairman's self-indulgence that is the greatest single barrier to the success of a meeting. His first duty, then, is to be aware of the temptation and of the dangers of yielding to it. The clearest of the danger signals is hearing himself talking a lot during a discussion.

One of the best chairmen I have ever served under makes it a rule to restrict her interventions to a single sentence, or at most two. She forbids herself ever to contribute a paragraph to a meeting she is chairing. It is a harsh rule, but you would be hard to find a regular attendee of her meetings who thought it was a bad one.

There is, in fact, only one legitimate source of pleasure in chairmanship, and that is pleasure in the achievements of the meeting—and to be legitimate, it must be shared by all those present. Meetings are *necessary* for all sorts of basic and primitive human reasons, but they are *useful* only if they are seen by all present to be getting somewhere—and somewhere they know they could not have gotten to individually.   (Jay, 1976:4)

Among the elements of a mature team are the following:

1. Clarity of goals and acceptance of purpose. This also implies commitment, not only to the status quo but also experimentation and participation in new ideas.
2. An ability to manufacture the roles required in a decision or situation. This also includes capacities for assuming both leader and follower roles. There are various levels in a decision-making process or stage of group life, whether the problem be development, action

decisions, evaluation, or implementation. It also means using one's expertise as well as resources.

3. A sense of equanimity. This refers to an awareness that the group will sometimes be too loose, sometimes be too tight, and may need help to rebound or come back to a middle range, often an uneven equilibrium among task, maintenance, and personal work, and toward mutual support and respect. In a sense, the group needs to learn and recognize when it has gone too far and is becoming unproductive.

4. The ability to utilize a number of decision-making and problem-solving strategies, ranging from the idealistic participative consensus model to the expert-, leader-, or small-group-centered when each is necessary.

5. An ability to face and examine differences without becoming guided or coerced by them. This is related to a group's ability to tolerate uncertainty and ambiguity. It implies an ability to use reasonable tensions for work.

6. An ability to stretch its zone of tolerance within the task, each other, or between one another.

7. The ability to take on other's roles, although not to the point where too many defenses are shaken or disturbed. One can stand a sociopath only for so long without setting limits.

8. An appreciation of the team's limits within the context of the organization or its purview. Teams never exist in a vacuum.

INTERPROFESSIONAL TEAMWORK AND DECISION MAKING

A large proportion of health care delivery organizations and an increasing proportion of human service organizations employ a staff that comprises people trained in a variety of disciplines. Among health professionals, physicians, nurses, and social workers work together especially frequently. What are the factors specific to teams or working groups composed of people trained in different professions or disciplines? Kane (1975) noted that much teamwork literature "unfortunately" emphasizes decreasing tensions and disagreements, even "honest disagreement" (16). Ephross and Ephross (1984) have emphasized the problem that different professions define success differently. This may introduce dissonance when members of various professions work together as a team.

An interprofessional team is in every sense a working group, and the principles outlined in this chapter apply to such teams. Other kinds of working characteristics of such teams should also be highlighted. One is that how one is educated as a professional has a great deal to do with one's normative expectations of the professional role. If one wishes to do interprofessional teamwork as an important part of professional practice, that kind of teamwork should begin as early as possible in the process of professional education.

A second point worth noting is that interprofessional teams, like all working groups, need to go through processes of formation. It is not productive to throw together a collection of individuals trained in various professions and announce to them that they are henceforth to function as a team, without providing opportunities for the group formation processes to take place, relationships to form, and early stages of group development to be completed successfully. Interprofessional teams need to be provided with histories or, rather, with the opportunities to develop their own history. One way to approach this is by having a series of training experiences before teams are let loose, as it were, on patients or clients. Another is to assign the role of facilitator to a worker, staff, or resource person of an interprofessional team, at least in the early stages. A third is to schedule periodic in-service training experiences for the team to help it develop its capacities as a working group.

We do not question the benefits of interprofessional teams. In fact, the discussion earlier in this chapter of the processes of working groups and their general superiority in decision making suggests that teamwork is essential in both the delivery of health and human services and the administration of organizations that deliver these services. What we are arguing here, rather, is that putting people together in the same time and space doesn't immediately produce an effective group. Interprofessional teams involve members who belong to professions that vary in power, prestige, and status. This is a fact that needs to be understood by each team member. It cannot be treated as taboo and therefore avoided. Neither should it be taken for granted that the various team members will bring their differential statuses from the outside world and function effectively as a team. McLeaurin (1982) noted that "in many teams the concepts of equality, knowledge, profession, marginality, task and domain are perceived differently by the various professions. . . . For instance, substantive rationality is violated when a team espouses equality, but functions in a non-egalitarian manner" (5). In a similar vein, Ephross (1983) observed that relationships within a service delivery organization tend to be based on the realities of administrative behaviors, not the stated ideals of a profession.

In summary, teamwork needs to be taught, practiced, facilitated, and undergirded by a supportive climate within an organization. The development of effective service delivery teams may require more attention to the front end—the early stages of group development—than is the case in other kinds of working groups. Such a view presupposes, of course, that the team is really new and not simply a reformulation of parts of past teams, as may sometimes be the case. Parenthetically, the ability to facilitate a service delivery team requires a particular background and attitudinal set on the part of the facilitator. The facilitator need not necessarily be a member of any of the professions involved but must be highly skilled in working with groups and in sympathy with, if not highly knowledgeable about, the various professions and disciplines represented in the team. Familiarity with the clientele of the service delivery team may also be helpful.

The Particular Role of Staff

Helping working groups with problem solving and decision making is a central part of a staff person's work. An interactional perspective that encompasses individuals, subgroups, and organizations is vital. It involves paying attention simultaneously to:

1. The subject of the decision-making enterprise. This means, for many staff, being able to educate oneself quickly about the dimensions of the issues involved.
2. The processes through which the group is engaging in a decision-making process. Struggles over decisions both create strengths and leave scars in groups. The first needs to be maximized and the second minimized.
3. The significance of the decision-making process for the organizational and external environment. Decisions that are real have an impact on a wide range of systems, subsystems, and individuals. If a staff person can train himself to think through the consequences of group actions in regard to decisions, he can be helpful to the group in the process.

We suggested earlier that group members should avoid exclusive investments in the outcome of decisions but should retain a basic commitment to the value and processes of democratic decision making. We repeat this advice, if anything with greater emphasis, to staff persons who are professional practitioners in working groups. The ability of a group to reach a thoughtful and apt decision is a much more important outcome, in most cases, than the features of the decision that is reached. The function of the staff person is to help a group learn, operate, and gain in its capacity for decision making. Only occasionally is it to advocate a particular point of view.

When a staff person does advocate a particular point of view, he owes the group open communication about why this is so and an acknowledgment that he is leaving the boundaries that usually circumscribe the staff role. There are certainly times when, whether because of personal values, a conviction about issues, or an assessment of the group's need, it is appropriate for a staff person to become an advocate for a particular point of view. In our opinion, these occasions should be relatively few. If they are not, the staff person—and perhaps the group as well—needs to examine why. The requirement of loyalty demands that the staff person, at least as much as the members, be clear about his or her responsibility for helping the group to implement decisions whether or not the staff person agrees with them. A loyalty to the group should outweigh loyalties to particular points of view, with rare exceptions. Following up on groups' decisions is essential, and much of the responsibility for orchestrating the follow-up, if not actually executing it, commonly falls within the responsibilities of a staff person.

We conclude with a list of practice principles in working with teams that is adapted from the work of Bales (1983).

1. Group size is an important consideration. To promote maximum interaction between each and every member, keep the size of the group below eight. In larger groups, strong members take up air time and quiet members can get lost.

2. If possible, when considering group composition, try to include some individuals who are assertive in order to build in energy for work.

3. To develop teamwork, aim for group membership that includes both those who value friendly behavior or closeness and those who value task orientation. Sometimes, these are designated as interpersonal and authority themes. One may expect tendencies among the membership to feel comfortable with one or the other of these two frameworks and, conversely, to show ambivalence toward the one they don't favor. Staff will need to explore these differences and build bridges between and among members with diverging frameworks.

4. Different kinds of situations and conditions within the group require that the staff person fulfill different roles. High performance, for example, needs a combination of particular staff, chair, and member

behaviors that balance both task and interpersonal orientation. Overemphasizing either one or the other can slow down and complicate the work of the group. In terms of composition, it is wise to choose personalities who can provide energy in each of these areas.

5. Encouraging and legitimizing a certain amount of dissent is important for high performance in group problem solving. This may raise negative feelings, but conflict clears the air and sharpens issues.

6. Conflicts can also be destructive, especially those that are intractable. To help a group develop better teamwork, start with the least difficult conflicts, while at the same time supporting common ground among group members.

7. The staff person should share power and leadership functions in order to develop the abilities of group members so far as this is compatible with high performance. Staff should do those things that are necessary but not possible at the time for other group members to handle.

8. In those situations where sharp differences threaten to overwhelm a group, the staff person needs to encourage members who can function as mediators. Frequently, these may those members who are uncommitted regarding a particular issue. Setting up and developing a coalition that can bring together sharply divided parties is a key function of staff. Such coalitions are useful in dealing with the uncommitted.

9. Do not let groups achieve internal solidarity by attacking one of their own or others on the outside. It is an unstable solution and damaging to the value of teamwork.

10. There are usually important reasons based either in personalities or the functional requirements of the group for members to behave as they do. Attacking symptoms directly can exacerbate group problems. One needs to try to deal with the underlying reasons. Individual behavior in the group may relate to the problem the group is facing, as well as to the personality needs of the members.

11. Difficult tasks may have to be redesigned to maintain teamwork. Starting with the least difficult conflicts is helpful, and in the process staff should consider whether its role is exacerbating polarization.

In general, these principles are directed toward developing a democratic microcosm such that the group can conduct its affairs and work at the same time that it is experiencing tensions. Problem solving and decision making are two central functions through which group issues of productivity and development can be approached.

Among the most relevant strategies people use to gain power that staff need to be aware of are the following:

1. Coalitions and cliques, especially in between-group meetings of members.
2. Expertness, intellectual arrogance, irrelevant asides or speeches.
3. Scapegoating, excluding, bullying.
4. Communicating in conclusions or declarative statements.
5. Foreclosing discussion.
6. Accepting but not responding to someone's affective responses.
7. Withdrawing after talking a lot. Withholding praise or support after someone has done a nice job or praising subservience.
8. Interrupting someone else's comments.
9. Consistently arguing with or avoiding the leader or other members.
10. "Yes, but . . ." disagreement masquerading as agreement.
11. Setting up conflicts or pointing out sharp differences between other members.
12. The "innocuously brutalizing" shrug or smile.
13. Citing a celebrity or noted authority as a model in support of a position, as in, "I don't think Dr. Freud would buy that, either."

To summarize, it can be overwhelming to consider all the possible complexities and scenarios in working with groups, interprofessional teams, and the like. For example, what is one to make of the thirteen power strategies? As a general rule, building pathways between coalitions means paying attention to both cognitive and interpersonal domains in order to provide opportunities for cooperation and group strength. Group leaders do have authority, some of it agency based and some of it deriving from internal group factors and the credibility given them by members, for performance and assistance toward group goals. All these support the authority of the leader.

In general, these power strategies are essentially self-defeating and damaging to the group. The problem the staff member faces is to convert negatives into positives, or at least to neutralize them. Simply put, one has to be aware of the potential for these power strategies to come into play, look for them, and proceed to deliver the cognitive-interpersonal lubricant to maintain group and members' composure and momentum.

II

ORGANIZATIONAL SETTINGS
AND STYLES

TWO IMPORTANT TOPICS that may seem unrelated at first glance are the place of a group within an organizational setting and the culture of the organization. One of these, place, is a structural concept. The other, culture, often appears to be less basic to an organization. Yet the two are intimately related.

In our view, culture refers not only to faddish or modish aspects of what takes place within an organization but also to the typical form or type of which a particular organization is an example. Garland, Jones, and Kolodny (1965) referred to this characteristic as a "frame of reference." Each organization views itself and is viewed by others as an example of a particular subset of organizational types. Which subset it falls into has important implications for the working groups within it; as we discuss below, among these are styles of interpersonal relationships, forms of normative and deviant behavioral definitions, preferred styles of conflict definition and resolution, and various other characteristics of organizational life. These characteristics are important for the members of a group and for the ways in which a group operates. Some illustrations may help clarify this point.

In example C, the Mount Williams Community Hospital group is made up of hospital department heads. The prototype is that of an industrial organization. The group's members are being paid to attend the group meetings, the group is meeting during work hours, and the business of the group is a serious part of the lives of its members. More specifically, the group is a serious part of the professional careers of its members. As might be expected, given its industrial prototype, the group is serious. Societal norms about work as opposed to play demand that humor be kept within bounds, interpersonal interrelating be viewed at best as a secondary outcome, and limits be set on the extent to which any one individual may be the recipient of exclusive attention in a particular meeting. The staff function in this group is likely to be limited, since a staff person, when there is one, probably lacks the professional identity, qualifications, and status of the group members. One might expect, all other things being equal, that members will come to meetings of this group dressed appropriately for their professional work. Furthermore, it would not be unusual for group members, especially at times of stress or tension, to address each other as "Dr.," "Mr.," or "Ms."

In example B, the Avon Friendly Society Board of Directors presents a different kind of organizational pattern. This is a fiduciary group, to which members are appointed by virtue of their standing in the community at large. The members are volunteers; the group meets during leisure time, not work time. The group is thus likely to adopt a more informal style. The staff person is likely to be more active and more central to the operation of the group, if only because the organizational setting is the full-time workplace of the staff person while it is only the part-time interest of the other members, including the chair. The culture of the organization has two prototypes. The first is a club, a group to which one belongs by virtue of the agreement of the other members. The second is charity or philanthropy: the group's members are donating their time for a worthy and altruistic cause. Attendance at meetings is an expression of philanthropy rather than a responsibility of job or career. Patterns of attendance may be expected to vary widely depending on how salient this group is to the total life pattern of each member.

The Mayor's Task Force of example A has as its prototype a political organization. Getting one's point across is important in such a group, and winning a vote tends to be important in citizens' groups in general. The parallel with a political group is clear. In a political group, having one's opinion adopted by the group amounts to winning. Both winning and losing may be experienced as crucial in such groups.

A final example might be a university faculty committee. Consider a committee on appointment, tenure, and promotion.[1] The prototype of such a group is a collection of "friends of the court." In this case, the court is that of a university administrator, and the friends are faculty who have been appointed or elected by their colleagues. This group may have a relatively low position on the list of professional priorities for each individual member, except for one thing: membership is the result of having been appointed by a powerful administrator or having been elected by one's colleagues. At worst, members may serve on such a group reluctantly, because they have been asked to do so and cannot refuse. At best, the reward for serving on such a group is the confirmation of one's senior status in the eyes of an administrator or one's colleagues. The actual work may be experienced by members as a sort of indentured servitude in return for being able to list membership on the committee among their accomplishments.

One might expect a wide variance in the way such groups function, and, indeed, this is the case in our experience. The reason is that members lack a clear frame of reference and therefore have to develop their own style of operation. Thus some members and chairs will bring an industrial frame of reference with them and take the work output of the committee very seriously. Others will bring with them the prototype of a club and avoid making deep or serious long-term commitments to the work of the group. Still others will identify more deeply with the candidates than with the work of the committee and will sit through meeting after meeting with the attitude of "there but for the grace of God go I."

Any attempt to list prototypes and styles exhaustively runs the risk of oversimplification. Not only will particular organizations have their own individual styles, but the membership of a group within an organization, particularly at the outset, may not behave according to the style of the organization as a whole. In fact, this is one difficulty that can be encountered in the formation and contracting processes. If each member of a group comes with a different view of the organization that sponsors the group and therefore of the group itself, there needs to be a meeting of the minds. To paraphrase Schwartz (1994), the group must search out a common ground before it can truly form. Anyone starting a working group should ask, what is the prototype of the group and that of the organization that sponsors it? If nothing else, this question is a useful spur to thinking about the group.

THE PLACE OF THE GROUP IN RELATION TO THE ORGANIZATION

Regardless of the culture of a particular organization, there are questions about the place of a particular working group in relation to that organization.

It is useful to think of the place of a working group in a vertical progression within the structure of the organization. Here are some examples:

1. A working group may have governance responsibility, sometimes including fiduciary responsibility for an organization. The working group, which in this instance is likely to be called a board of directors, governors, or electors, is the organization in a legal sense. This is often a difficult fact for staff trained in a health or human services profession to grasp. In our highly specialized society, in which the division of labor is well advanced, it seems to go against common sense that a school committee made up of elected or appointed laypersons, for example, is the school system, rather than the highly skilled and credentialed superintendent of schools and his staff. In fact, however, it is the professional staff who work for the school committee, not the other way around. Similarly, the legal existence of a hospital is vested in its board of trustees, not in its professional staff; a social agency legally is its board of directors, not its professional staff; and the government of a jurisdiction is its elected officials and ultimately its voters, not the professional staff employed by, say, the planning department.

2. A working group may be composed entirely of employees of a single organization. These may be high-ranking and powerful employees (as in example C) or relatively low-level employees of a particular department or subdivision.

3. A working group may be a council, that is, a body made up of representatives of various organizations, agencies, or constituencies. Councils, and a variant called coalitions, have particular dynamics of their own. One of them is the tension caused by the fact that each council member is also accountable to a sponsoring group or organization. Group members may be laypersons, professionals, or a mixture of the two. One of us recalls an instance in which a staff member of a social agency carried three different statuses simultaneously. She was (a) a member of the professional staff; (b) a long-time resident of the community served by the agency; and (c) the parent of a young person who was being served by the agency. At different times, then, this staff member was speaking under one or more of her "three hats," and this fact had an impact on the processes of the group. For this reason, she took pains to acquaint the other members of the staff with the fact that she was representing three different sets of concerns.

4. Another characteristic place for a group within an organization is that of an advisory group. (Such is the case in example E's Winterset Advisory Committee.) Advisory groups vary greatly in the extent to which they are

purely advisory. They range from merely serving to channel organizational propaganda to a broader constituency, on the one hand, to filling an essential and highly regarded role in the overall organizational structure, on the other. In general, however, it seems safe to generalize that advisory groups' gain freedom as they lose power. That is, its position as an advisory body confers on the group as a whole a freedom to express itself because it is not subject to any form of administrative discipline. At the same time, unless the group gradually carves out for itself a position of power, it lacks the influence to insist on any of its recommendations being translated into action. We suggest that freedom and power form a zero-sum; this is a useful hypothesis for further investigation.

Freedom and power vary with other aspects of organizations. The differences between a "staff" group and a "line" group are well known and have been documented elsewhere (e.g., Katz and Kahn, 1978). Working groups in branches, located at a distance from the headquarters or central office of an organization, tend to have certain characteristics in common; so do groups that are part of the headquarters or central office of an organization.

Power in Organizations

Power, prestige, the ability to affect one's future and that of others (Lasswell, 1951), and the ability to command deferential behavior from others or their organization are vital (and sometimes taboo) subjects. Organizational secrets, carefully guarded privileges and ambitions, and news about changes in the organization are emotionally loaded subjects. This may be especially true in organizations whose products are less tangible, such as those whose output consists of health care or human services. In such organizations, there is often a dissonance between a staff person's status in the professional group and the same person's status in the organizational hierarchy. An assistant director who holds several graduate degrees may be subject to being overruled by a low-ranking clerk when it comes to a minor purchase of supplies, for example. Knowing how to manage organizational trivia, then, may be as important, for a few moments at least, as knowing how to perform a complex organizational task. These two frames of reference interpenetrate each other during the course of organizational life. In addition, the people who staff health and human services organizations tend to share an egalitarian ethos, to some extent, at the same time that they are organized in hierarchical, bureaucratic ways.

The organizations with which we are concerned are typically dependent on outside sources for all or a significant part of their resources. Such organizations live in a world in which "they," outside the organization, support "us.""They" may be public legislative bodies, voluntary contributors, philanthropic entities, or programs of grants-in-aid. "They" often do not truly understand "us," as "we" see it.

These organizations also share a service ideology. They view themselves, at least formally, as working from a desire to be of service, to help, to educate, or, in the motto of many police departments, to "serve and protect." Because the formal organizational objectives are humanitarian, such organizations can exercise a good deal of influence over the inner lives, self-perceptions, and life patterns of the human beings who work for and in them. Identification with the organization, something that is expected of many professionals, is one mechanism for this influence.

Certain features of organizational life can be oppressive to employees, including those who staff working groups. This is hardly a new idea. The relationship of the worker to the organization has been studied by many sociologists for more than a century (e.g., Weber, 1947; Goffman, 1961). The alienation of workers from the products of their labor, because of the way work is organized, is a central concept for many sociologists and social critics (Seeman, 1959).

The nature of human experience within organizational contexts in general, and within contemporary, postindustrial, human service delivery organizations in particular, is understudied. There are two reasons why this has not been a popular subject. As has been suggested elsewhere (Ephross, 1983), a form of machismo can characterize such organizations. Organizational ideologies, which insist that the needs of clients/patients/consumers come first, tend to generate an unresponsive toughness with regard to the needs of staff. Concern with the hidden agendas and interpersonal needs of staff members is sometimes treated with scorn and often dismissed as irrelevant. Essentially, what a consumer gets from a service organization, however, is the attention of one or more staff members; thus ignoring the needs of staff is, in effect, ignoring the quality of the consumer's experience as well.

A second reason for the relative lack of attention to the needs of staff in such organizations is a tendency toward what may be called stigma generalization: the stigma attached to certain client groups may affect, by association, those who serve them. For example, human service organizations, at least generally, do not serve the powerful strata of our society. They serve disproportionately the poor, the old, the very young, minority groups, convicted offenders, recent immigrants, people who are sick, and the like. Add to this the fact that some of the human services professions are traditionally staffed by women and that sexist attitudes and perceptions often prevail, and the stigma may be doubled.

POSTINDUSTRIAL HUMAN SERVICE ORGANIZATIONS: SPECIFIC ASPECTS

To attempt a comprehensive discussion of all aspects of contemporary human service organizations, let alone to trace all of their effects, is beyond the scope of this book. We shall confine ourselves to discussing briefly five organizational phenomena: greedy organizational identities; the effects of annual budgeting and funding; the management of communication; the expansion of vertical resource patterns; and policy formulation through accounting and auditing mechanisms. Our emphasis is on the effects of these phenomena on working groups within the organization, rather than on organizations as wholes or on the interaction of these phenomena with broader societal developments.

Greedy Institutions

Coser (1967) has discussed the concept of "greedy institutions," institutional forms that demand that a person submerge his or her individual identity in the work role. Examples may be found in the military, in which one's identity becomes that of one's rank, or in certain kinds of religious organizations, in which one symbolizes membership in the organization by adopting a new name. Persons who serve greedy institutions are often called by only part of their names or are referred to only by their work titles, rather than by their names. Coser points out both the importance of such language and the inherently asymmetrical and often unstable relationships between these institutions and the people who belong to them. In return for their services, people who work for greedy institutions gain considerable power and general anonymity.

Many health and human services organizations share the characteristics of Coser's greedy institutions. One common pattern is to restrict communication outside the organization, unless one is at a supervisory or administrative level. Speeches of major administrators are often written by nameless staff members whose work is not credited. Announcements and press releases supposedly emanating from presidents of boards of directors may be news to them until they receive copies of what they are supposed to have said. Chairs of committees frequently have in front of them an information sheet prepared by a sometimes powerful but anonymous staff member.

Such patterns produce results not very different from those noted by Coser. First, the role of servant to a greedy organization may include severe limitations on personal behavior outside work, as the person becomes viewed as merely an extension of the organization. The relevance of greedy organizations for working groups is that the identity of the group—like the identity of the individual—may be submerged, supposedly for the greater good of the organization but also as a means of control. Statements and even inquiries by groups may need to be cleared with successively higher levels of administrators and governance bodies, to the point where the group is seriously handicapped in its attempt to fulfill its mission. When this happens, the group needs to focus inward and rediscuss its charge and its resources. If it does not, a mounting sense of frustration may bring the life of the group to a premature end.

The Budgeting Process

Budgeting in many organizations occurs annually. In theory, each year, a decision-making process concerning the organization's survival for the next year takes places. As experienced by working groups within the organization, of course, budget decisions determine whether group members will have jobs the following year and, if so, at what salary. Periodically, rationalists urge a truly zero-based approach, one that involves a fresh look at an organization's existence each year. Rarely is such an approach genuine or sincere, since "zeroing out," or doing away with an organization, is rarely an option. To the extent that an organization is dependent on outside resources—whether philanthropic, public, or a mixture of the two—resource provision through budgeting involves a political process in the true sense of that term. Obtaining resources becomes largely an issue of power relationships, although, admittedly, service obligations form part of the power equation.

The importance of this for working groups is that their actions, if they are viewed as potentially jeopardizing the following year's budget, become viewed as serious violations of organizational norms and standards. Conversely, actions that are thought to enhance the organization's position in budget negotiating are highly valued and rewarded. The working group thus faces continual evaluation according to criteria irrelevant to its particular mission. Democratic decisions, reached in good faith, may be viewed as potentially treasonous because of their real or presumed effects on sources of funding. Furthermore, behaviors and performances of groups are sometimes evaluated by budget criteria, which may have little or nothing to do with the formal service goals of the organization. Health and human service organizations that close because of lack of funding are not necessarily those whose staffs have practiced poorly. Rather, they may be those whose staffs have simply paid more attention to the quality of professional practice than to resource development and the political skills necessary to surviving the budgeting process.

Managing the News

Organizations are faced with the problem of managing the news, both internally and externally. Public relations practice has developed for this purpose. An administrator is never dismissed; she "has made the decision to return to practice" or "been offered a position elsewhere he could not refuse." Ineffective staff leave "to seek a new challenge." Many organizations make use of the language of diplomacy, language sometimes designed to obfuscate rather than to reveal and to educate. New service programs are always presented as creative responses, never as attempts to justify an organization's continued existence. Sophistication is sometimes required to interpret hidden meanings in public communications. This aspect of organizational functioning has serious implications for working groups. One must make sure that the group understands (although not necessarily adopts) the language of the organization. If it does not, tension will grow between the group and its sponsor. Groups also need to understand that organizations behave as they do because they view themselves as living in a threatening and turbulent environment.

Vertical Resource Patterns

Increasingly, health and human service organizations have become dependent on vertical resource patterns, that is, on resources that come from larger, centralized bodies (Warren, 1972). Of course, such resources are welcome and necessary. The process of obtaining them involves cost, however, both for the organization and for the working groups that live within them. Applying for grants and negotiating contracts involve another process of being judged, of trying to put the best face on the organization and the groups within it, of covering weaknesses and leading from strengths. The process of funding is rational only in part. The esteem ascribed to particular working groups, and sometimes the jobs of group members, may be in the hands of impersonal, distant forces. The further away the funding source, the less rational the process of judgment may feel.

Accountability

The last twenty-five years have been marked by a proliferation of systems designed to ensure what is usually called "accountability." In our view, the accountability sought is often very limited. For the most part, it is not an accountability to consumers; rather, the term is often used as a synonym for fiscal control. Such accountability can mean spending less, keeping better records, and increasing the importance of auditing.

The conventional wisdom is that auditing and accounting systems operate independently of policy decisions. They are designed to measure efficiency in the use of resources. In fact, however, the increasingly pervasive fiscal control to which service delivery organizations are subject has two (possibly) unintended effects. The first is entropy. In organizations, this means that increasing amounts of effort, energy, and resources are devoted to meeting the needs and demands of audits. For working groups in organizations, the effect may be a need to devote considerable energy to providing data to those in the organization who furnish data to funding sources and outside checkers. This process not only subtracts from the energy of the working group; it also may serve to inhibit the democratic microcosmic forces that we identified in chapter 4 as being vital to the operation of a productive group. Working groups generally do not perform well when they are reminded at frequent intervals that people are looking over their shoulders.

On the other hand, a caveat is in order at this point. Sanctioning bodies are necessary to provide teeth to the expectations and performances of stakeholders in an organization in order to protect and advance the interests of employees and customers. When the lines of responsibility and accountability are blurred by moral lapses by those in charge, such as CEOs, boards of directors, and participating independent accounting bodies, then one could argue that the "looking over one's shoulder" phenomenon is vital. Given the negative experiences with large organizations such as Enron and WorldCom, whatever democratic microcosms are at work, they should not be viewed as insulated or separate from what is happening in other organizational domains.

In summary, we recommend a stance about contemporary service delivery organizations that is neither cynical nor naive. We share the concern that new and less distorting ways be found for complex organizations to operate. We suggest that the leadership of working groups in organizations needs to be clear about all the various constraints and issues defined by their particular organizations' settings, styles, funding patterns, and other characteristics. One may not be able to change a group's external environment; one does have a responsibility to be clear and forthright about what it is.

THE WORKING GROUP AS MEDIATOR

Sometimes, working groups are only parts of the organizations in which they are located. This may be true of a staff committee, for example. In other situations, however, a working group carries a mediating function. That is, it mediates between an organization and the environment that surrounds it.

> Much of the discussion in the Winterset Advisory Committee (example E) consisted of members of the committee interpreting to the higher-prestige board members how residents of the housing project actually viewed various aspects of the community, including the board and the neighborhood center. The committee served as a forum where widely disparate views and judgments were communicated, their sharp edges rubbed off, and a common language developed. While the board might not have listened to the abstraction called "the community," the group provided board members with an opportunity to listen to specific individuals who represented points of view found in the community.

A working group may serve as a mediator between individuals of widely disparate backgrounds and the organization that sponsors the working group. The function of the staff member as mediator has been discussed elsewhere (Shulman, 1984). We are emphasizing the operation of the group as a whole in a mediating function. This ability to mediate is one of the major assets an organization gains by having a rich panoply of working groups that involve members who come from both inside and outside the organization. Such groups are ideal data transfer mechanisms and as such may be invaluable for the organization.

IMPLICATIONS FOR PROFESSIONAL PRACTICE

As has been discussed above, working groups are structured and symbolic. That is, they have legal and/or professional and/or administrative and/or task-determined realities and at the same time may be viewed symbolically as stages on which a complex drama of interpersonal relationships and needs is enacted. It is important for staff, chairs, and members to reach agreement and understanding about organizational opportunities and constraints. The place of a group within an organization's structure needs to be clearly understood in terms of its effects on both group actions and the self-definition of the group. Groups may or may not like the places they occupy within organizations. They may accept those places and work within them, or they may seek to change them. But they must understand the structure. There must be an understanding that is shared among the actors in the group drama so that each is not acting a different part in a different play in a different house before a different audience.

Organizations are human creations. They are subject to change stemming from both internal and external evolution. Just as it is a mistake for working groups to ignore organizations' existence, constraints, resources, and structures, it is also a mistake to view organizations as fixed for all time. There are many examples of working groups that have brought about major and significant changes within the organizations of which they are part.

As a closing note, sometimes it is important, both in groups and in organizations, to consider the positive aspects of mild and thoughtful resistance to change. Such resistance can be helpful, insofar as it promotes stability. Those who consider the implications of change or innovation most thoughtfully may turn out to be the most reliable supporters of change once a group or organization has made a commitment to it.

Boards of Directors

Boards of directors, usually composed of prominent lay citizens but sometimes including professionals as well, are governing bodies in organizations; their major functions generally include resource development, hiring and evaluating senior executive staff, legal responsibility for organizational use of resources, and the development and maintenance of organizational policies. Effective board function is essential if an organization is to adapt to its environment, cope with changes, and anticipate alternative outcomes. Boards provide continuity and connections with organizational history and traditions. In planning for the future, boards legitimate both present and future activities. In addition, boards perform an evaluative function with regard to services, leadership, staff, and community and interorganizational relationships.

Boards are generally composed of members who represent different publics and different points of view about relevant issues. Often, members are chosen to represent various racial/ethnic groups, schools of thought, political philosophies, professions, political subdivisions, levels of financial resources, and a mix of provider and consumer perspectives. An effective board thus brings together in one forum the differing values, commonalities, interests, and conflicts that exist in a given community.

Boards can be very large, with formal board meetings conducted according to parliamentary rules of formal procedure. Most of the work of boards, however, is conducted by their subunits, which include both standing and ad hoc committees, task forces, subcommittees, and similar bodies. These generally form and function as working groups in every sense. Many of them are staffed by professionals, with the echelon from which the staff is drawn serving as a rough indicator of the status of the subunit within the organization as a whole. For example, it is customary for the chief executive of the organization to staff the executive committee of a board.

The behavior and life of a board of directors and its subunits may reflect influences and methods of reaching decisions that are both rationalist and political (Greenwood and Jenkins, 1981). In the rationalist tradition, technical expertise is often a significant factor. Emphasis is placed on logic, facts, and reasoned arguments. When complex issues arise, however, as is often the case when major policy issues are being addressed, emotions may run high, and rational methods of decision making may give way to a political frame of reference, one that is sometimes deeply entwined with emotional and less rational attachments.

When a board is driven by political influences rather than by purely rational evaluations of ideas and proposed policies, decision making may be based on, more than anything else, personal or organizational commitments, interests, and identities. Reaction, compromise, and negotiation, which are key elements in political arenas, become crucial processes. Thus boards and their subunits are likely to utilize both rational and political decision-making processes as well as some mixed forms that combine the two, depending on the issues and the atmosphere that surrounds them. In all these instances, the life of board subunits as small groups includes cognitive, valuative, and affective spheres, in various constellations. A board unit may act as a kitchen cabinet with respect to a staff executive. At other times, it may guard with great perseverance the organizational interests it represents. There are dangers as well as strengths in both patterns. The dangers have been well documented by Janis (1972) and Janis and Mann (1977).

Boards are generally composed of persons who are connected to other important groups. Members may bring in information from these other groups and may influence relationships with them. One can think of the participation of each member of a board or a subunit as though it were influenced by the internal committee the board member brings into the board. Membership in these other committees (such as the family) may consciously or unconsciously influence role behavior within the board. Thus psychosocial influences may have an effect on what looks like an administrative process of developing policy. The converse may also be true; that is, policy content may influence group processes. For example, the need to take positions, for policy reasons, that are unpopular in a community may produce a sense of strain among board members.

To extend this point further, a board committee member's involvement in a policy-making process—for instance, in initiating ideas, considering alternatives and consequences, and making, implementing, and evaluating decisions—may influence that same member's behavior in the group. It may either free or restrain participation depending on how it is received by other members, especially some who may feel competitive. This is a specialized case, sometimes a dramatic one, of the interrelationship between task and process in groups. Because of this interrelationship, boards and their units benefit particularly from the development of a democratic microcosm and suffer particularly when such an atmosphere of safety and mutual respect is not fully developed. It is especially in governance bodies that diversity needs to be fostered and diverse points of view respected, in order to avoid the deterioration of the board into a rubber stamp for approving administrators' actions, decisions, and perspectives.

Organizational contexts always have major implications for boards of directors. Fiduciary constraints and responsibilities, emergent social issues, religious positions of segments of a community, and political controversies enter regularly into the consciousnesses of boards and their units. Health and human service organizations deal with issues, such as child abuse, delinquency, intergroup relations, unwanted pregnancy, sexually transmitted diseases, and care of the aged, that polarize segments of a community and bring out deeply felt positions. Staff interests, often expressed as concerns on behalf of clients, patients, and consumers, can generate severe pressures on boards. So can the demands of suppliers of resources, whether from voluntary philanthropic or from public funds. Both internal and external influences merge, oppose each other, and intertwine in diverse and complicated ways, often creating crises that influence both roles and outcomes in the governance groups that need to deal with them.

Boards work best when their atmosphere permits the widest expression of citizenship values such as altruism, free participation, diversity of ideas, and mutual respect. Both political cooperation and the cultivation of roles of worthy adversaries are essential to a democratic process, and democratic process is in turn essential to effective board function. Such process enhances both pragmatic and principled operations and leads to equitable and meaningful production and task accomplishment as well. For boards as well as for other types of working groups, a well-cared-for democracy is not a luxury but a necessity in the long run.

Fiduciary Responsibility

The inadequacy and perhaps lack of fiduciary responsibility of corporate boards have exacerbated corporate fraud and lack of representativeness to shareholders. Indeed, the boards of directors of many organizations have acted more like rubber stamps, both commending and participating in the corporate inequities.

As the country responds to corporate greed by passing tough laws to deal with present and avoid future misdeeds, the composition and operation of boards takes on central importance, as does the practice of leadership that assists boards to operate as independent policy-making and oversight groups.

To help boards exercise the full measure of their responsibilities and authority, a staff person will need to be prepared in at least two ways. The first involves understanding the major issues that are current and the policies that they affect; the second consists of developing a working group equal to its task in the context of the various complementary and challenging roles required of each member.

One of the major issues that affects group process and development is group composition. How many (if any) insiders in the organization should be members of the group? A major concern here is conflicts of interest, which can compromise the full measure of review and recommendation. Another feature of an independent board is the capacity to accumulate all the organizational and personal skills essential to the proper exercise of leadership. An independent board of directors must shape a management structure that infuses an organization culture with honesty and integrity. Given the lure of money and status, it is no small task to embed unimpeachable standards of operation in a group's cultural way of life. This orientation requires support and reaffirmation to contain the tension between formal and informal influences. In this context, the pressure to inhibit risk taking will be enormous. Risk taking is a strong feature of executive behavior, and an independent board needs to deal with it most judiciously. Boards may well be overly leery of the potential failures attendant on risky behavior. Finding a proper balance requires skilled leadership.

A board of directors, in its processes and procedures, stands at the pinnacle of an organization as a model of moral character. A leadership group can impose powerful moral guidelines on an organization, not only through exercising its formal authority but by influencing informal pathways, as well as promotional, financial, and training regimens, in order to fortify a democratic point of view. On the other side of the equation, the board of directors needs to be open to various influences from inside the organization. Information and influence have to move both ways. As a further advantage, this practice acts as a definite morale booster.

In the best of worlds, there could be sharp differences between staff and the board. Final authority rests with the board, but this does not exclude negotiation. Bitter strife can cause staff to leave and injure an organization's public image. Reasoned conflict, however, can foster an atmosphere of electric anticipation and lead to worthwhile models for future behavior. In other words, depending on how they are handled, conflicts can yield positive results.

In a settlement house, issues of health, education, and environmental concern had festered to the point that residents, with staff help and having exhausted a series of other mediating devices, decided to march through the city's main street to the mayor's office, armed with a set of demands. The staff, which had been involved with the initiative for over a year and were invested in it both professionally and personally, was prepared to march alongside the residents. The board felt otherwise and stated its position that staff had done its job by guiding the tenants' association to this next step and should applaud from the sidelines. The staff, however, felt a deep, moral commitment to participating in the march, particularly since they felt their presence might mitigate the vulnerability of the residents, who were indirectly beholden to local politicians for their living arrangements in the housing development. Feelings were strong on both sides, and in the steamy negotiating sessions, it was formally agreed that the staff could join the march only if they were at the end of the procession. As it turned out, the staff were asked to step up in the line and march arm in arm with the residents for about a mile. There were no repercussions for staff, and a strong message was sent to the larger community about the agency's role.

Clearly, for the staff in this situation, solidarity to the community it served took precedence over obedience to the board. It is relevant to note that the board, which was quite independent of the agency though led by its director, was essentially tied to high social status, money, fund raising, and banking interests and had no feel for the staff's work with families and tenants in poverty or the struggles these constituents faced every day. The staff's backgrounds, by contrast, were rooted in the working class, by education, family, and so forth. This is not to say that no efforts were made to educate the board. They were, in small group meetings. Even with the best of intentions, however, communication may have been evasive.

The central question is, whom does a board represent and protect? Composition takes on a very important dimension here, even if perfection in this regard is impossible. Board members need to be selected for their particular abilities to respond to agency/organization needs and culture, while what liabilities they may also carry need to be contained. Personal issues aside—although these may be quite relevant—it is important to consider their organizational backgrounds, their political and economic clout, their sense of morality and character, their ethnic and racial identities, and their experience in other types of policy groups. While composition is more art than science, there is every reason to distill through the processes of judgment just what the potential is. It is also important to consider who makes the judgments as to who will serve on the board and who will interview the candidates. Will the search committee comprise staff from each and every level of the organization? What effect will this have? All these factors are important to consider.

In the final analysis, boards of directors need to separate legal from illegal, ethical from unethical, promise from frivolity. In a large sense, the board of directors needs to shape and reinforce policies that are within a normative range of social parameters. Whether in the realm of personality, behavior, ideas, or policies, transformation takes place very gradually. Change rarely occurs as epiphany. The process of transformation is the hardest of the practitioner's art. Sometimes, maybe most of the time, members (and leaders) are not fully aware of it.

Among the smaller but no less important issues for boards of directors are entrance and exit procedures for individual members and decisions as to whether board members should belong to more than one board. In organization theory, the chief executive officer usually staffs the board of directors and operates as the mediating influence between the board and the rest of the organization under his direction. Balance between the board and management is imperative for both continuity and innovation (development) and requires a sharing of power and governance,. powerful issues embedded in the purpose and operating culture of the group. When the chair of the board is also the chief operating officer, board independence and operative relationships may strain the governance and legal parameters. Both boards and chairs need to develop principles for self-evaluation and to affirm independence. To further this, it may be wise for boards to have regular meetings without the presence of the chair.

Sonnenfeld (2002), comparing well-managed boards to those that failed, observed that issues such as composition, expertise, age, independence, and executive sessions, while important, were not sufficient to account for the differences. The critical issue seemed to be not structure as much as the development of a robust social system. A strong and well-functioning board requires good chemistry, a spirit of give and take, the ability to manufacture necessary roles, including but not limited to those with differing opinions, and a system for evaluating personal and peer performance. Fostering honesty, trust, and mutual respect requires a group culture where these expectations flourish. Within this context, the spirit of inquiry and independence of mind are necessary to challenge fellow members, whether this involves questioning the basis of the information they supply, the clarity of their ideas, the quality of their analyses, or other issues of similar importance. Sonnenfeld summarizes the components of high-functioning boards in the following way:

> We all owe the shareholders, activists, accountants, lawyers, and analysts who study corporate governance a debt: In the 1980s and 1990s, they alerted us to the importance of independent directors, audit committees, ethical guidelines, and other structural elements that can help ensure that a corporate board does its job. Without a doubt, these good-governance guidelines have helped companies avoid problems, big and small. But they're not the whole story or even the longest chapter in the story. If a board is to truly fulfill its mission—to monitor performance, advise the CEO, and provide connections with a broader world—it must become a robust team—one whose members know how to ferret out the truth, challenge one another, and even have a good fight now and then. (113)

The widening problem of corporate misdeeds has affected more than large business organizations. In our view, many nonprofit groups are facing a shortage of qualified candidates to serve as members of boards of directors.

The lack of the leadership necessary to carry out governmental and management responsibilities may be weakening organizations' abilities to fulfill their missions.

Professional social work practitioners either at midlevel or executive positions as administrators are likely to come into conflict with boards of directors. There will always be cross-currents of interest between boards and service employees, including midlevel managers. The social work administrator's position is simply to mediate between these parties while maintaining and exercising his/her responsibilities within the context of a democratic microcosm applied at various levels. Developing and maintaining a generalized frame of reference adaptable to various constituencies within an organization (and perhaps external to it) may be the most valuable quality or skill of the executive as "change master" (Kanter, 1986).

12

TECHNOLOGIES FOR GROUP MAINTENANCE, OPERATION, AND PRODUCTIVITY

IN THIS CHAPTER, we shall be considering technologies useful to working groups, appropriate for use by staff members, chairs, and frequently individual group members. Who uses them is less important than that they are used. We shall discuss technologies under three headings. First, we shall briefly review some that can be used to manage working groups in general. In the next section, we shall discuss a sample of leadership role behaviors that are appropriate for particular types of groups, group situations, tasks, and stages of group development. Finally, we shall provide an extensive—though admittedly incomplete—list of leadership role behaviors, in the hope that this list will stimulate the widest possible consideration of alternative behaviors and skills in groups.[1]

TOOLS AND DEVICES FOR MANAGING GROUP LIFE

Tropman (1980) has done an excellent job of discussing various tools and devices managing group life. These devices are not just peripheral adjuncts, to be used or not as the fancy strikes. Rather, each of them is an essential element of the skeleton of a working group. Whether one follows Tropman's prescriptions precisely or not, to neglect them is to court failure.

Agendas are important for two reasons. They focus the attention of the group, and developing them particularly focuses the thinking of the person whose task it is to prepare them. In all but the most formal groups, agendas are to be viewed as relatively tentative. Crises, unanticipated developments, and organizational demands will modify them. Agendas need to be drawn with care. Group members should know the process by which one gets an item on the agenda for a particular meeting. Agendas distributed at the beginning of a meeting are better than nothing; agendas distributed in advance, so that members may come to a meeting prepared, are better. The major point is that agendas should be distributed enough in advance that members can think about the items on them but not so far in advance that they have been considered and forgotten.

Minutes are essential for maintaining a record of group decisions. In some fiduciary groups, minutes may be mandated by law. In all groups, however, keeping a record of actions is essential. One should not confuse minutes with process recordings or professional records of any kind. Minutes record decisions and certain formal aspects of decision making such as votes. Occasionally, it may be useful to summarize the major points made in a decision-making process. Often, it is also useful to include minority positions as well as the one that ultimately prevails. The precedents contained in minutes can serve as building blocks for a group.

Some organizations have developed a habit of having professional staff take minutes. There is much to be said both for and against this practice. Staff are usually sophisticated minute takers and also have access to the machinery for distributing minutes. On the negative side, though, the minute taker exercises considerable control over the group's perception of the meeting; it is often possible in writing minutes to frame a discussion or decision in one way or another. Thus having a staff person take minutes gives that person considerable power to influence the group's perception of itself and others' perceptions of it. In addition, a responsibility for taking minutes can inhibit the participation and thinking of the staff person. When one is writing, one has proportionately less attention to give to understanding and influencing the group's processes. Whether or not taking minutes makes good use of professional time is something that each organization—and, perhaps, each group and each staff person—needs to decide for itself.

Notices of meetings seem trivial at first glance but often carry considerable symbolic meaning. At issue is not only when the notices are sent out—the timing should correspond to the scheduling and life space of members—but also the messages conveyed by how the notices are sent and what they say. Engraved invitations have different connotations from scrawled postcards or hurried telephone calls. Incidentally, nonattendance should be followed up on a routine but serious basis. It ought not to be easy to miss meetings of working groups, and the reasons for missing a meeting should be known to the entire group.

All three of these items have value for staff members and chairs. Agendas provide an opportunity for structuring meetings in such a way that the group is faced with tasks that can be accomplished in a sequence that makes sense.

The usual advice is to hold knotty or difficult issues for the middle of the meeting, when the group's attentiveness and energy are at their height. Minutes provide a valuable resource for both staff and group members, as well as an opportunity for staff to recalibrate their short-, intermediate-, and long-term goals for the group. Attendance patterns provide a valuable means of feedback since, as has often been said, group members vote with their feet by attending or not.

Working between meetings is important. The assumption that such work will take place is implicit in the discussions in previous chapters. As a general rule, one should allocate two to three times as much time for between-meeting work as for the actual meetings themselves. Such work, both for chair and for staff, includes:

1. Follow-up of decisions reached by the group.
2. Facilitation of minutes and their distribution.
3. Contact with individual group members, initiated either by staff or chair or by the members themselves.
4. The accumulation of data requested by the group for its work.
5. Testing the waters in the form of informal discussions of issues with individual members, between staff and chair, or with relevant subgroups.
6. As appropriate, contact with other groups or salient publics outside the group on behalf of the group.
7. Perhaps most important, thoughtful reflection about what has been happening with the group and about its expectations.

Physical space is worthy of consideration and attention. As more and more is learned about the relationships between behavior and physical and spatial surroundings (Brower and Taylor, 1985), it becomes clear that groups need to be concerned with the temperature, humidity, size, and table shapes of their meeting space. One should remember, too, that the group's work skills will be of little relevance if the group gathers on a cold winter's evening and no one has the key to open the building.

Specific Technologies

"Technologies" refers to what the staff, chair, or group member does. The "when" of an action is very important, but the beginning point is the "what."

The next questions are empirical: When does staff member X or chair Y use technology Z? Why? For what intended effect? How do they know that the technology was effective? Collectively, the technologies performed by a person in a group constitute that person's role behavior (Biddle and Thomas, 1966). Staff perform roles in groups because they are needed. The roles may be prescribed, or no one else in the group may be able to perform them. "Technologies" also refers to entering into an "ongoing system of relationships, to come between or among persons, groups ... for the purpose of helping them" (Argyris, 1970:15).[2]

There is no comprehensive list of appropriate leadership role behaviors in groups. Neither the discussion that follows nor the listing that concludes this chapter is complete. In any group situation, the possible technologies are many. It is our experience that not being able to think of something to do is a sign of emotional blockage or lack of clear thinking or assessment rather then an indication that the group has exhausted its possibilities. The problem in working groups is not to think of a way to do things but rather to choose among the many means available. The range of choices of technologies available depends on the staff person's ability to take on the role of learner and listen to what the group needs.

There should be a clear connection between assessment and technology, between what one is thinking and what one does. However, this connection may not be simple or linear. Two different practitioners may well assess the same group event in exactly the same way (lack of group maintenance role behavior, for example) and conclude that support between and among members is the necessary first step for group progress. In the end, however, each may use a different technology to achieve this goal. There is an interacting, two-way relationship between assessment and technology. What one does in a group needs to be related to what one thinks is going on and will be going on; the converse is also true.

Here are some specific technologies:

Silence

Silence means not saying anything while behaving nonverbally in an interested and attentive way (for example, folding one's arms and paying attention, looking stern, smiling). Waiting and not talking permits the group members to work on the group's task. After all, the task is their responsibility, and silence can be a way of demanding work from them. Silence does not mean that one is not thinking. One's thoughts may range from observations and perceptions about one member, a subgroup, the group as a whole, or the task, on the one hand, to what one's next actions might be, on the other. Silence can offer the opportunity to scan the group and its environment.

Silence is linked with the use of time. Groups, as well as individuals, differ in their abilities to tolerate silences of different durations and to use them constructively. Silence and nonresponsiveness may also have particular cultural, gender-based or class-limited significance to a group membership. Responses vary by type of group and composition of membership. Waiting in silence can generate anxiety. For example, some members may jump in to make comments, while others may sit back and looking puzzled or simply bored. Each of these responses gives clues for assessment. The way group members respond to silence also gives some indication of the dynamics and controls within the group. Some members may deliberately not participate in order to slow down the pace of the group's discussion. By waiting, they give themselves time to process events and develop responses that express their particular interest.

Empathy

Empathy is connected not only with the affective domain (feelings) but also with the cognitive (what one knows). A French proverb referring to this phenomenon translates as, "To understand everything is to forgive everything." In other words, the more one knows about another person, situation, or experience, the more likely it is that one will be able to empathize with the people involved. This connection between feeling and knowing underlies the need for group participants to understand more about other group members and their experiences. Of course, one does not gain an understanding of a group all at once. Each member has the responsibility constantly to seek new information and examine the implications of new learnings.

> In example C, the following interchange took place at a meeting of the chiefs of service of the Mount Williams Community Hospital: The head of the Department of Buildings and Grounds said to the chair: "I wish you'd do something about the adolescent psychiatric unit and the trash it generates. It is everywhere: on the floor, on the steps, and even in front of the building, in messy plastic bags. My staff has enough to do without cleaning up all that filthy mess." The chair, Dr. Dudley, responded, "It's no fun being taken for granted. Keeping the building looking reasonable must seem like a never-ending job. I'll do what I can to help and talk to the unit administrator about this." The chair had taken the complaint seriously, treating it nonjudgmentally and respectfully, and offered to help.

In working groups, one also needs to be sensitive to the possibility of what may be termed "empathy overkill." Empathizing with the difficulties that group members face to the point that task accomplishment is neglected is a favor neither to the group nor to the individual member. An empathic stance needs to be balanced with a realistic assessment of what it takes for the group to get its jobs done. One without the other is not useful.

Reflecting Feelings (Mirroring)

This technology refers to responsive playback of verbal or nonverbal communications. Examples include responses such as, "It seems to me that you feel the plan won't work"; "Your face tells me you're not sure of the question"; and "Everyone looks a little puzzled about what's going on." Reflecting feelings (mirroring) is intended to draw members into a discussion, to maintain their participation when they've become unsure of how to proceed, or to expose them to how their communication has been experienced by others.

Feedback

Feedback is related to mirroring but takes it one step further. Clarity of understanding and meaning is very important in discussions of group issues. Sometimes, one may seek feedback from silent, expressive, or boisterous members, in order to try to get a clear sense of what's going on. At other times, various group members, including but not limited to staff and chair, may seek to stimulate members to use feedback. This may be the case when there are private sentiments that need to be made public. The process of obtaining feedback has a clarifying and testing aspect. Those who give feedback also need to receive it.

Situations often develop in working groups in which feedback is given to one group member, the chair, or the staff person. It is important to enable such feedback to be expressed openly and without fear. It is also important to limit the extent to which the particular sentiments being aired are allowed to dominate the meeting. The time needs to be sufficient to ensure that the feedback is heard but not so long that the group feels it is being inundated.

Exploring, Probing, and Questioning

Sometimes in group meetings, especially early in a group's history, members tend to become more oriented more toward solutions than problems. That is, they try to achieve closure before an adequate amount of discussion and consideration has taken place and before there has been adequate exploration of alternative ways of problem solving. Open-ended questions are one way of maintaining a problem orientation. Examples are, "Could you expand on that, please?" or, "How does this problem strike you?" or, "Are there other people here who see things differently?" The major reason for avoiding premature closure is that such action can result in a decision being made to which the group does not feel commitment or that does not adequately address the problem. Exploring, probing, and questioning can help develop a point that is incomplete, get more information, or invite members to expand ideas in greater detail. In this way, the group can arrive at a decision that is truly its own. Such a solution is more likely to be implemented.

Giving Direction or Advice

Sometimes, groups need advice, facts, or data. For example, a group may need to know who would be a good resource person or speaker, how other systems work, what the statistics on delinquency are in a particular census tract, or just what someone thinks about an issue. Schwartz (1976, 1994) has referred to this as "contributing data" and identified it as one of the central tasks of a staff person. Giving direction or advice in a working group is not a simple act. Giving too much or repeatedly using this technology may result in withdrawal on the part of group members. The unexpressed reaction of group members in such instances may be, "If you're such an expert, then you solve the problem."

Fulfilling an expert role may also mobilize what Benveniste (1972) has referred to as "the politics of expertise." There is a danger that the expert may be tempted to give inaccurate data, data that are partially correct, or data that reflect only one particular point of view as a way of managing a desired outcome. Participants in working groups have a responsibility to contribute their truly expert knowledge, particularly in interdisciplinary or interprofessional situations, in which the expertise owned by one profession may be a significant contribution to the group's overall process and task accomplishment. Perhaps a good rule of thumb is that if one finds oneself giving direction or advice more than twice in any one group meeting, one should examine closely the motivations and effects of one's behavior.

Universalizing

"Universalizing" refers to generalizing a communication or comment from one member to the group as a whole. One nonverbal technique for doing this is to direct one's gaze quizzically to the entire group after a member raises a point. When a member verbalizes a fear about dealing with an outside organization, for example, one might respond by noting, "Most of us have feelings about taking on difficult tasks. How do some others feel about this?" or "What are some of the ways of dealing with it?" These responses may make more sense after a group has had an opportunity to express its feelings about an issue.

Confrontation

The term "confrontation" has been overused. We use it here to refer to helping groups and group members face what appear to be discrepancies between what has been said and what is being done. It also refers to facing the possible consequences of action and/or decision making. Sometimes, helping members, subgroups, or the group as a whole face the reality of how others perceive them can become a method for developing a strategy for dealing with others' assumptive worlds.

Confrontations are most useful in the work phase of group development and may be directed at avoidance techniques. They are helpful only if group members are prepared to use them constructively. When a group ventilates its feelings against a person in authority, one constructive way of using confrontation is to role-play or ask how the group members would feel were they in the other's shoes. Unquestionably, some persons feel more comfortable in confrontation situations than others. Staff members and chairs, especially, have a responsibility to assess whether confrontation is used legitimately as a method to move the group along or as an expression of personal needs. In the latter case, the use of this technology merits close examination.

One of the major findings of an early study by Lieberman, Yalom, and Miles (1973) is that leadership that is confrontational and challenging and ignores the principles of gradual change can be destructive. The study also notes that not everyone benefits from confrontation. Some members may need help in learning to contain their tendencies to be confrontational. Here are some guidelines for the use of confrontation:

1. Changing ideas or attitudes and developing plans requires patience and time.
2. Maintaining an open mind to alternatives and other perspectives can be useful.
3. Confrontations should be preceded and followed by support and empathy.
4. Confrontation can be applied to a member's or a group's strengths as well as weaknesses. Group members can be challenged to perform in areas in which they are strong.

5. Confrontation based on anger needs to be used with care. While expressing anger directly can be very useful, distorting it into confrontation can lead to serious and long-lasting consequences within a group.

6. Repeated confrontation can produce the opposite of the intended behavior and can encourage rebelliousness.

7. Part of the function of leadership in a group is to be frustrating, in the sense of clarifying and protecting the group from reaching decisions that are not fully thought out.

8. Confrontation can be carried out on conceptual, emotional, or behavioral levels. Nonverbal cues such as voice tone, posture, and speech can be useful indicators of a discrepancy between overt and covert meanings.

Let us consider some variations of confrontation as a technology. The first is a response to erroneous or insufficient information. Group members may simply lack knowledge about a particular issue, and it is the leader's responsibility to bring this out. This may be considered a sort of "didactic confrontation."

Another example of a situation that may call for confrontation is a failure on the part of the group to consider alternatives. Some groups develop tunnel vision, which precludes flexible and creative consideration of alternatives. It may be useful to confront the discrepancy between the group's convictions and the fact that other alternatives exist. In doing so, one may even want to question why the group has become locked in to only one alternative.

Confrontation may also be useful group members are masking their real feelings. For example, one or more members of a group may say that no problem exists as a way of avoiding debate. Pointing out this discrepancy constitutes a use of confrontation. Done with skill, it is useful not only for the parties involved but for the group as a whole.

Our final example relates to manipulative behavior, subtle or overt maneuvering to gain a covert end. A group member may use charm, flattery, or even threats to achieve such an end. One way to deal with this is to keep issues as overt as possible. This need not mean that a group member's efforts need to be exposed; rather, the process itself needs confronting. To the extent that this can be done with humor, such confrontation may proceed with less hurt to individuals and less interruption to the process of the group as a whole. Whether done humorously or seriously, however, confrontation is an appropriate way to deal with a pattern of dysfunctional manipulation.

Support

Support is a general technology that can be divided into several types. One type involves restoring or strengthening a person's or a subgroup's skills, abilities, or capacities so that they can be exercised in the group. Another type refers to giving support to the group qua group. An example is, "This meeting has been most productive even though it's been exhausting." Support includes activities such as encouraging members to talk, expressing acceptance of feelings, and expressing confidence in comments or decisions. As a technology, it can decrease feelings of tension, guilt, or uncertainty and can be used to emphasize one side of an ambivalence. For example, a member's statement that something really deserves to be done even though the member is very busy can be met with a response such as, "I'm really happy that you feel committed to solving this problem."

Cautions should be kept in mind with this technology as well as the others. Anything overdone becomes counterproductive; too much of a "good parent" response can produce excessive dependence. Other questions also deserve consideration: Should one express support for the group or for an individual, when there is tension between the two? With respect to individuals, just which capacities or opinions are to be supported? Support needs to be based on a realistic assessment. It is not supportive—and often the opposite—to accept as the best the group can do a product that is poor in quality. In such a situation, one is saying that the group lacks capacity. The comment is thus deprecating rather than supportive.

Modeling, Coaching, and Shaping

These technologies are related but distinct from each other. They are similar in that each contains an instructional component. They are different in that modeling means showing others how to do something, coaching means providing cues when members are being trained for a particular event, and shaping is the use of selective attention and inattention to various member and group behaviors. Any group member may model and coach, and both techniques are particularly useful for between-meeting contacts between staff and chair, whether in person or by telephone. Shaping, however, is the domain of the group leader. Making sure that less verbal or relatively low-participating members have a chance to say something may require controlling verbose members, either by not giving them the chance to speak or by limiting the amount of time they are allowed to do so. Creating an environment where participation is at least somewhat equitable is important because greater or lesser input by one or a few members does affect process and structure. Shaping through selective inattention to side conversations is one way of trying to reduce the occurrence of this behavior; if this doesn't work, an outright confrontation may be necessary.

Role-Playing

Role-playing and role rehearsals are either on the-spot or planned activities in which a member or an entire group plays out a scenario of a problem situation that the group faces. The roles should be accurate, to the extent possible, and should be related to the current or anticipated experiences of the group. Roles can be played by group members or by staff, with the caution that one should be sensitive in assigning roles to people that may cause them personal pain. The value of role-playing and role rehearsal as activities is that they can focus attention on the cognitive, affective (feeling) aspects, actions, or combinations of these in a given situation. Another use of role-playing may be called role reversal, wherein members learn about others' points of view by experiencing others' roles. Role-playing is an important tool for training group members about the processes that help or hinder group performance in general, and skill in its use is particularly important for staff in working groups (Maier, 1971).

Role-playing can be used with individuals, subgroups, the group as a whole, or between two groups, to rehearse negotiations. It may be carefully scripted, minimally sketched, or, in certain cases, spontaneous. Members should be given choices of roles, in case any particular role is distasteful to a member for any reason. Role-playing is probably chiefly useful as a stimulus for discussion; unexamined role-playing is rarely worth doing.

Suppositions

This term refers to the use of hypothetical suggestions, or "what ifs?" These can be useful in clarifying alternative problem solutions and considering the consequences of an action. They can also be useful when a staff person, or anyone else, is interceding or mediating between any two parties, who may or may not be members of the same group. This technology can be very useful for negotiating roles, mediating conflicts, and avoiding breaches of confidentiality by making situations hypothetical.

Suppositions involve what might be called "dealing in the subjunctive." At times, staff may and should provide factual data and advice. The more usual prefixes to staff comments, however, are "perhaps," "might," and other such introductions. The ultimate decisions of working groups lie with their members. Use of the subjunctive keeps it that way, while at the same time giving staff a way of injecting comments, suggestions, and perceptions and stimulating consideration of the consequences of decisions.

Summarizing

At the end of a discussion, it is often useful to summarize its major themes. At the end of meetings, summarizing is a useful technology because it can encompass emphasis and direction for further work. During meetings, summaries can provide a transition from one agenda item to another. Summary statements may serve as precedents that can be referred to later. They can also be used to bridge, that is, to provide a carryover from one meeting to the next and thus help to set the agenda for the next meeting.

Working in the Members' Idiom

This is less a technology, perhaps, than a stance. By the "members' idiom," we mean that idiosyncratic types of individual or community behavior that must be accepted. Groups may use language in particular ways or approach decision making in their own idiosyncratic way. Some of the idioms used may be conceptual and symbolic, localized, or specific to a particular ethnic group. One should also be prepared to utilize terms and concepts that fit into the members' frames of reference. In groups, one needs to be sophisticated both about the dictionary meaning of a term (the denotation) and the attitude and perceptions that are linked to it (the connotation). To put it simply, you have to know the territory you're working in.

Idiosyncratic words not only characterize various citizen groups, such as members of certain socioeconomic, racial, or ethnic backgrounds, but they also characterize the argot of various professionals. For example, physicians express themselves in a certain vocabulary to which they have been socialized as a result of their professional education. So do nurses, social workers, public administrators, and members of other professions. In each case, knowing the idiom of group members is essential both for effective communication and for being able to participate in the conversation of the group.

Focusing, Partializing, Sequencing, Pacing, and Grading

Each of these technologies is related to a logical "bits and pieces" approach to problem solving. "Partializing" means breaking down a complex problem or issue into a series of doable, task-specific actions. "Focusing" refers to helping members come to terms with significant feelings and ideas and separate the core content from the peripheral. "Sequencing" refers to collecting bits and pieces of tasks into larger clusters and then reaching conscious decisions about what needs to be done first. (Some working groups will utilize modern management technologies such as Management by Objectives or PERT (Program Evaluation Review Technique) in planning their own work.) "Sequencing" also refers to conceptualizing the work of a staff person or chair over a period of time. It suggests a connection between short- and long-term goals. "Grading" refers to arranging activities in order from the simple to the more complex. "Pacing" is related to timing and to what have been called "critical moments." Each participant in a group process needs to be concerned with how much anxiety can be permitted to exist within the group for the group still to produce good work. A related question is, "How much resistance can be allowed to exist within a group for the group still to accomplish its tasks?" In working groups, no one, including the staff person, can control anxiety and resistance entirely. Each participant, however, can affect these variables and should be aware of methods for doing so.

Decentering

There are several forms of this technique, which refers to getting apathetic groups off dead center, encouraging criticism so as to open the boundaries of a situation, and encouraging risk taking either by the group as a whole or by members. Decentering carries with it the possibility of introducing content that may help move the group along. Introducing divergent thinking is an important professional function in working groups; it may also be undertaken by group members. Sometimes, a useful method for decentering is to pose issues as paradoxes to be resolved.

Setting Limits

Limits often need to be set. For example, insistent and continued interruptions or bickering among members may have to be stopped. Groups may need to be reminded of the realistic limits of a situation: for instance, the time available; the presence of others, which restricts the amount of noise that can be made; or even the limits set by good taste and convention to language that may be used during a meeting. When the right moment comes (and the timing of that moment is always a judgment call), the staff, or chair, or a member may simply have to point out the deleterious effects of an action. There is an element of closure to the limit-setting process that differentiates it from confrontation.

Necessity is not the only reason for setting limits; there are positive aspects as well. Limitless situations produce unbounded anxiety. Various writers have pointed out that limits and boundaries are essential to productive group operation (e.g., Somers, 1976). The ambivalence that beginning staff persons often feel about setting limits may reflect their own concerns about their place in the group rather than a realistic assessment of the group's needs. This may be particularly true when the staff person is younger, or less experienced in life, or an outsider in the community from which a group's members are drawn.

Dividing into Subgroups

When groups are either hostile or apathetic, it is difficult for them to work. It may be more worthwhile to divide the group into smaller parts so that the problem-solving process may be carried on. When subgroups simply cannot agree, it may be useful to appoint a steering committee. For example, in large groups with overwhelming agendas, the steering committee may be directed to bring back a workable agenda the following week and to arrange agenda issues into lists of pros and cons. Generally subgroups or "buzz" groups— short-term or time-limited discussion groups—are asked to report back to the group as a whole so that all may benefit from their work. A variety of audiovisual methods, some of them using available computer software, can help buzz groups report back.

Cognitive Restructuring or Reframing

Reframing means reorganizing bits and pieces, as in a puzzle. into a different pattern so that they make more sense and provide leads for further action. Sometimes, groups get stuck or fixed on a particular point or issue. For whatever reasons, a different perspective may be needed for the group to move ahead. Providing this new perspective is what reframing is all about. It is not the same as a strategic retreat or taking a break when the group's process gets tough, although time-outs can be valuable in steamy sessions. For instance, when a group defines a problem as being caused by others outside of the group, which can be a dead-end or an example of scapegoating, it is often possible to reframe the problem so that various actors, including the group, are viewed as having responsibility for parts of the problem. Group members can thus be enabled to see ways in which their actions can contribute to a solution. Reframing a problem may help groups think of resources in addition to those on which they usually draw. It may also help groups define differently the interests and objectives of other groups with whom they may feel themselves in conflict or competition.

Building or Structuring

One of the most productive, attractive, and desirable phenomena in groups takes place when various members' comments and suggestions seem to build on each other. Staff and chair may have roles in this process by supplying missing pieces or assembling threads based on the various abilities and contributions of group members. This progressive pattern of building may not be apparent to group members who are participating at the time, because each is eager to have his or her point of view expressed and given credence by the other group members.

Releasing Tension

A sense of humor goes a long way in groups. Whether at a tense moment or before, during, or at the end of a long meeting, an injection of humor can help members wind down and reduce the likelihood of jamming up or system overload. There are moments in groups when a proposed action may have a self-defeating component to it. An example is prematurely demanding someone's resignation. At such moments, it may be incumbent upon staff or chair to make a plea for reconsideration or to defuse the situation in some other way.

A staff member or chair may have to work with what the members provide. This implies working with and building on members' strengths and neutralizing or restructuring situations in order to reduce tension. For example, some members have strong intellectual abilities coupled with articulate defenses. Others have easily wounded sensibilities and sensitivities. Still others are good at nuts-and-bolts activities but become uncomfortable with conceptual approaches. With each of these, a balance needs to be struck. Clumsy and offensive attempts at humor may be counterproductive and may introduce tension rather than reducing it. When a member locks himself into an assertive stance, it may be more rather than less difficult for the group to consider the wisdom of what he is saying because the viewpoint may be entrenched and any response reinforces a defensive stance. Accepting a group's first product may inhibit rather than advance a group's problem-solving capacity. There is little substitute for common sense, tact, and sensitivity in dealing with tense group situations.

It may also be useful for staff and chair, at times, to take on themselves more of the responsibility for tension than they actually think they deserve. For example, a staff member may introduce reconsideration by suggesting that he/she had not been clear at the previous meeting, as a way of dealing with a situation in which in fact members did not hear properly. It is not the prestige of staff or chair that needs to be guarded but rather the group's problem-solving capacity and its self-esteem.

Muddling Through

There are times, perhaps more than one would like, when one simply doesn't know what's going on or what a group should do. The first approach is to stop the group and find out. If it is still not possible to achieve the desired clarity, keep muddling along and keep thinking. By all means, reflect afterward on the group with a supervisor, a colleague, or a trusted friend. But remember that talented and skilled staff members, chairpersons, and group members are not afraid of being learners. In fact, it is our observation that the more secure and competent a person feels, the easier it is for them to admit to flying by the seat of their pants.

Muddling through is defined by a continual process of exploring present ambiguities with group members at the same time that one tries to conceptualize a theme related to the task or the process. In essence, the ability to work under this sort of tension is a skill that one learns in incremental steps. It is an important aspect of sound practice in groups.

Pointing to History

This is less a technology than a function for the group. It refers to the role of staff or chair in remembering precedents, which issues were left unresolved earlier in the group's history, and the like. Taking notes can be useful. These notes often serve not only as a record of what has happened but as a source for conceptualizing and designing future work. This useful historical function should be differentiated from the behavior of the naysayer, which is often destructive to groups. The naysayer is the person who knows that everything has been tried before and won't work. Staff persons may need to try to neutralize this negative behavior at the same time that they make productive use of accurate material from the group's history.

Evaluating

Groups have several products: programs, learnings, decisions, reports, negotiations conducted with other parties, among others. There need to be measures or criteria against which productivity can be assessed. Periodic assessment of group process and outcome, formal or informal, is useful. Leading the process of evaluating and taking stock is an important technology for staff persons and chairs. Groups should experience the evaluation process as helpful rather than threatening or destructive. Unfortunately, the word "evaluation" somehow strikes terror into the hearts of many people. Our suggestion is that periodic evaluation be undertaken, but where possible a more neutral term be substituted, such as "taking stock," or "seeing where we are."

Self-Disclosure on Behalf of Authenticity

How personal should a staff member become? How. much of one's own inner processes ought one to reveal? No precise answer is possible, but, in our view, a staff person should be able to be personal enough to admit mistakes and learn from them. On the other hand, staff persons should not become so undisciplined as to forget their role. Self-disclosure, if overdone, is counterproductive. One other fact to take into account is the time span of the group. A staff person who participates in fifty consecutive meetings of a group becomes less constrained about self-disclosure than someone who is participating in a tense, time-limited group experience with a deadline by which a product needs to be produced.

Reaching for Feelings (Desensitizing and Sensitizing)

Reaching for feelings legitimizes the affective responses of group members. Members' feelings can be valuable to a group. Desensitizing them when they are overdone is related to modeling and coaching; it refers to a situation in which group members—perhaps primarily the chair or leader—learn to take criticism as valuable feedback rather than as destructive disapproval. Sensitizing group members to others' points of view may be thought of as the active teaching part of empathy. It attempts to induce individuals to take on the roles of others through various means, from the direct to the indirect. A direct method may include asking the group to think about where others are coming from. An indirect way may involve a joint meeting with those who hold another point of view. Both means may be especially valuable when the others are salient publics outside of a group who have a stake in the problem or issue with which a group is dealing.

Moving with the Group's Flow or Situation

This technology consists of tuning in to the flow and mood of a group and at the same time playing a part in this flow. Staff need to be able to change gears in midstream so as to affect a process of discussion, interpersonal transmission of feelings, or task accomplishment. Moving with the flow also refers to a mildly opportunistic stance: being willing to use what occurs naturally in a group as grist for the mill in order to help a group achieve its objectives.

Clarifying

This technology refers to straightening out what might be distorted perceptions or communication. Another use of clarifying is to check the meaning of what has been said in the immediate context. An example is, "What I hear you saying is that you disagree with John's analysis of the case. Is that correct?" Care needs to be taken that clichés are not overused in the process of clarification. Some clichés can draw negative responses because they have been overused. It is not necessary to "have one's head in a particular place" in order to question whether one has understood a comment correctly.

Synthesizing

This technology refers to finding and stating a theme common to separate but related thoughts among group members. Finding a common theme, or what one influential writer has referred to as "a common ground" (Schwartz, 1971), is essential for group formation, let alone group progress. While synthesizing may sound like summary and review, it goes beyond these technologies by putting together various points of view into a comprehensible, conceptual scheme or rationale. The synthesizer has to identify what parts of group discussion or process are central. One also has to identify which pieces are extraneous, notice what's missing, and package the entire collection into comprehensible form. Synthesizing reduces ambiguity as well as setting the stage for broader discussion because it moves a group forward to the next level of concern.

Listening

We have save what might be the most important of these technologies for last: listening. Listening includes not only the physical act of hearing but also a dynamic responsive stance. This stance aims at connecting with as many levels of communication as possible, in as great a depth as possible, in order to understand what group members are saying and doing. Nonverbal cues such as eye contact, body language, posture, head nods, and the like can be useful in conveying the fact that one is listening. Listening is a demanding activity that requires physical and mental alertness. Group participants need to be aware of their own limits in active listening and need to develop the ability to ask for breaks, seek refreshments, or otherwise return themselves to being able to listen actively. The ability to hear is probably the most vital single skill in enabling one to work effectively in and with working groups. It is a skill that demands close attention over a long period of time, and no one ever masters it completely.

A Listing of Skills

To aid the student of groups to develop a repertoire of leadership role behaviors, table 12.1 presents an incomplete list to serve as a rough guide. We list these role behaviors, more or less arbitrarily, under four general headings: problem solving, dealing with feelings, supporting, and inducing change. Several deserve to be listed under more than one heading, but space constraints prevent this. Readers may wish to add to or extend this list or to contribute to future, more complete typologies.

I'm Staffing, You're Chairing, Who's Leading?

The relationship between a staff person and a chairperson can impact the functioning of the group. The following vignette, written from the perspective of the staff person, demonstrates some of the difficulties that can arise when the staff and chairperson have not clearly defined their respective roles and responsibilities. In the example below, the committee, composed of community volunteers, was charged with planning an agency's fall community education series. The primary purpose of the meeting was to select a featured speaker.

> I passed the agenda (which I had written) around the table. Before calling the meeting to order, I looked at the chair to confirm that she wanted me to proceed. She was looking back at me, waiting, as was the rest of the committee.
>
> The first agenda item was "housekeeping." I shared a press release that I had drafted based on the outcome of the previous meeting.
>
> The second item was "speaker selection." I told the group that I had been contacted by a "human service friendly" political candidate who was a longtime friend of the agency. He wished to address our group as a featured speaker. Rachel, a committee member, immediately jumped in, saying that she did not want the staff training to be a campaign platform for anyone. Tuning in to her tone and body language, I surmised that she was interpreting the information I had relayed as my wish for the group. I felt the need to reiterate that I was not recommending the candidate but rather was relaying relevant information. Rich, the only male committee member, had an idea for a speaker, but it was immediately rejected by the chair, who felt strongly that the speaker needed to be a resident of the

TABLE 12.1   *An Incomplete List of Leadership Role Behaviors in Working Groups*

PROBLEM SOLVING

*Focusing	*Using suppositions	Identifying resources
*Contracting	*Exploring, probing, questioning	Setting priorities
Scouting	Participating	*Reframing and restructuring
*Synthesizing	*Partializing and sequencing	*Clarifying
*Receiving feedback	*Framing	*Giving feedback
*Pointing to consequences	*Scanning	Understanding liaison mission
and alternatives	Providing information	*Pointing to history
Identifying subgroup	Supervising voting	Preparing written statements
positions		
*Dividing into subgroups		

DEALING WITH FEELINGS

*Researching for feelings	*Sharing and self-disclosure	*Remaining silent
Responding directly	Providing perspective	*Amplifying weak or
*Turning down strong	*Mirroring and reflecting feelings	confusing messages
messages	Absorbing	Bridging
		Containing
		*Using humor

SUPPORTING

*Listening	*Exercising empathy and	Providing encouragement
*Referring to precedents	reflectingunderstanding	*Dealing with dysfunctional
*Translating members'	*Working in group members'	behavior styles
idioms (universalizing)	idioms	Supporting part of a position

INDUCING CHANGE

*Modeling	*Rehearsing behavior	*Maintaining silence
*Decentering	*Giving direct advice	*Amplifying weak or
Planned ignoring	*Confronting	confusing messages
*Summarizing	*Setting limits	Bridging
Engaging differences	Interpreting	Containing
Appealing to broader	Participating forcefully	*Using humor
the societal, institutional,	*Evaluating	
or sociocultural context		
in cases of value		
conflict		

*Behavior discussed in the text.

Note: We are grateful to Professor Emerita Ruth Middleman of the Kent School of Social Work of the University of Louisville, Kentucky, for sharing with us her earlier list, to which we have made additions.

community. I reported information relayed to me by an absent committee member who had attended a conference and heard a great speech. I read pieces of the speaker's biographical statement to the group.

I recommended that the committee begin ranking the speakers in the order of their preference, as had been done in previous years. This process went relatively quickly, and I repeated back to them what I heard to make sure I had understood them correctly. I asked the group what kinds of topics they wanted me to ask the speaker to address. The chair was active during this part of the discussion, saying that she wanted someone who could discuss the conflicts and changes facing the agency and provide a message of hope.

We then began to pick our next meeting date. I suggested a date. Rachel said something else about picking a speaker. Several others joined in, and it became clear that half the group thought that I would go through the list they had developed and would use my judgment, based on the criteria they had identified, to invite a speaker. The other half of the group thought that I would be doing more research and that we would be meeting again to discuss the results and make a group decision. Rich (who was among the first half) became visibly frustrated and remarked that he did not want to "micromanage" me or "be talked to death at meetings." His frustration was apparent in his tone of voice and gestures. Rachel (who was among the second half) said, "Why have a committee?" Rachel conveyed her irritation through her tone of voice and refusal to make eye contact with Rich. Rich then explained that he thought that the committee had accomplished a lot and that he trusted me to implement what was discussed. The chair and Rachel were vocal about wanting more information with which to make a decision.

Since time was an issue and tensions were mounting, I suggested that I gather more information and fax it to them and that they fax me back their choices. If an obvious group consensus did not emerge, we would have a meeting ten days from then to reach a group decision. Otherwise, I would act based on their faxed responses to me. The subgroup that originally did not feel the need to meet again was vocal in its approval of this plan. The chair and Rachel still seemed irritated with Rich for suggesting that I have more authority but agreed that I should fax them information. Rich also appeared very irritated at the hair and Rachel for their inability to respond decisively at that time.

I waited for the chair to adjourn the meeting and reminded them all to fax their responses to me as quickly as possible so that we could avoid meeting again in ten days.

Both the staff person and the chair made a number of obvious mistakes at this meeting. These began long before the start of the meeting, when the staff person, rather than the chairperson, distributed the agenda and called the meeting to order. The staff person and the chairperson should have been meeting regularly before meetings to plan and coordinate their efforts. These before-meeting communications should have been used to clarify the roles each party would play and the boundaries of each person's decision-making arena. If the chairperson did not have the time or skill to compile the agenda, the staff person should have done so in consultation with her. The staff person should have been working with the chairperson to develop her leadership skills and to strengthen her position in the committee. Regardless of the skill level of the chairperson, the staff person should have helped her maintain the appearance of leadership to prevent the further erosion of her status.

The most significant conflict during this group meeting mirrored the tension between the staff person and chairperson. Neither the staff nor the chairperson was confident about how much of a leadership role each should be asserting or about which decisions fall within the realm of the staff person. These precise issues were acted out in the group, mostly through Rich and Rachel. Had the chairperson and the staff person come into the meeting with these issue resolved, they would have been able to mediate the conflict between Rich and Rachel more successfully (and comfortably) Admittedly, these are difficult issues that need to be examined on a case-by-case basis; however, one should always view the staff person as implementing committee decisions. It is important for the committee to trust that the staff person will use authority wisely and fairly.

There were several instances when the chair attempted to assume a leadership role. At these times, the chair would assert in absolute terms what she wanted the particular outcome to be (e.g., the speaker must be a resident and address the topic). The committee chose to let her assert her power in this manner, until she tried to dictate an extra meeting. By neglecting opportunities to facilitate a discussion, she failed to convert what was left of her positional power into referent power, causing her to be even weaker when the more difficult argument began. Had she been a more effective leader, she would have sought to facilitate a discussion and build consensus among committee members.

Finally, one must look at the organizational environment within which the group was working. The staff person felt herself accountable for the group outcome and not the group process. Both should have been her concern. She felt responsible for the outcomes of decisions that properly belonged to the committee. This caused her to take on more of a leadership role to protect her own interest in a positive job performance evaluation. If the staff person believed that she would be evaluated by performance measures that included the quality of the group process, she may have felt more comfortable about relinquishing some of her authority and sharing her expertise with the chair. Instead, she felt accountable for outcomes beyond her proper control. Staff members should be rewarded for aiding groups as they strive to become democratic microcosms.

In closing, both the staff member and the chairperson failed to develop a positive working agreement outlining the proper roles, responsibilities, and boundaries of authority. Their failure to develop such an understanding negatively affected the group. In addition, the staff person's failure to develop the leadership of the chairperson, or at least to assist in maintaining an appearance of leadership, greatly diminished the chair's influence over the group.[3] Technologies are tools guided by purpose. The purpose is guided by the staff member's own sense of purpose and the specifics of a particular organization and history. The group leader may have taken more responsibility for the outcome than was necessary. Finding a balance is part of the learning process of the group leader, who learns to make whatever adjustments are necessary.

13

RECURRING PROBLEMS IN
GROUPS AND SUGGESTED
STAFF RESPONSES

O NE IMPORTANT KIND of recurring problem in groups is caused by deviant, difficult, or ambiguous behavior on the part of group members. A staff person needs to assess the meaning of such behaviors and, on the basis of this assessment, plan meaningful responses to help a group to cope with them. There is rarely just one appropriate response to any one pattern of behavior. One must understand, in some depth, the meaning of an individual's behavior before one knows whether or how to respond.

The responsibility for dealing with these various behaviors is not exclusively the staff's or the chair's. Each member of a working group carries some of the responsibility for dealing with behaviors that may divert the group from accomplishing its purpose as well as for recentering it on the task at hand. This can be thought of as the gyroscopic function in working groups. It may be the particular responsibility of a group's chair or staff person to deal with such behavior, assuming that the group as a whole has not been able or willing to do so. Each of the roles to be discussed contains positive, neutral, and negative elements, depending on the type of group, its attributes, and the extent to which the behavior is modulated to fit a group's circumstances.

INDIVIDUAL VIGNETTES

The Quiet Person
The quiet person in the group may be engaging in calm, contemplative listening, which can be constructive, or withdrawal, which can be destructive because it subtracts from the group's ability to obtain its members' perspectives and participation in decision making. How is one to know the difference? This assessment needs to be based both on the cues given by the per-

son and on the responses of the other members of the group. Nonverbal signs of engagement and thoughtful listening should be valued. Similar kinds of cues in the opposite direction should also be given attention. The situation within the group, the nature of the agenda, and the stage of group development all play parts in the assessment of the quiet member. If listening seems appropriate, then a person who is listening is hardly a problem. Quiet people often make good process observers, and this may be what a member is doing.

Assuming that it is important to elicit participation from a quiet member, there are several ways of doing this. One is to direct questions toward that member that cannot be answered by "yes" or "no" but require a statement of fact or opinion. A second approach is to communicate a message of expectancy toward the quiet member about his participation in discussion of those issues to which he seems particularly attentive. A third is to ask a direct question: "Mr. Brown, I wonder where you stand on this issue?"

The Excessive Talker

Excessive talkers may be divided into two subcategories: those who talk a lot and have something to say and those who talk a lot and do not have much to say. Often, the chair or staff should try to get some sense of how the rest of the group is experiencing the talkative person. If the group's experience is that the verbalizations are useful, then the group leadership may need to deal with its own responses and ask members whether they are appropriate. If the group seems visibly annoyed by the verbosity, then one needs to think about affecting the behavior. As with each of the behaviors in this chapter, the group's part in eliciting excessive verbalization needs to be examined. Talkers are useful to groups because they fill space and keep things moving; they are destructive when they monopolize time and energy and prevent others from participating.

There may be points at which excessive talkers simply need to be cut off. This should be done with as much sensitivity as possible. It may be possible to communicate to a member that silence is indicated with a smile and with regard for the person's feelings, rather than with anger or annoyance.

The Critic

Critics come in two major forms. One type genuinely enjoys playing the devil's advocate, raising objections to clarify group thinking or answer genuine questions. This is a very useful and functional role, especially in a group that has a tendency to jump to closure prematurely. The second major type of critic proceeds on the basis of personal rather than group needs. For some reason, a negative, cynical, or critical stance is functional for the way such a person defines himself in a group or for the person's intrapersonal needs.

Negative critics are risks both to themselves and to the groups of which they are a part. For themselves, they run the risk of making themselves available to a scapegoating process that can be destructive to all concerned. For the group, the risk is that they will drain the group of positive affect, self-esteem, confidence in its own capabilities, and belief in the importance of the group's task. In working groups, leaders should hesitate before putting themselves in the position of protecting members from the consequences of their own behavior. One exception to this is in the instance of scapegoating, because of the destructive effects this process can have on the group as a whole. One is reminded that Shulman (1967) has prescribed "preemptive intervention" to prevent scapegoating, as has Kolodny (1973). Although it may sound harsh, for a group to turn on a negative critic temporarily may be helpful in the long run. Our informal rule is to wait for the third instance of negative behavior in a meeting before intervening. Drawing an analogy with baseball, one should respond decisively to the third strike.

The Formalist-Theoretician

Formalist-theoreticians discuss issues in the abstract, lecture, and seem to be concerned with communicating how much they know rather than how much they can contribute to the process of the group. They consistently confuse the expert role with the member role. (Occasionally, of course, this is appropriate, when a member has genuine expertise in a particular area or subject.) Such patterns of participation exacerbate the effects of differences in style, social class, and level of education within the group. Sometimes, the formalist-theoretician may be seeking recognition for past group experiences or academic expertise. Or the roots of his behavior may lie in a sense of status deprivation. Once the background and ability of the person are recognized, his need to operate in this manner may or may not dissipate.

Working groups can use formalist-theoreticians by utilizing their education or standing in the community for relationships with other groups and outside organizations. Frequently, such members make excellent committees of one for preparing written documents or bylaws or representing the group to certain groups and publics in the external world. Our general tactic would be to try to utilize the strengths of such a person rather than to emphasize his weaknesses. One should also guard against a simplistic formulation that says that a particular member is only looking for attention. Further, if this is the case, what effects would one expect a denial of attention to have on the behavior of the member?

The Fence-Straddler

This pattern of participation can arise from a variety of motives. One is a frank desire to ingratiate oneself with the leadership of the group. It is all too easy to condemn this motive. Particularly if one has extensive experience in working groups, it is easy to forget how important approval from the group's leadership can be for a particular member at a particular time. A variant of this pattern is exhibited by the member for whom winning and losing are extraordinarily important. Much fence-straddling stems from such a definition of the situation. Unlike the professional politician, who knows that elections are lost as well as won, losing a vote or not gaining the group's agreement may be extraordinarily painful for such a person.

Of course, one should seek opportunities to utilize whatever strengths the fence-straddler has, including the possibility of having this person serve as the observer or representative in intergroup situations. It is also important, however, for such a person to learn that positions can be taken in a working group without fear of reprisal. This fear sometimes motivates behavior of the sort noted. As it becomes clear that one's contribution is valued rather than one's always being correct, some of the repetitive fence-straddling behavior may disappear.

The Ideologue

Ideologues come in various forms. There is the radical ideologue, for whom all issues are recast in terms of ultimate social change. There is the extremist, who sees in any proposal to help people a decline of moral fiber that he or she, presumably, is in a position to assess better than anyone else. There is the fanatic, who sees salvation as dependent on each group vote. There are also dedicated followers of many single issues, both in the outside world and within the group. The basic rule we suggest in dealing with ideologues is to avoid being intimidated. Ideologues often have the ability to cast issues in terms so black and white that many group members, and staff persons, are intimidated because they do not live up to the implied standards.

The functions and purposes of each group need to be kept in mind. In many cases, the attempt of an ideologue to reframe a group situation does violence to the purpose for which the group exists. Policies and perspectives of the sponsoring organization need to be kept in mind as well. Whatever the virtues of radical social change, for example, they are usually not relevant to the specific purposes of a committee that meets annually because of its limited scope. Attempted intimidation is sometimes part of the conscious baggage of ideologues. That is, intimidating the majority can be a planned step toward having one's own point of view carry the day.

Both because of their impact on groups and because of the broader social values in which group work is embedded, one should pay particular attention to the dangers of single-issue politics or approaches. Single-issue politics can be deeply destructive to the concept of the democratic microcosm that we have stressed throughout this book. Individual group members have a right to their beliefs. They do not, however, have the right to substitute their agendas for the group's agenda, unless this substitution can be supported by the chair, the staff person, and ultimately by the membership as well.

The Domineering Member

Individuals may find themselves in dominant positions in groups for many reasons. One possibility is that they have sought such a position and derive satisfaction from controlling, overawing, or otherwise demonstrating their supposed superiority to the other members. A second, especially in fiduciary groups, is a stereotyped member who is treated with awe by the other members of the group. He himself may not desire this. The big giver on a philanthropic board may find himself in this position, as may a highly respected community figure on a community council. If a position of dominance has been given to a member by the group, then the problem really is the group's. The individual involved may be uncomfortable with the role and may try repeatedly to get out of the position of dominance that has been handed to him. If, on the other hand, the dominance has been sought by the individual, then the staff person and chair have particular parts to play. Those parts, after reflection, may be put into operation by pointing out that the reason for having a group is that several opinions need to come together and that any one opinion, no matter how important, cannot solve the problem by itself.

One of the unfortunate effects of initiating a pattern of dominance/submission in groups is the introduction of fear. Fear has no place in an effective group. Group members cannot contribute to a common solution if they are afraid. Neither can chairs or staff members. A staff member who is an employee of an organization may experience the same kind of fear that other group members do, whether for the same or for different reasons. Staff persons cannot operate out of fear and remain helpful. Should this problem arise, there should be appropriate people in the organization—colleagues or supervisors—from whom help can be sought.

The Structuralist

The structuralist is the self-appointed guardian of the treasury, the bylaws, parliamentary procedure, historic ways of doing things, or other rules or prohibitions that prevent a group from taking proposed actions. Sometimes, the relationship between the structuralist's internal need for control and the member's behavior in a group is evident. At other times, since a certain amount of structuralism is necessary for a working group to accomplish its purpose, it may take a span of several meetings before one becomes aware that structuralism is the preferred activity for a particular group member. One tactic for dealing with structuralism is to help put this group member in a position in which devotion to rules and procedures will be of help. Sometimes, such a person makes a good treasurer of a fund-raising drive, for example.

The basic point, however, is that the rules and procedures of a working group should be designed and used to facilitate task accomplishment, not to frustrate it. Formal parliamentary bodies occasionally ignore deviations from stated procedures when the nature of the task or situation warrants it. The use of rules and procedures to frustrate the group's purpose is an element to be confronted. This is best done by the group itself, though the group's leadership needs to be prepared to take a firm stand if the group is not able to deal with the particular member's behavior.

What we have described are pure types. No one of the characteristics discussed will appear singly in any one member. At different times, various members may exhibit a combination of these behaviors. Nor is this brief listing comprehensive; rather, it represents some general observations about common, recurring individual problems. One should guard against trying to categorize group members too neatly in closed categories, and one should avoid diagnosis for its own sake. This last is particularly important if a worker or chair is a member of one of the clinical professions.

> In example C, the chair of the Mount Williams Community Hospital group is also the chair of the Department of Psychiatry. When she is chairing the chief's group, she is operating as the chair of a work group and not as its psychiatrist.

Timing, quick thinking, and civility are always useful in working groups, especially in muddling through. Group leaders need to be able to think on their feet. While it may be helpful, at times, to share one's own feelings, including negative and angry ones, it is not useful to lose control in a group, no matter how provocative the circumstances. One should also remember that members of the group share responsibility for its work. They may be able to deal with problematic behavior more easily and more directly than can the group's leadership. Finally, groups belong both to their members and to the organizations that sponsor them. They do not belong to their chairs or to the person who provides staff services for them.

Given all these caveats, in the final analysis, one acts in a group as one thinks best. "I thought about it and decided to act in that way" is a valid justification for any reasonable action on the part of a staff person or chair. On the other hand, not thinking about one's behavior or considering its consequences invalidates the most creative of responses.

Group Vignettes

We turn next to a series of eight vignettes that describe realistic group events. For each, we shall indicate a possible solution; we invite the reader to consider other possible solutions. For advanced thinking about groups, one may put together any of the recurring problematic member behaviors discussed above with any of these vignettes.

1. It is the first meeting of a group of representatives of local public and private organizations called together for the purpose of developing a citywide referral system to deal with the mental health needs of children and youth. You, the staff person, have worked hard and diligently in pregroup interviews and in other ways to help develop an acceptable agenda for the group meeting. Just after the halfway point in the meeting, one group member, a well-respected agency executive, asserts aggressively that he is totally displeased with the agenda and wants to proceed with his own important issues. The other members turn and look at you for the next move. What do you do?

The pressure on you, as staff person, to answer and to defend the agenda that you developed may be nearly irresistible. We recommend, however, that you resist it. If the group has gone along with the agenda beyond the halfway point in the meeting, it has, in effect, adopted the agenda as its own. We suggest that you wait for the group to respond and, by so waiting, indicate to the group that it, not just you, should deal with the member's question. In fact, the member's question may mean any of a number of things, and it is important to sort these out.

If the group is not yet sufficiently formed at this first meeting to deal with the member's question, after some thought, you may decide to respond as follows: "No agenda is perfect. Since we've gotten the discussion under way, why don't we put your question under 'new business'? We can then discuss ways in which the agendas of future meetings will be developed."

2. You are a staff person who has been assigned to develop a program for dealing with perceived neighborhood concerns about a lack of recreational facilities for the children and youth of a community. In response to a general flier that was mailed to over a hundred families, eight adults appear at a meeting. You introduce yourself, and the others introduce themselves. Then everyone turns and looks at you expectantly. What do you do?

In hindsight, necessary pregroup work was probably omitted here. Either it was not thought of or it was not feasible. In any case, the reality of the situation is that there are eight people present. The process of group formation needs to be started. A beginning working contract needs to be negotiated, the purposes of the group reviewed, plans for future meetings made, and other beginning steps of group life undertaken. Many successful community efforts have begun with eight people plus a staff member. Another way of stating the same point is that exploration and the beginning development of group themes are important, as important as the number in attendance.

3. A neighborhood association spends much of its third meeting talking about politics. No one appears to be displeased with the discussion, and it looks as though it may continue for the remainder of the meeting. The chair is part of the discussion and appears to be enjoying it. As a staff person, what do you do?

The group's behavior has some meaning. It may be that members are utilizing this discussion to take each other's measure and get to know each other better. Members may also be using this discussion in order to avoid the stated purpose of the group because that purpose is somehow uncomfortable or alien to them. We suggest that a first step would be for you to translate your feelings into a form in which they can be shared with the group: "I'm wondering whether we're just having a nice discussion because we want to or because we're avoiding talking about something else." If the group responds that this is the way they wish to spend their time, and they know that there is lots of time ahead in which to get the group's work done, then the members have a right to so decide, particularly since their chair is joining in the discussion.

4. It is the fourth meeting of a planning committee made up of both members of the staff and the board in a human services agency. One member comes in fifteen minutes late for the third consecutive time. No one says anything about it, including the chair. The late arrival is also the highest-status member of the group and represents a large department in the organization. What do you do?

Our initial suggestion is that you as the staff person do nothing. Tardiness may or may not be perceived as a problem by the group. If the group does perceive it as a problem, it will find a mechanism for dealing with it, possibly in the form of some mild ribbing or teasing following the meeting or in some other form. You may feel uncomfortable about not taking a stand in relation to this potentially destructive behavior. If you take on the responsibility for dealing with this situation at this time, however, you run a risk of going outside the idiom of the group and outside your prescribed role in the group. Whether you want to join in some generalized group expression that urges everyone to come on time next time is up to you.

Another possibility is to deal with this incident obliquely, by introducing the question of starting time at the end of the meeting: "Is this a good meeting time for everybody in the group?" This may make it possible to raise the issue of lateness indirectly and to stimulate some discussion about the need for members to arrive on time. A more theoretical analysis might identify the situation as part of the power and control struggles within the group. One would, in that case, have to raise the question of whether this is an issue around which power and control struggles should take place.

5. Sharp factionalism exists between two subgroups in an interorganizational committee within a community mental health center. The purpose of the committee is to develop guidelines and procedures in order to apply for a fairly substantial federal grant to improve family life education programs at the center. It can almost be predicted that if one subgroup member says something, a member of the other subgroup responds in the negative. The chair is utterly at a loss because the group seems to be stalemated. What would you do if you were the staff person?

Though one might be tempted to promote a confrontation within the group, we suggest that this is the kind of problem for which structural approaches might prove useful. One such approach would be to set up a task force containing a limited number of members of each of the subgroups and in effect to put them in a room together and let them set up procedures and solve their conflicts. Another approach would involve some work before the next meeting in the form of an encounter that you set up with the group's chair and representatives of each of the subgroups where the issues could be discussed in depth. The line you take at this meeting may be that the project is too important to be stalemated in a battle between the subgroups. Moral judgments should be avoided, and emphasis placed on the way the current fight blocks task accomplishment.

6. After a series of meetings of a biracial community council, one of the minority members announces that she is going to quit the group because it doesn't seem to be going anywhere. She has been forceful in trying to get group support and approval for a neighborhood petition to fire the local school principal but has not received this approval to date. The chair appears to be astonished by her declaration, as do other members. What do you do?

One of the difficult aspects of this situation is that as staff person you may now be aware that you have missed some earlier cues. Racial tensions may have been building for quite a while and may need to be addressed. It is also possible that the expressed intention to quit may be simply an announcement of strong feelings rather than an actual commitment to action. It is important to clarify this last point before proceeding. In our experience, it is sometimes useful for a group leader to take responsibility for an error in process even when that is not fully justified. "Perhaps I didn't express myself clearly" is sometimes easier for groups to hear than "How come you didn't hear what I said?" It may be possible to reframe the issue in such a way that the member's comment is redefined as a positive rather than negative expression: "I'm really glad that you've shared your frustration, because I think you're expressing what several of us are feeling. Can anyone help us understand why it seems to be so difficult to move ahead?" What seemed to be a personal issue may be reframable as a group issue.

7. You chair a committee composed of charge nurses in a hospital. The group is receiving a report from its subcommittee on the orientation of newly hired R.N.s. The meeting is attended by the hospital's administra-

tor, who keeps interrupting the meeting with personal and emotional statements about what he liked and what he didn't like about past orientation programs. Since his comments are largely irrelevant to the subcommittee, members are getting increasingly upset, drumming their fingers on the table or looking out the window. As chair, what do you do?

Although you may feel quite threatened in your position as chair, your obligation to the group as a whole demands that you appear in control and relatively calm. After waiting to see whether other members of the group are going to challenge the visitor and deciding that they are not going to, it becomes incumbent upon you as chair to do so. One way to initiate such an interchange would be turn and ask the administrator, "Your sharing all these opinions with us suggests that you're looking for some response." Another, perhaps to be undertaken with a sense of perspective if you can summon any at that point, would be to remark in a humorous way, "I didn't realize that you were a member of the subcommittee." There is no easy way out of this situation. There may be a fight coming, and you need to trust your own skill and the integrity of the group to be sure that the group will survive such a fight. Maintain control. Reflect on all the past group disagreements and conflicts that you have survived.

8. You are subexecutive of a large human services organization. Your administrative superior has instructed you to get the department head's group to agree to a particular plan for distributing summer vacations. You had told your superior that the department heads would not go along with the plan, but your report was ignored and the order repeated. As it turns out, the department heads unanimously express opposition to the scheme you are proposing and instead counter with a plan they have developed. How do you deal with this dilemma?

Since you are caught in the middle, you might as well make this fact overt by sponsoring a meeting between the administrator and either a representative subgroup or the entire body of department heads. Rather than carrying messages from one side to the other and incurring the wrath of both, at this meeting you can define its purpose as being to solve what seems like a difficult dilemma.

We have sketched only a few recurring problems in this chapter; and there are certainly many solutions to both the individual behavioral and the group-situational problems in addition to those we have discussed. One of our reasons for posing these problems is to point out that there are always several possible solutions for any problem. Group leaders can also use these vignettes and descriptions of patterned roles as reference materials when they are stuck or looking for different options in dealing with situations equivalent or similar to those mentioned. You are likely to face a large cohort of tricky situations involving burdensome members whose activities seem to erode the group's confidence. If these are left unaddressed, members could walk away saying to themselves, "What's the use?" or, "There's no sense of competence or enjoyment in maintaining membership." This material can be useful for developing preliminary empathy or understanding and planning a strategy that transforms negatives into positives (no small task). Such conversions are a significant feature of group work. Sarcastic humor can be derailed by a leader's self-deprecating comments regarding similar incidents. Oppositional behavior can be transformed into investigative work or new ideas. These and other coping strategies make up individually or collectively the lubricant group workers need to move the group along.

One question that has we have not discussed here deals with idiosyncratic issues, regarding a chair's or staff person's style. Do age, gender, racial/ethnic background, number of years of experience, or other personal characteristics of the staff person or chair affect the ways in which problems will be approached and solved? Such characteristics are important in the development of individual styles. The relationship between person and style is not a simple one and needs to develop over a long period of time.

14

Perspectives for
Professional Practice
with Working Groups

Skill in staffing, leading, and being a member of working groups is essential for all health and human service professionals. Some of the most skilled group members and leaders we know are not group specialists but have learned their skills in the group equivalent of the school of hard knocks. Some people are naturals at working in groups; others have accumulated their skills through experience and reflection. For many, the crucial learning laboratory may not have been a group connected with the practice of their professions but another group experience in which they participated as part of their personal lives or a training group or course in small groups. However the skills are acquired, it is important to develop curricula, both formal and informal, to teach them in working groups to students of the various helping professions.

We shall discuss the development of such curricula in this chapter. First, we shall comment briefly on some of the theoretical points of view that we think should undergird training programs and curricula in work with groups. Then, we shall discuss somewhat more specifically some of the content that specialists in working groups need to learn. Finally, we shall attempt briefly to sketch a research agenda that needs to be undertaken if professional practice with working groups is to move ahead and accumulate empirically based findings that test some of the propositions put forth in this book and others.

Though this is not a book on developmental theory or on the social theory relevant to working groups, it does seem appropriate to begin by commenting briefly on several theoretical positions that are useful for understanding group life and the skills necessary for professional practice in groups.

THE EGO-PSYCHOLOGICAL LINKAGE

Ego psychology grew from psychoanalytic theory. As a personality theory, it provides useful guidelines for understanding how people work. Its major concepts help make sense of behavior that may be both reasonable and unreasonable according to different contexts and even, at times, self-defeating. The focus of ego psychology is concern for how people adapt to the demands and opportunities of their worlds in accordance with inner requirements. The theory emphasizes measures for adaptation and the many devices people have for negotiating their daily lives in a coherent way. In its broadest aspect, the theory emphasizes critical issues that need to be mastered at each of eight developmental stages, beginning with infancy and extending into old age. Innate forces or propensities are essential points in ego psychology; equally critical are the ways in which a person triggers, reacts to, and acts on them. The ego is simply a theoretical construct that provides a sort of window through which an understanding of a person's coping responses can be assessed.

Two streams involved in ego psychology deserve comment. The first is the influence of defenses, coercions, and other stubborn and unconscious patterns that can govern a person's behavior. These patterns, of course, can characterize staff as well as group members. An example might be members' hidden agendas, which can influence the ways they operate in groups. A second facet of the ego is its more rational and problem-solving aspects, such as moves toward self-actualization, mastery, the development of personal and social competence, and learning ways to engage the outside world. Useful functions of the ego that relate to adaptation and competence include the following, as listed by Caplan (1961):

1. Seeing, hearing, knowing, and perceiving are aspects of cognition that can start from either inside or outside the person. Included are acts of perception, selection, and attention, as well as the consciousness of one's needs.

2. Selection and integration are processes that endow certain feelings with meaning by connecting them with information that has been received in the past. Thus, once something is perceived, it is sorted into appropriate categories, and the meanings assigned to them can range and vary widely.

3. Planning is connected with problem solving. Once messages are connected with meaning, then the ego is faced with the need to do

something about the situation. Planning and deciding what one ought to do are important ego functions.

4. Control—meaning containing impulses and choosing one action over another—is another important ego function. Initiating and exercising action in the implementation of a plan are parts of control.

5. Synthesizing provides coherence to a response and also helps to compose an identity. That is, certain patterns of behavior that appear over and over again signal some predictability for people's behavior. This consistency really is a workable amalgam of pressures from the demands of a task, inner feelings, an organization's demands, and a person's external environment.

6. Object relationships are relationships with other people; the quality of these relationships, how they are formed, their types, and their intensity constitute a person's expression of self in an interpersonal context.

Table 14.1 outlines a set of person capacities, "those abilities that the individual may be helped to draw upon. . . . in order to deal with his current situation" (Ripple, Polemis, and Alexander, 1964:28). It provides a useful tool for assessing what abilities members have and bring to the group for services. While listed topically, their value is in the configuration presented and developed by the worker in pregroup interviews and confirmed by observations on the group process. For further discussion and elaboration of how these capacities fit to a group, see Balgopal and Vassil (1983:79–110).

The internal factors are cognitive, perceptual, and affective. The ability to plan, creativity, intellectuality, being able to wait and think, staying open to possibilities, demonstrating an ability to put ideas together, and appreciating events with humor, achievement, and a sense of optimism round out central features of the internal capacities.

At the interpersonal level, where building, cooperating, sharing, and flexibility are key elements, the ability to relate in various ways adds to the sense of "groupness" and helps construct the safety envelope necessary for work to proceed. For both, a range of internal and interpersonal capacities is necessary for meaningful mutual aid or work to take place.

The social dimensions extend the above elements to combine with person behaviors or roles that are integrated within and beyond the group to other collectivities reaching inside and outside the organization in public and private domains, such as volunteer activities, community groups, professional

TABLE 14.1 *Member Capacities**

INTERNAL	INTERPERSONAL	SOCIAL
Cognitive		
Intelligence	Empathy	Role adaptability
Logical reasoning	Authenticity	Role integration
Intellectuality—	Warmth	Role embracement
(ordering, simplifying,	Trust	Role distance
and classifying)	Ability to reciprocate	Role disparity
Planfulness	Social competence	
Creativity	Flexibility—to be assertive,	
Insight and awareness	submissive, or affiliative	
Self-identity	when appropriate	
Anticipation		
Intimacy and isolation		
Perceptual		
Tolerance of ambiguity		
Openness to new experiences		
Selective awareness		
Discriminating cues		
Affective		
Spontaneity		
Sense of pleasure		
Sense of competence		
Sense of humor		
Sense of optimism		

*Capacities included in this table are drawn from the works of social and behavioral scientists such as Bruner, Erickson, Piaget, White, Leighton, Rogers, and Mead, among others.

associations. These roles, such as active spokesperson, action figure, or con-templative listener, manifested in a few or wide range of contexts, keep members on task. Exercise of these roles also involves criticizing when the group loses focus, staying aloof from entanglements, being willing to take on additional responsibility, and keeping ideas and feelings in balance. In addition, being able to take criticism, learn, back off from unwanted demands to perform, and connect with other members contribute to the ability to perform in a number and variety of roles, which is essential and instructive to keep a group moving. When potential members can integrate these types of specific abilities, then value both inside and outside the group is enhanced.

Vaillant (1993) provides a useful update and wise perspective in a book aptly titled *The Wisdom of the Ego*. An awareness of defenses (the world of the unconscious) and the concepts we have presented can be useful in assessing how a person will react to new situations, solve problems, and deal with satisfying needs and choosing from the options the social world offers. Ego psychology is most helpful when one is dealing with individuals. It does not provide a conceptual means to represent adequately the interpersonal and larger social processes that provide the context for action. For this, one needs to turn to the social-psychological linkage.

Social Psychological Linkages

In order to function effectively and with satisfaction as a member of a democratic microcosm, group members need to have internalized in depth the values, advantages, and satisfactions inherent in membership in such groups. From the viewpoint of ego psychology, this requires considerable early experience in environments that are fundamentally stable. It requires learning in childhood and relearning in adolescence the skills and satisfactions of group life. The first group in a person's life, of course, is the family (or a family surrogate), supplemented by interpersonal experiences with peers. The second major setting for learning is one or a series of peer groups. From young adulthood on, both work and community groups are major settings for group experience. If one has not progressively integrated an ability to derive satisfaction from functioning as a member of a democratic microcosm into one's personality and role behaviors, it is difficult to learn how to do this, for the first time, as an adult. If one has, then democratic group participation seems a normal way of obtaining satisfaction of one's intrapsychic and interpersonal needs. Something like this was in the mind of Kurt Lewin and his early followers as they struggled with the relationship between group structure and group phenomena and the task of creating and providing foundations for a democratic society (see Lewin, 1948, 1951). Early group experiences may be the most important because they lay the groundwork for lifelong functioning in a variety of democratic microcosms and for the social capital necessary for democratic institutions to flourish.

Symbolic interaction theory casts valuable light on the same set of phenomena (Manis and Meltzer, 1972:43–57; Ephross and Greene, 1991:ch. 9). Symbolically, each member can experience a group as a safe arena for gaining a sense of personal effectiveness and self-worth or as a dangerous arena where personal ineffectiveness can be learned and self-esteem is likely to be drained at any time. The difference between these two sets of learning, it seems to us, is related to the sum total of one's earlier experiences in groups. The relationship may not be linear, because different experiences at different stages of life have different impacts, but it is real, nevertheless.

Detailed individual analyses of individuals are rarely attempted in working groups. Neither staff persons nor groups consider such analyses necessary, in most cases. Rather, there is a tendency for group members, chairs, and staff to assess the potential functioning of individual members on a global basis. One hears, "So-and-so is a good team member," or "So-and-so tends to go to pieces in a crises," or "So-and-so is only comfortable when he is in the position of chair." These are shorthand assessments, often stereotypical, of how members have integrated earlier personal experiences. Such assessments imply an intuitive understanding of the connections among past, present, and future group experiences for individuals. Moreover, groups often sense the connections between a person's intrapsychic processes and the ways in which the same individual is likely to take part in a particular working group situation. Some of the judgments are empirical, based on past experiences with individuals in comparable working group situations. Some are overly global, and some are contaminated by the admission of irrelevant criteria, such as class-linked factors that are viewed prejudicially in the broader society. In general, though, because there is rarely a surplus of group talent or group leadership talent, groups' assessments are roughly accurate.

Lewin's pioneering and seminal perspective provides a balance for the tendency to view individuals' behavior as consistent from one working group situation to another. Lewin's theory focuses on the field that surrounds an individual's behavior and, simply put, states that changing the rules changes behavior. From this perspective, the behaviors of individuals and groups are changeable. By contrast, developmental theory views the behavior of individuals—and thus of the groups they form—as consistent. Both these perspectives are necessary.

Individuals do tend to behave in consistent ways in various working group situations. On the other hand, different group compositions, organization linkages, tasks, and other characteristics can cause considerable variability in how the same person behaves in different groups. Thus, when it comes to consistency in behavior in various groups, the glass of water is both half full and half empty: individuals both behave consistently and behave differently.

PREPARING PROFESSIONALS FOR WORKING GROUPS

Knowledge Aspects

Ambivalence toward working in groups is pervasive in American society. Several reasons can account for this ambivalence, prominent among them, our cultural inheritance of an ethos based on individualism. This ethos can be traced to the theological roots of Protestant nonconformism and to the physical, economic, and human ecologies of the United States during its formative years. Students of health and human service professions share this ethos. At the same time, both their professional education and their lives as practitioners require a high degree of interdependence and extensive involvement in working groups.

The history of what has been called the "groups industry" over the past sixty years gives clear testimony to the ambivalence with which learning about groups has been approached. Lewin and his followers founded the groups industry with a basic truth: that effective human relations need to be taught and learned in settings designed for this purpose. This basic understanding and its dissemination were greeted by sensationalization, commercialization, overreaction, defensiveness, various forms of resistance, and considerable backlash. In the long run, however, work in groups has become a serious subject, spurred in recent years by concerns about issues that range from quality of work life to national productivity.

In many educational curricula, learning about groups, especially experiential learning, have been characterized as "soft" and thus somehow unworthy. Both theory and practice with working groups tend to fall between the cracks of various curricula. On the one hand, these topics may be treated as extraneous to curricula that prepare students for clinical practice, since they do not deal with direct work with patients/clients. On the other hand, the study of group work is sometimes viewed as lacking in rigor for those preparing themselves for careers as administrators and organizational technicians. A similar pattern may be found in many educational programs that prepare planners. The omnipresent committees are sometimes treated as subjects for complaint rather than instruction and research. Nursing and medical curricula have been increasingly cognizant of the need for developing interpersonal skills in working with various types of patients; job skills in working in groups with other professionals have received a lower priority. Curricula in public administration and related fields sometimes either omit working group skills or assume that somehow students will develop skills with such groups on their own, during internships or elsewhere.

There are signs, however, of an interesting process of rebirth of concern about working groups. Role-playing as a learning and teaching technique, for example, has made its way back into some programs of professional education via its translation into case study methods in schools of business administration and elsewhere. For example, one university offers a program leading to a graduate degree in administrative science. This program is often recommended to nurses and social workers who have reached administrative positions as a vehicle for learning "hard" management skills. Part of the program emphasizes the acquisition of working group skills through intricately designed role-playing experiences. Those nursing or social work graduates who never encountered basic group work concepts in their own professional education can encounter them in translation, as it were.

What should professional practitioners know about working groups? They should know the basic structuralist, symbolic interactionist, and dramaturgical positions about the nature of group life (Hartford, 1972; Douglas, 1979). They should be familiar with the pioneering work of Lewin (1948; 1951) and the classic group dynamics experiments of Asch (1951), Bavelas (1973), and others. They should be exposed to some of the vast literature on social stratification and its effects, as well as the literature in social psychology about group structure, communication, and task accomplishment (Ofshe, 1973; Hare, 1976). They should understand, in depth, recent perspectives on pluralism and cultural differences and on the effects of racism, sexism, and discrimination in all their ugly forms (Gordon, 1981; Weiss and Ephross, 1986). On a related track, concepts of legitimacy and authority, as well as specific knowledge about organizational structure and governance arrangements for service delivery organizations, are important underpinnings about which to learn.

Attitudinal Aspects

One of us once had the valuable opportunity of hearing a noted scholar present what later became chapters in a book about adult personality. The presentations were organized around the major roles of adult life, defined as the marital/sexual, the vocational, and the parental. In each session, the point was made in discussion that the role of citizen/community member/polity member had been omitted. The presenter agreed, each time, that this role, or cluster of roles, has enormous importance for many adults. Publication of the book, however, confirmed the presence of a lingering resistance to this notion. It contains no chapter about the adult as community member or citizen. Nor does it contain any significant mention of the importance of group membership for adult life. These omissions are widespread in both scientific and popular literatures about adult life.

Psychological views of the nature of the human condition should not be deprecated. An understanding of the workings of human psyches is essential for practice in any of the health and human service professions. Though members of working groups have the same psychological processes, needs, and characteristics as do all people, a psychologically based view of human behavior is often not the most helpful for the practitioner in working groups. Sociologically based views that identify social processes operating on and within groups are often more valuable. Views drawn from microsociology and the sociology of daily life, as well as from research and theory in social psychology, can be especially useful.

Political and economic views of group and organizational behavior are often effective for understanding working groups and their settings. Budgets, for example, need to be understood as political and economic documents, not only as projections of the values of members of budget committees. Money means many things to many people, but how it is used in service delivery organizations can often best be understood from a political, interorganizational perspective.

Health and human services are very big business in contemporary society. Partly for this reason, many persons and institutions of wealth and power are involved in decision making about them. To resist learning about the perspectives of such actors and how to influence them can be self-defeating. To learn to mobilize community power and resources on behalf of needed services is an important professional skill, as is learning about the grant-writing process and other ways to trip the levers of power and resources. One place where attitudes and knowledge interact is the arena of technical information about organizations' structure, services, and clientele. Such information is extremely valuable for working groups. Working groups that need it also need professionals who can provide it and help groups understand it. The point is not that professionals should serve as walking data banks but rather that they need the knowledge and skills necessary for rapid and accurate data retrieval in a variety of fields and from a variety of data bases.

Skill Aspects

The skills required for effective working group practice can be divided roughly into two kinds: the analytic and the interpersonal. Often these blend and interface. It seems to us that those who are engaged in educating and training practitioners have a responsibility to develop lists, categories, and typologies of the skills that need to be learned and taught. We have provided a step toward such a list in chapter 9. While we noted there that this list is hardly exhaustive, we suggest that it provides a good starting point for curriculum development and for guiding the content of in-service training and professional development learning experiences.

In addition to these two broad categories of skills, there is another that is, perhaps, harder to operationalize. It is a variant of one of the core skills listed by Helen Phillips (1975); her term was "skill in using the reality of the present" (116). It seems more precise, to us, to talk of skill in *relating* to the reality of the present. We have in mind the ability of a professional person, whether member, chair, or staff, to become involved in and relate himself to the reality of a working group's mission, task, composition, and place in the organizational cosmos and to invest in the importance of that involvement and relationship. Perhaps another way of describing this would be *skill at supporting the importance of a working group's life*. Experienced practitioners will recognize this skill, but we need to work toward more precise operational definitions of it.

RESEARCH

Professional activity, in our view, includes three essential (functional) roles: those of theoretician, practitioner, and empiricist. The connections among these roles have been noted by Thelen:

> For much policy making, the dialects and roles to be included in the group are those of practitioner, theorist and empiricist. The concern and responsibility of the theorist is with universal propositions: the framework of assumptions and, by implication, values that are to be adopted by the group and that will give it its identity. Once agreed upon, these became the authority for group functioning and for individual self-discipline. The theorist is the purest representative and conveyor of the group's centripetal tendencies. In sharp contrast, the concern and responsibility of the practitioner is to find better ways to do his thing in his own local and idiosyncratic situation. Practitioners continually confront the group with diverse inputs and demands; they best convey the individualistic or centrifugal tendencies of the system. In order to resolve the conflict between these opposing tendencies, the group has

to find some compelling and accessible authority that can mediate between the propositions of the theorists and the "needs" of the practitioners. This authority is nature itself: the way the world "is," as distinct from the way the theorist encapsulates it or the practitioner selectively perceives it. Hence the empiricist is needed. We can see that the theorist needs the empiricist's help to convince the others that his propositions do indeed illuminate existential reality. The practitioner likewise needs the empiricist's help to convince others that his accounts and allegations about his experience are dependable, that is, that they are in line with what has already been established about similar classes of situations and phenomena. The opposing forces are conciliated by confident agreement that what is to be done (empirical) has a chance to be done because the practitioners see it as a better means to their goals; and that it will be socially and humanely significant because it reflects propositions that (theoretically) should capture enduring long-range values and aspirations.   (1981:60–61)

These three roles were also proposed in a slightly different form by Schwartz (1994). A theory of change and one of changing, while related, are not quite the same. Knowing how a person learns does not necessarily tell us how to teach that person. Schon (1983) presents a scheme in which professional practitioners are depicted as those who develop a thoughtful and ongoing dialogue with the consumers of their services. Such practitioners act on the basis of the consumers' responses to their original interventions.

Knowing, according to Schon, is in our acting. And, in a sequential sense, actions lead to thoughts and back again to action. However, as Schwartz (1994) has pointed out, the transition from knowing to doing is complex and, further, is not always easy to describe. In a sense, one may do a lot more than one can talk about, or even know, although one's actions are not haphazard. Practitioners are always using what they think will be helpful and modifying their actions based on feedback. It is in this sense that art and science exist side by side in each and every practitioner. The potential range of activities in action, then, include theorizing (trying to explain an event), practicing (doing something personal, ways of acting), and empiricizing (testing of ideas in action in relation to all the work). Introducing and bringing together these three roles in teaching/learning situations is an important mission for professional education.

There is a long and important research agenda for professional practice with working groups. The variables to be studied are many. In our view, one preferred research strategy at this point needs to be sophisticated but largely naturalistic observation and the systematization of those observations. Longitudinal studies that record, with the use of video technology, the development of working groups over time should be high on the research agenda. Cross-sectional studies are of limited value in studying the phasic qualities of group life. Some use of instrumentation is also indicated, especially instrumentation that helps to catalog in systematic fashion the perception and experiences of participants in working groups. Nor do we wish to rule out a limited amount of manipulation of significant variables, as, for example, in studying the many unresolved issues that still surround the question of group composition.[1]

Fortunately, ethical problems in research on working groups do not appear to be major obstacles because much of the most-needed research need not be hidden or its purposes concealed. The purposes of these studies can be shared honestly, even though it may sometimes seem preferable to state them in a general way. Informed consent can and, we believe, will be given freely by the members of most working groups.

Both structuralist and interactionist perspectives on group life need to be employed in working group research. Each generates important variables for study, as does a dramaturgical perspective. The research done to date is small in volume, and a great many gaps in our knowledge about groups remain. Besides the needed naturalistic observations, we have stated many hypotheses for testing throughout this book. Other lines of inquiry are not hard to find. Working groups provide a superior arena for the study of the effects of cultural, ethnic, class, racial, and gender differences; beginnings have been made in this direction by Davis (1984) and Reed and Garvin (1983) and by their colleagues. Still, a great many propositions drawn from practice experience badly need empirical testing; practitioners are a fertile source of such researchable issues.

The practice of social work with groups is complex simply because in a small group of persons led by a professionally trained worker all the parties involved are affected by their various personalities. The influence of the group and the salient publics of organization, culture, and broader community in which groups are imbedded add to the complexity of the work. It appears to be a breathtaking task to attempt to understand what presents itself as a cornucopia of feelings, ideas, and behaviors with roots and branches in other domains. The step from observation, to influence, to understanding inevitably leads to the question of predictability. Real-life groups never sit still too long, as anyone who has attended even just one meeting can readily attest.

Considering the person–group construct as the nucleus to the study and practice of group work, Bales (1970) makes the distinction between individual personality and an individual's group role, defined by the situation. For the practitioner, the distinction is important because attention needs to be directed to the key determinants of both, which are not necessarily similar. This distinction was raised earlier by Chaiklin (1969) in discussing differences between personality and social systems and later on in a classic sociology text by Smelser and Smelser, *Personality and Social Systems* (1970).

Bales's point is that prediction is too lofty a goal and argues, with John Stuart Mill, that knowledge insufficient for prediction may be most valuable for guidance. Bales quotes Mills to support the extent and limits of knowledge:

> It is evident, that Sociology, considered as a system of deductions *a priori* cannot be a science of positive predictions, but only of tendencies. We may be able to conclude, from the laws of human nature applied to the circumstances of a given state of society, that a particular cause will operate in a certain manner unless counteracted; but we can never be assured to what extent or amount it will so operate, or affirm with certainty that it will not be counteracted; because we can seldom know, even approximately; all the agencies which may coexist with it, and still less calculate the collective results of so many combined elements.
>
> It is not necessary for the wise conduct of the affairs of society, no more than of any one's private concerns, that we should be able to foresee infallibly the results of what we do. We must seek our objects by means which may perhaps be defeated, and take precautions against dangers which possibly may never be realized. The aim of practical politics is to surround any given society with the greatest possible number of circumstances of which the tendencies are beneficial, and to remove or counteract, as far as practicable, those of which the tendencies are injurious. A knowledge of the tendencies only, though without power of accurately predicting their conjunct result, gives us to a considerable extent this power.[2] (cited in Bales, 1971:20–21)

Working groups are a central and largely understudied part of the professional (as well as personal) lives of many people. The time seems to us to be ripe to reclaim them as legitimate objects for theory development, professional education, skilled professional practice, and research. It is our hope that this book has made a contribution toward this end.

Population of Self-Descriptive Q-Sort Statements

Thelen and his colleagues at the University of Chicago Human Dynamics Laboratory (Stock and Thelen, 1958) carried out a series of studies to explore and understand the bilateral operations between individuals and groups. Basing their work on the theoretical formulations of W. R. Bion, the research group developed an array of instruments to assess relationships between and among members, subgroups, and the group as a whole, as well as developmental changes in the group process over time.

While Bion's formulations were developed working with patients suffering from combat fatigue, his ideas and constructs were believed to be applicable to human relations training groups. Bion's observations of patient groups led him to conceptualize three central emotional states—dependency, fight-flight, and pairing—that reflected unconscious expressions of the group as a whole. They were perceived to be intimately related to the work aspect of the group, a reality-based and consciously determined goal activity. Bion's theoretical constructs were expanded to include counterdependency. In addition, the research group developed specific behavioral items to describe positive, neutral, and negative features for each theoretical construct.

The value of this effort, described below in the Q-sort instrument, are threefold:

1. They are theory based, drawn from Bion's conceptualizations.
2. They represent positive, negative, and neutral behavioral components, each of which is related to the work aspect.
3. They provide a useful and realistic checklist applicable to individuals, subgroups, or taken together as reflective of the group as a whole. The intricacies of the operation between and among members and the group thus become accessible for description, assessment, and intervention.

Fight

Fight-Neutral (FN)
I enjoy a good argument in the group.

When someone attacks me, I fight back.

When I'm annoyed, I feel free to say so.

I am impulsive in expressing feelings against others.

I get angry quickly but get over it just as quickly.

I feel angry that my role is that of critically evaluating the progress of the group.

Fight-Supportive (FS)

My expressions of impatience help when the group is apathetic.

I think it helps to say what you feel even though it may hurt someone's feelings.

When the group is following some task blindly without much interest, I point it out.

When people talk in vague terms, I ask them what they really mean.

When someone makes an irresponsible suggestion, I point it out.

When a group adopts a suggestion without looking into it, I think it should be acknowledged.

Fight-Destructive (FD)

I tend to question the decisions the group makes.

I question whether the group really knows what it's doing.

I resent it when people say, "Let's get back to the problem."

When I'm mad at the group, I refuse to make suggestions.

I stand by my position regardless of what the group thinks.

I refuse to work on insignificant problems.

DEPENDENCY

Dependency-Neutral (DN)

I am inclined to go along with the way the group as a whole feels about something.

I feel most comfortable when the leader actively gives direction.

I feel curious about why the leader makes the comments he does.

I feel self-conscious about what the leader is thinking of me.

I'm willing to follow the suggestions of other group members.

I would rather let others set the direction of the group.

Dependency-Supportive (DS)

I try to help establish a working routine for the group.

I try to make sure I know what's wanted before I present a plan or suggestion.

I'm willing to discuss whatever issues the group thinks important.

I feel the leader's role is to indicate the direction he wants the group to follow.

I'm inclined to support the suggestions the leader makes in the group.

When the group bogs down, I'm likely to ask for suggestions.

Dependency-Destructive (DD)

I feel that others are better qualified to make suggestions to the group.

I feel a group shouldn't begin work on a problem until it knows what others
did in the same situation.

I don't like to commit myself on an issue until I know how others stand.

I think the leader should handle the group so that those who don't want to
contribute don't have to.

I feel it's the leader's job to prepare an agenda for the group.

I don't think a group should discuss things within itself it wouldn't say outside.

PAIRING

Pairing-Neutral (PN)

I enjoy talking about my personal reactions in the group.

I feel closer to some members than to others.

I feel warmly about the group as a whole.

I'm inclined to make warm friends among group members.

I want to know some of the other members of the group intimately.

I get especially attached to one or two particular members.

Pairing-Supportive (PS)

I try to see that everyone who wants to participate gets a chance to do so.

I enjoy planning group activities with certain other members.

I think a large group can get more done by breaking up into small subgroups.

I try to suggest procedures that most members will feel comfortable with.

When the group can't seem to get ahead, I try to be sensitive to everyone's
feelings about the situation.

I like to work out solutions cooperatively with other members.

Pairing-Destructive (PD)

I feel the group shouldn't discuss issues likely to divide the group.

I like to exchange private comments about what is happening with certain
other members.

I try tot keep up a friendly, polite atmosphere in the group.

The approval of others is important to me.

I feel it's important for all the members to think well of each other.

My attempts to discuss personal matters seem to bother other members.

FLIGHT

Flight-Neutral (FLN)
I keep myself from expressing strong feelings in the group.
I prefer keeping relations with others on an impersonal level.
I don't like to show my real feelings in the group.
I tend to feel that what goes on in meetings is pretty unimportant.
I like group discussion to have a light touch.
During group discussion, I become interested in following my own train of thought.

Flight-Supportive (FLS)
I can discuss issues best in abstract rather than personal terms.
When the group can't get ahead, I change the subject.
I can work best if I maintain an objective attitude toward the group.
When I want really to understand group operation, I withdraw from participation for a time.
When a touchy issue comes up, I think the group ought to think about it overnight.
I'm interested in the philosophical implications behind group actions.

Flight-Destructive (FLD)
I lose interest when people make heavy demands on the group.
I feel there's not much use in going on when the group doesn't know what it wants to do.
When the group can't seem to make progress, I feel it should disband.
Other members don't seem to see what's happening in the group the same way I do.
I find it hard to see the "problem" that the others are talking about.
I find it wiser not to try to participate when strong feelings are expressed in the group.

COUNTERDEPENDENCY

Counterdependency-Neutral (CDN)
I play an active, influential role in the group.
I think the leader should participate only minimally in the group.
I like a leader who acts like just another member.
I don't pay much attention to what the leader does.
I insist on making my own decisions.
I think experienced members are looked up to too much.

Counterdependency-Supportive (CDS)

When the group can't get started, I'm not afraid to stick my neck out with a suggestion.

I think the group shouldn't accept a leader's plan any more readily than a member's.

I feel that group members can solve their own problems without help if they really want to.

I like to get my own suggestions into the discussion before the group decides anything.

I feel the leader shouldn't intervene when the group is working hard on a problem.

When the group is bogged down, I like to be the one who takes over.

Counterdependency-Destructive (CDD)

I enjoy arguing with the leader of the group.

I enjoy testing my leadership skills against those of other members.

Group members who control things irritate me.

I feel that a lot of a leader's activity is intended simply to keep control of the group.

I tend to suggest alternatives to plans proposed by the leader.

I feel some members have to get together to keep a check on the leader.

NOTES

3. Toward a Model of Working Groups

1. Concepts are ideas. They are useful, intellectually, in analyzing the processes of a group. Concepts don't live; people do. One should never forget that a group is formed by live people, not by a collection of intellectual concepts. What this means is that the feelings and the sense of humanity of group members must always be taken into account, no matter which concept is being used for group analysis or for planning the behavior of a staff person in a group.

2. The term "democratic microcosm" was taught to both of us by Professor Herbert A. Thelen, then of the School of Education, University of Chicago. Like other terms of Thelen's devising, it strikes an immediate chord for any one who has thought extensively about the life of groups.

3. We have borrowed the terms "simple," "covalent," and "coordinate covalent" from chemistry because we find these words so graphic and evocative.

4. The preceding discussion is taken from an unpublished dissertation (Vassil, 1975).

5. Leadership Theory

1. Suitably disguised, this represents a real experience with a real group.

6. Leadership in Working Groups

1. In this chapter, the term "leadership" will be used to denote all persons who carry leadership functions for groups, regardless of whether they are staff, chairs, or members. As the chapter will make clear, we view leadership as a shared function carried throughout the group's life by many different members and even subgroups within a working group.

2. It is questionable whether passivity is an appropriate stance for a leader in any group. For discussion of this subject, see Balgopal and Vassil (1983), chap. 7.

9. Stages/Phases of Group Development

1. Evidence for the existence of both phases and cycles may be found in Williamson (1977).

2. In general, we continue to be guided by the phases of group development put forth by Margaret Hartford in her book *Groups in Social Work* (1972).

11. ORGANIZATIONAL SETTINGS AND STYLES

1. We are indebted to Dr. S. Michael Plaut for suggesting this example, as well as others.

12. TECHNOLOGIES FOR GROUP MAINTENANCE, OPERATION, AND PRODUCTIVITY

1. Concerned with groups of all kinds, Northen and Kurland (2001:81–108) have constructed what they call "clusters of interventive skills," which we consider directly useful or for working with and in working groups (or modifiable for such use).

2. Argyris was referring to consultants' roles; we have in mind the behavior of staff, chairs, and group members.

3. This record and analysis were prepared for this volume by Raymie Wayne, M.S.W., J.D. The authors gratefully acknowledge her contribution.

14. PERSPECTIVES FOR PROFESSIONAL PRACTICE WITH WORKING GROUPS

1. In this regard, Bales (2002) has developed a scheme to assess personal, interpersonal, group, and organizational factors which he calls "field theory." SYMLOG (an acronym for Systematic, Multiple Level Observations of Groups) is intended to be a milestone in developing an integrated theory of personality and group dynamics. It is designed to be used to assess and change behavior in small groups. This work has been applied to a variety of settings including clinical, working, and managerial groups, classrooms, and teams.

2. Bales was quoting from John Stuart Mill, *A System of Logic, Ratiocinative and Inductive: Being a Connected View of the Principles of Evidence and the Methods of Scientific Investigation*, book 6, *On the Logic of the Moral Sciences* (London: Longmans, Green, 1936).

BIBLIOGRAPHY

Alissi, A. S. and C. C. Mergins, eds. 1997. *Voices From the Field: Group Work Responds*. New York: Haworth.

Anderson, J. 1997. *Social Work with Groups: A Process Model*. New York: Longman.

Argyris, C. 1970. *Intervention Theory and Method*. Reading, Mass.: Addison-Wesley.

Argyris, C. and D. A. Schon. 1974. *Theory in Practice*. San Francisco: Jossey-Bass.

Asch, S. E. 1951. Effects of group pressure upon the modification and distortion of subjects. In H. Guetzkow, ed., *Groups, Leadership, and Men*. Pittsburgh: Carnegie.

Association for the Advancement of Social Work with Groups. 1999. *Standards for Social Work Practice with Groups*. Akron, Ohio: AASWG.

Bales, R. F. 1970. *Personality and Interpersonal Behavior*. New York: Holt, Rinehart, and Winston.

——. 1983. *Hints for Building Teamwork*. Weston, Mass.: Symlog Consultants. Typescript.

——. 2002. *Social Interaction Systems: Theory and Measurement*. New Brunswick, N.J.: Transaction Publishers.

Bales, R. F., S. P. Cohen, and S. A. Williamson. 1979. *Symlog: A System for the Multiple-Level Observations of Groups*. New York: Free.

Bales, R. F. and F. Strodtbeck. 1956. Phases in group problem solving. In D. Cartwright and A. Zander, eds.,. *Group Dynamics*. 2d ed. Evanston, Ill.: Row, Peterson.

Balgopal, P. R. and T. V. Vassil. 1983. *Groups in Social Work: An Ecological Perspective*. New York: Macmillan.

Barlow, C., J. A. Blythe, and M. Edmonds. 1999. *A Handbook of Interactive Exercises for Groups*. Boston: Allyn and Bacon.

Baugh, S. G. and G. B. Graen. 1997. Effects of team gender and racial composition on perceptions of team performance in cross-functional teams. *Groups and Organization Management* 22 (3): 366–383.

Bavelas, A. 1973. Communication patterns in task-oriented groups. In R. J. Ofshe, ed., *Interpersonal Behavior in Small Groups*. Englewood Cliffs, N.J.: Prentice-Hall.

Beck, D. 1997. *Advances in Small Group Research: Contributions from the German-Speaking Countries Between 1984 and 1995*. European Psychologist 2 (4): 368–376.

Benne, K. D. 1976. The Moral Orientation of Laboratory Methods of Education and Changing. In W. G. Bennis, K. D. Benne, R. Chin, and K. Corey, *The Planning of Change*. 3d ed. New York: Holt, Rinehart and Winston.

Bennis, W. E. and H. A. Shepard. 1956. A theory of group development. *Human Relations* 9 (4): 415–437.

Bennis, W. E., G. M. Spreitzer, and T. C. Cummings, eds. 2001. *The Future of Leadership*. San Francisco: Jossey-Bass.

Benveniste, G. 1972. *The Politics of Expertise*. Berkeley: Glendessary.

Berger, R. 1996. A comparative analysis of different methods of teaching group work. *Social Work with Groups* 19 (1): 79–89.

Berne, Eric. 1964. *Games People Play*. New York: Grove.

Bernstein, S. B., ed. 1965. *Explorations in Group Work*. Boston: Milford House.

Bertcher, H. J. 1996. *Creating Groups*. Thousand Oaks, CA: Sage.

Bertcher, H. J., L . F. Kurtz, and A. Lamont, eds., 1999. *Rebuilding Communities: Challenges for Group Work*. New York: Haworth.

Biddle, B. and E. Thomas, eds. 1966. *Role Theory: Concepts and Research*. New York: Wiley.

Bion, W. R. 1961. *Experiences in Groups*. New York: Basic.

Blumer, H. 1971. Social problems as collective behavior. *Social Problems* 18 (3): 298–306.

Bond, H. H. and W. Y. F. Shiu. 1997. The relationship between a group's personality resources and the two dimensions of its group process. *Small Group Research* 28 (2): 194–217.

Bradford, L., D. W. Stock, and M. Horwitz. 1970. How to diagnose group problems. In R. Golembiewski, ed., *Sensitivity Training and the Laboratory Approach*. Itasca, Ill.: F. E. Peacock.

Brandler, S. and C. P. Roman. 1999. *Group Work: Skills and Strategies for Effective Interventions.*, 2d ed. New York: Haworth.

Breton, M. 1990. Learning from social group work traditions. *Social Work with Groups* 13 (3): 21–34.

——. 1992. Liberation-Theology, group work, and the right of the poor and oppressed to participate in the life of the community. *Social Work with Groups* 15 (2–3): 257–269.

Brill, N. 1995. *Working with People: The Helping Process*, 5th ed. New York: Longman.

Brower, A. M. 1996. Group development as constructed social reality revisited: The constructivism of small groups. *Families in Society* 77 (6): 336–344.

Brower, A. M. and S. D. Rose, eds. 1990. *Advances in Group Work Research*. New York: Haworth.

Brower, S. and R. Taylor. 1985. Home and near home territories. In I. Altaian and C. Werner, eds., *Theory and Research*. New York: Plenum.

Brown, A. G. 1990. British perspectives on groupwork: Present and future. *Social Work Groups* 13 (3): 35–40.

Brown, A. G. and T. Mistry. 1994. Group work with "mixed membership" groups: Issues of race and gender. *Social Work with Groups* 17 (3): 5–21.

Brown, L. N. 1991. *Groups for Growth and Change*. White Plains, N.Y.: Longman.

Brown, R. 2000. *Group Processes: Dynamics Within and Between Groups.* 2d ed. Malden, Mass.: Blackwell.

Bums, J. M. 1980. *Leadership.* New York: Harper and Row.

Campbell, M. M. and L. Shulman. 1994. *Social Group Work in the 1990's.* New Orleans: Tulane University Press.

Caplan, G. 1961. *An Approach to Community Mental Health.* New York: Grune and Stratton.

Carter, S. L. 1998. *Civility.* New York: HarperCollins, Harper Perennial.

Chaiklin, H. 1969. Social system, personality system, and practice theory. In *Social Work Practice.* New York: Columbia University Press.

Chau, K. L., ed. 1991. *Ethnicity and Biculturalism: Emerging Perspectives of Social Group Work.* New York: Haworth.

Cnaan, R. A. and H. Adar. 1987. An integrative model for group work in community organization practice. *Social Work with Groups* 10 (3): 5–24.

Cohen, A. M. and Smith, R. D. 1976. *The Critical Incident in Growth Groups: A Manual for Group Leaders.* La Jolla, Calif.: University Associates.

Cohen, M. B. and A. Mullender. 1999. The personal in the political: Exploring the group work continuum from individual to social change goals. *Social Work with Groups* 22 (1): 13–31.

Congress, E. P. and M. Lynn. 1997. Group work practice in the community: Navigating the slippery slope of ethical dilemmas. *Social Work with Groups* 20 (3): 61–74.

Corey, M. S. and G. Corey. 2001. *Groups: Process and Practice.* 6th ed. Pacific Grove, Calif.: Brooks/Cole Publishing.

Coser, L. 1967. *Continuities in the Study of Social Conflicts.* New York: Free.

——. 1974. *Greedy Institutions.* New York: Free.

Cox, E. O. 1991. The critical role of social-action in empowerment oriented groups. *Social Work with Groups* 14 (3–4): 77–90.

Coyle, G. L. 1930. *Social Process in Organized Groups.* New York: Richard R. Smith.

——. 1954. Social group work. In *Social Work Year Book.* New York: American Association of Social Workers.

Davis, L., ed. 1984. Ethnicity content in group work practice. Special issue, *Social Work with Groups* 7 (3).

Davis, L. E., L. C. Cheng, and M. J. Strube. 1996. Differential effects of racial composition on male and female groups: Implications for group work practice. *Social Work Research* 20 (3): 157–166.

Davis, L. E., M. J. Galinsky, and J. H. Schopler. 1995. RAP—A framework for leadership of multiracial groups. *Social Work* 40 (2):155–165.

Deutsch, M. 1973. Factors influencing the resolution of conflict. In *The Resolution of Conflict.* New Haven: Yale University Press.

Dimock, H. G. 1987. *Groups: Leadership and Group Development.* San Diego, Calif.: Pfeiffer.

Douglas, T. 1979. *Group Processes in Social Work.* New York: Wiley.

Druskat, V. N. and S. B. Wolff. 2001. Building the emotional intelligence of groups. *Harvard Business Review* (March): 80–92.

Edelwich, J. and A. Brodsky. 1980. *Burn-Out: Stages of Disillusionment in the Helping Professions.* New York: Human Sciences.

Ephross, P. H. 1983. Giving up martyrdom. *Public Welfare* 41 (2).

Ephross, P. H. 1986. Group work with work groups: A case of arrested development. In P. H. Glasser and N. S. Mayadas, eds., *Group Workers at Work: Theory and Practice for the '80s.* Totowa, N.J.: Rowman and Littlefield.

Ephross, P. H. and J. E. Ephross. 1984. Some theoretical and practical issues in intraprofessional teamwork serving retarded children and their families. Typescript.

Ephross, P. H. and R. R. Greene. 1991. Symbolic interactionism. In R. R. Greene and P. H. Ephross, eds., *Human Behavior Theory and Social Work Practice.* New York: Aldine de Gruyter.

Ephross, P. H., C. Polak, and O. Westgaard. 1998. Designing work groups, jobs and work flow. *Social Work with Groups* 21 (1–2): 167–169.

Ephross, P. H. and T. V. Vassil. 1993. The Rediscovery of Real-World Groups. *Social Work with Groups* 16 (1–2):15–25.

Ephross, P. H. and J. C. Weiss. 1985. Sexual interactions in the workplace: From affirmation to harassment. Typescript.

Falek, H. S. 1988. *Social Work: The Membership Perspective.* New York: Springer.

Fatout, M. and S. R. Rose. 1995. *Task Groups in the Social Services.* Thousand Oaks, Calif.: Sage.

Feldman, R. A. and H. Specht. 1968. The world of social group work. In *Social Work Practice.* New York: Columbia University Press for the National Conference on Social Welfare.

Follett, M. P. 1920. *The New State.* New York: Longmans Green.

Galinsky, M. J. and J. H. Schopler, eds. 1995. *Support Groups: Current Perspectives on Theory and Practice.* New York: Haworth.

Garland, J. A. ed. 1992. *Group Work Reaching Out: People, Places and Power.* New York: Haworth.

Garland, J. E., H. E. Jones, and R. L. Kolodny. 1965. A model for stages of development in social work groups. In S. B. Bernstein, ed., *Explorations in Group Work.* Boston: Charles River.

Garland, J. E. and R. L. Kolodny. 1967. *Characteristics and resolution of scapegoating.* In *Social Work Practice.* New York: Columbia University Press for the National Conference on Social Welfare.

Garvin, C. D. 1987. *Contemporary Group Work.* 2d ed. Englewood Cliffs, N.J.: Prentice-Hall.

——. 1991. Barriers to effective social actions by groups. *Social Work with Groups* 14 (3–4): 65–76.

——. 1997. *Contemporary Group Work.* 3d ed. Boston: Allyn and Bacon.

Garvin, C. D. and B. A. Seabury. 1984. *Interpersonal Practice in Social Work: Processes and Procedures.* Englewood Cliffs, N.J.: Prentice-Hall.

Getzels, J. W. and H. A. Thelen. 1960. The classroom group as a unique social system. In *The Dynamics of Institutional Groups.* Chicago: National Society for the Study of Education.

Gilbert, M. C. and A. Gitterman. 2000. Spirituality in work groups: Practitioners speak out. *Social Work with Groups* 22 (4): 67–84.

Glassman, U. and L. Kates. 1990. *Group Work: A Humanistic Approach*. Newbury Park, Calif.: Sage.

Glidewell, J. 1972. A social psychology of mental health. In S. E. Golahh and C. Eisdorfer, eds., *Handbook of Community Mental Health*. New York: Appleton-Century-Crofts.

——. 1975. A social psychology of laboratory training. In K. D. Benne, L. P. Bradford, J. R. Gibb, and R. O. Lippitt, eds. *The Laboratory Method of Changing and Learning*. Palo Alto, Calif.: Science and Behavior Books. a Social Psychology of Lab Training, 1975.

Goffee, R. and Jones, G. 2002. Why should anyone be led by you. *Harvard Business Review* (September–October): 63–70.

Goffman, E. 1961. *Asylums*. New York: Doubleday, Anchor.

Goleman, Daniel. 2000. Leadership that gets results. *Harvard Business Review* (March–April): 78–90.

Gordon, M., ed. 1981. America as a multicultural society. Special issue, *Annals of the American Academy of Political and Social Sciences* 454.

Greenwood, R. and W. Jenkins. 1981. Policymaking groups. In R. Payne and C. Cooper, eds., *Groups at Work*. New York: Wiley.

Greif, G. L. and P. H. Ephross, eds. 1997. *Group Work with Populations at Risk*. New York: Oxford University Press.

Gummer, B. 1987. Groups as substance and symbol: Group processes and organizational politics. *Social Work with Groups* 10 (2): 25–39.

Gumpert, J. and J. E. Saltman. 1998. Social group work practice in rural areas: The practitioners speak. *Social Work with Groups* 21 (3): 19–34.

Hare, A. P. 1976. *Handbook of Small Group Research*. 2d ed. New York: Free.

Hare, A. P., H. H. Blumberg, M. F. Davies, and M. V. Kent. 1994. *Small Group Research: A Handbook*. Norwood, N.J.: Ablex.

Harris; J. J. 1976. Status as a moderator of job satisfaction and role ambiguity. D.S.W. diss., University of Maryland, Baltimore.

Hartford, M. E. 1972. *Groups in Social Work*. New York: Columbia University Press.

——, ed. 1964. *Working Papers Towards a Frame of Reference for Social Group Work*. New York: National Association of Social Workers.

Hartsock, S. 1997. The effects of organizational climate on the behavior of children in residential care. Ph.D. diss., University of Maryland, Baltimore.

Henry, S. 1992. Group skills. In *Social Work: A Four-Dimensional Approach*. 2d ed. Pacific Grove, Calif.: Brooks/Cole.

Hopps, J. G. and E. Pinderhughes. 1999. *Group Work with Overwhelmed Clients: How the Power of Groups Can Help People Transform Their Lives*. New York: Free.

Janis, I. 1972. *Victims of Groupthink*. Boston: Houghton Mifflin.

Janis, I. and L. Mann. 1977. *Decision Making*. New York: Free.

Janis, I. L. 1997. *Groupthink*. Notre Dame, Ind.: University of Notre Dame Press.

Jaques, E. 1970. *Work, Creativity and Social Justice*. New York: International University Press.

Jay, A. 2003. The good meeting. *Harvard Business Review* (April): 126.

Johnson, D. W. and F. P. Johnson. 2000. *Joining Together: Group Theory and Group Skills*, 7th ed. Boston: Allyn and Bacon.

Kane, R. 1975. *Interprofessional Teamwork*. Syracuse, N.Y.: Syracuse University School of Social Work.

Kanter, R. M. 1986. *The Joys and Tensions of Teamwork*. *Bryn Mawr Alumnae Bulletin*, winter: 3–9.

Katz, D. and R. Kahn. 1978. *Social Psychology of Organizations*. New York: Wiley.

Klein, A. F. 1953. *Society, Democracy, and the Group*. New York: White-side, Morrow.

——. 1972. *Effective Groupwork: An Introduction to Principle and Method*. New York: Association Press.

Kolodny, R. L. 1973. The handicapped child and his peer group: Strategy for integration. In S. B. Bernstein, ed., *Further Explorations in Group Work*. Boston: Charles River.

Kurland, R. and R. Salmon. 1992. The interplay among social group work, community work and social action. *Social Work with Groups* 15 (1):35–50.

——, eds. 1995. *Group Work Practice in a Troubled Society: Problems and Opportunities*. New York: Haworth.

Lassner, J., K. Powell and E. Finnegan, eds. 1987. *Social Group Work: Competence and Values in Practice*. New York: Haworth.

Lasswell, H. 1951. The policy orientation. In D. Lemer and H. Lasswell, eds., *The Policy Sciences*. Palo Alto, Calif.: Stanford University Press.

Leavitt, H. J. 1980. Suppose we took groups seriously? In L. L. Cummings and A. Dunham, eds., *Introduction to Organizational Behavior*. Homewood, Ill.: Richard D. Irwin.

Lee, J. A. B. 1994. *The Empowerment Approach to Social Work Practice*. New York: Columbia University Press.

——, ed. 1989. *Group Work with the Poor and Oppressed*. New York: Haworth.

Leighton, A. H. 1982. *Caring for Mentally Ill People*. New York: Cambridge University Press.

Lewin, K. 1948. *Resolving Social Conflicts*. New York: Harper and Row.

——. 1951. *Field Theory in Social Science*. New York: Harper and Row.

Lewin, K., R. Lippitt, and R. W. White. 1939. Patterns of aggressive behavior in experimentally created social climates. *Journal of Social Psychology* 10:271–299.

Lewis, E. 1991. Social-change and citizen action: A philosophical exploration for modern social group work. *Social Work with Groups* 14 (3–4): 23–34.

——. 1992. Regaining Promise—Feminist Perspectives for Social Group Work. *Social Work with Groups* 15 (2–3): 271–284.

Lieberman, M. A., I. Yalom, and M. Miles. 1973. *Encounter Groups: First Facts*. New York: Basic.

Lincoln, Y. S. 1985. Organizational theory and inquiry. Introduction to Y. S. Lincoln, ed., *The Paradigm Revolution*. Newbury Park, Calif.: Sage.

Lipman-Blumen, J. and H. J. Leavitt. 1999. *Hot Groups*. New York: Oxford University Press.

Lowy, L. 1965. Group decision making. In S. B. Bernstein, ed., *Explorations in Group Work*. Boston: Charles River.

Luft, J. 1970. *Group Processes: An Introduction to Group Dynamics*. 2d ed. Palo Alto, Calif.: National Press Books.

McLeaurin, D. 1982. Three behavioral strategies for increasing levels of productive conflict resolution among tripartite (medicine, nursing, social work) groups functioning as problem-solving health teams. Typescript.

Maier, N. R. F. 1963. *Problem Solving Discussions and Conferences: Leadership Methods and Skills*. New York: McGraw-Hill.

——. 1971. Assets and liabilities in group problem solving. In B. Hinton and H. J. Reitz, eds., *Groups and Organizations*. Belmont. Calif.: Wadsworth.

Malekoff, A. 1999. *Group Work with Adolescents: Principles and Practice*. New York: Guilford.

Manis, J. G. and B. N. Meltzer. 1972. *Symbolic Interaction: A Reader in Social Psychology*. 2d ed. Boston: Allyn and Bacon.

Mann, R. D. 1967. *Interpersonal Styles and Group Development*. New York: Wiley.

Manor, O. 2000. *Choosing a Groupwork Approach: An Inclusive Stance*. Philadelphia: Jessica Kingsley.

Mead, G. H. 1934. *Mind, Self, and Society*. Chicago: University of Chicago Press.

Menefee, D. T. 1990. Toward a functional model of problem solving in social service work groups. Ph.D. diss., University of Washington.

Miles, M., ed. 1964. On temporary systems. In *Innovations in Education*. New York: Teachers College Press of Columbia University.

Mills, J. S. 1936. *A System of Logic, Ratiocinative and Inductive: Being a Connected View of the Principles of Evidence and the Methods of Scientific Investigation*. Vol. 6, *On the Logic of the Moral Sciences*. London: Longmans, Green.

Mills, T. 1984. *The Sociology of Small Groups*. 2d ed. Englewood Cliffs, N.J.: Prentice-Hall.

Mistry, T. and A. Brown, eds. 1997. *Race and Groupwork*. Concord, Mass.: Paul and Co. Publishers' Consortium.

Napier, R. and M. K. Gershenfeld. 1993. *Groups, Theory and Experience*. Boston: Houghton Mifflin.

New York Times. 1982. *Everyday Dictionary*. Ed. T. M. Paikeday. New York: New York Times.

Northen, H. 1969. *Social Work with Groups*. New York: Columbia University Press.

——. 1998. Ethical dilemmas in social work with groups. *Social Work with Groups* 21 (1–2): 5–18.

Northen, H. and R. Kurland. 2001. *Social Work with Groups*. 3d ed. New York: Columbia University Press.

Ofshe, R. J., ed. 1973. *Interpersonal Behavior in Small Groups*. Englewood Cliffs, N.J.: Prentice-Hall.

Oichi, W. G. 1981. *Theory Z*. Reading, Mass.: Addison-Wesley.

Patton, M. Q. 1975. *Alternative Education Research Paradigms*. Grand Forks: University Of North Dakota Press.

Phillips, H. U. 1975. *The Essentials of Social Group Work Skill*. New York: Association Press, for the University of Pennsylvania School of Social Work.

Polley, R. B., A. P. Hare, and P. J. Stone, eds. 1988. *The SYMLOG Practitioner: Applications of Small Group Research*. New York: Praeger.

Ramey, J. H. 1992. Group work with practice in neighborhood centers today. *Social Work with Groups* 15 (2–3): 193–206.

——. 1998. *Bibliography on Group Work*. Akron, Ohio: Association for the Advancement of Social Work with Groups.

Randel, D. 2002. *The Force of Argument. Chicago Magazine* 95 (1): 11.

Redl, F. 1942. Types of group formation, group emotion, and leadership. *Psychiatry* 5 (4).

Reed, B.G. and C.D. Garvin. 1996. Feminist psychodynamic group psychotherapy: The applications of principles. In B. DeChant, ed. *Women and Group Psychotherapy: Theory and Practice*. New York: Guilford.

——, eds. 1983. Group work with women/group work with Men: An overview of gender issues in social group work practice. Special issue, *Social Work with Groups*, 6 (3/4).

Regan, S. and G. Lee. 1992. The interplay among social group work, community work and social-action. *Social Work with Groups* 15 (1): 35–50.

Ripple, L. B. Polemis, and C. Alexander. 1964. *Motivation, Capacity, and Opportunity*. Chicago: University of Chicago Press.

Robinson, E. A. R. and H. J. Doucek. 1994. Implications of the pre/post/then design for evaluating social group work. *Research on Social Work Practice* 4 (2): 224–239.

Rose, S. R. 1998. *Group Work with Children and Adolescents: Prevention and Intervention in School and Community Systems*. Thousand Oaks, Calif.: Sage.

Rose, S. D. and A. M. Brower, eds. 1989. *Advances in Group Work Research*. New York: Haworth.

Rose, S. D. and J. L. Edleson. 1991. *Working with Children and Adolescents in Groups*. San Francisco: Jossey-Bass.

Sarri, R. C. and M. J. Galinsky. 1967. A conceptual framework for group development. In R. D. Vinter, ed., *Readings in Group Work Practice*. Ann Arbor, Mich.: Campus.

Schiller, L.Y. 1995. Stages of development in women's groups: A relational model. In R. Kurland and R. Salmon, eds., *Group Work Practice in a Troubled Society: Problems and Opportunities*. Binghamton, N.Y.: Haworth.

Schon, D. 1983. *The Reflective Practitioner*. New York: Basic.

Schopler, J. 1987. Interorganizational groups: Origins, structure, and outcomes. *Academy of Management Review* 12 (4): 702–713.

Schutz, W. C. 1956. *The Interpersonal Underworld*. Palo Alto, Calif.: Science and Behavior Books.

Schwartz, P. and J. Ogilvy. 1979. *The Emergent Paradigm in Changing Patterns of Thought and Belief*. Menlo Park, Calif.: SRI International.

Schwartz, W. 1971. On the use of groups in social work practice. In W. Schwartz and S. Zalba, eds., *The Practice of Group Work*. New York: Columbia University Press

——. 1994. The social worker in the group. In *Social Work: The Collected Writings of William Schwartz*. Ed. Toby Berman-Rossi. Itasca, Ill.: F. E. Peacock. Originally published in *The Social Welfare Forum: Proceedings of the National Conference of Social Welfare* (New York: Columbia University Press, 1961).

———. 1976. Between client and system: The mediating function. In R. Roberts and H. Northen, eds., *Theories of Social Work with Groups*. New York: Columbia University Press.

Seeman, M. 1959. On the meaning of alienation. *American Sociological Review* 24:783–791.

Shapiro, B. Z. 1991. Social-action, the group and society. *Social Work with Groups* 14 (3–4): 7–21.

Shulman, L. 1967. Scapegoats, group workers, and preemptive intervention. *Social Work* 12 (2): 37–43.

———. 1984. *Skills of Helping Individuals and Groups*. 2d ed. Itasca, Ill.: F. E. Peacock.

———. 2001. *The Skills of Helping Individuals, Families, Group and Communities*. 4th ed. Itasca, Ill.: F. E. Peacock.

Silber, J. 1995. *Obedience to the Unenforceable*. Commencement address, Boston University.

Siporin, M. 1986. Group work method and the inquiry. In P. H. Glasser and N. S. Mayadas, eds., *Group Workers at Work: Theory and Practice in the '80s*. Totowa, N.J.: Rowman and Littlefield.

Smelser, N. J. and W. T. Smelser. 1970. *Personality and Society Systems*. 2d ed. New York: Wiley.

Somers, M. L. 1976. Problem-solving in small groups. In R. Roberts and H. Northen, eds., *Theories of Social Work with Groups*. New York: Columbia University Press.

Sonnenfeld, J. A. 2002. *What Makes Great Boards Great*. Harvard Business Review (September): 106–113.

Steinberg, D. M. 1993. Some findings from a study on the impact of group work education on social work practitioners work with groups. *Social Work with Groups* 16 (3): 23–39.

Stempler, B. L. and M. S. Glass, eds. 1996. *Social Group Work Today and Tomorrow: Moving From Theory to Advanced Training and Practice*. New York: Haworth.

Stock, D. and H. A. Thelen. 1958. *Emotional Dynamics and Group Culture*. New York: New York University Press.

Stogdill, R. M. 1974. *Handbook of Leadership: A Survey of Theory and Research*. New York: Free.

Sullivan, N. 1995. Who owns the group? The role of worker control in the development of a group: A qualitative research study of practice. *Social Work with Groups* 18 (2–3): 15–32.

Thelen, H. A. 1958. *Dynamics of Groups at Work*. Chicago: University of Chicago Press.

———. 1981. *The Classroom Society*. New York: Halsted.

Thompson, L. L., E. A. Mannix, and M. H. Bazerman. 1988. Group negotiation: Effects of a decision rule, agenda, and aspiration. *Journal of Personality and Social Psychology* 54 (1): 86–95.

Tolman, R. M. and C. E. Molidor. 1994. A decade of social group work research—Trends in methodology, theory, and program-development. *Research on Social Work Practice* 4 (2): 142–159.

Toseland, R. W. 1995. *Group Work with the Elderly and Family Caregivers.* New York: Springer.

Toseland, R.W. and P. H. Ephross, eds. 1987. *Working Effectively with Administrative Groups.* New York: Haworth.

Tropman, J. E. 1980. *Effective Meetings.* Beverly Hills: Sage.

———. 1996. *Effective Meetings: Improving Group Decision Making,* 2d ed. Thousand Oaks, Calif.: Sage.

Tropp, E. 1976. A developmental theory. In R. Roberts and H. Northen, eds., *Theories of Social Work with Groups.* New York: Columbia University Press.

Tuckman, B. 1965. Developmental sequence in small groups. *Psychological Bulletin* 63:384–399.

Tuckman, B.W. and M.A. C. Jensen. 1977. Stages of small group development revisited. *Groups and Organizational Studies* 2 (1): 419–427.

Underwood, W. 1977. Roles that facilitate and inhibit group development. In R. T. Golembiewski and A. Blumberg, eds., *Sensitivity Training and the Laboratory Approach.* 3d ed. Itasca, Ill.: F. E. Peacock.

U. S. Census Bureau. 2004. http://factfinder.census.gov/home/saff/main.html?_lang=en

Vaillant, G. 1993. *The Wisdom of the Ego.* Cambridge: Harvard University Press.

Vassil, T.V. 1975. Factors influencing role perceptions of adolescents in social work problem solving groups. Ph.D. diss., University of Chicago.

Verdi, A. F. and S. A.Wheelan. 1992. Developmental patterns in same-sex and mixed-sex groups. *Small Group Research* 23 (3): 356–378.

Vinik, A. and M. Levin, eds. 1992. *Social Action and Group Work.* New York: Haworth.

Warren, R. L. 1972. *The Community in America.* 2d ed. Chicago: Rand McNally.

Weber, M. 1947. *The Theory of Social and Economic Organizations.* Trans. and ed. A. M. Henderson and T. Parsons. New York: Oxford University Press.

Weick, K. E. 1995. Sense making in organization. In *Organizations.* Thousand Oaks, Calif.: Sage.

———. 2001. Leadership as the legitimation of doubt. In W. E. Bennis, G. M. Spreitzer, and T. C. Cummings, eds., *The Future of Leadership.* San Francisco: Jossey-Bass

Weil, M., K. L. Chau, and D. Southerland, eds. 1991. *Theory and Practice in Social Group Work.* New York: Haworth.

Weiss, J. C. 1988. The D-R model of of co-leadership of groups. *Small Group Behavior* 19 (1).

Weiss, J. C. and P. H. Ephross. 1985. Coalitions and councils: Specialized forms of working groups. Typescript.

———. 1986. Group work approaches to hate violence incidents: A rediscovered arena for practice. *Social Work* 31 (2): 132–136.

Wenocur, S, P. H. Ephross, T. V. Vassil, and R. K. Varghese, eds. 1993. *Social Work with Groups: Expanding Horizons.* New York: Haworth.

West, M. 1998. Social work. In F. P. Orelove and H. G. Garner, eds., *Teamwork.* Washington, D.C.: CWLA Press.

Whitaker, D. S. 2001. *Use of Groups to Help People.* 2d ed. Philadelphia: Brunner-Routledge.

Williamson, S. A. 1977. Developmental patterns in self-analytic groups. Ph. D. diss., Harvard University.

Wilson, G. and G. Ryland. 1949. *Social Group Work Practice.* Cambridge, Mass.: Houghton Mifflin.

Wilson, G. L. 2001. *Groups in Context: Leadership and Participation in Small Groups,* 6th ed. Burr Ridge, Ill.: McGraw-Hill.

Zaleznik, A. and D. Moment. 1964. *Dynamics of Interpersonal Behavior.* New York: Wiley.

Zander, A. 1982. *Making Groups Effective.* San Francisco: Jossey-Bass.

INDEX

Page references in italics refer to tables and figures.